ECONOMIC CRISIS AND NEW NATIONALISMS

GERMAN POLITICAL ECONOMY AS PERCEIVED BY EUROPEAN PARTNERS

P.I.E. Peter Lang
Bruxelles · Bern · Berlin · Frankfurt am Main · New York · Oxford · Wien

EUROCLIO is a scientific and editorial project, a network of research institutions and researchers, and an ideas forum. EUROCLIO as an editorial project consists of two aspects: the first concerns studies and documents, the second concerns tools. Both are aimed at making the results of research more accessible, and also at opening up paths through the history of European construction/integration/unification.

The EUROCLIO series meets a dual objective:

- to provide reference tools for research,
- to provide a platform for this research in terms of the publication of results.

The series thus consists of two sub-series that satisfy these requirements: the Studies and Documents series and the References series. These two series are aimed at general libraries and/or university history departments, teachers and researchers, and in certain cases, specific professional circles.

The Studies and Documents series consists of monographs, collections of articles, conference proceedings, and collections of texts with notes for teaching purposes.

The References series consists of bibliographies, guides and other tools. It thus contributes to the creation of a database making up a "Permanent catalogue of sources and bibliographies on European construction".

ECONOMIC CRISIS AND NEW NATIONALISMS

GERMAN POLITICAL ECONOMY AS PERCEIVED BY EUROPEAN PARTNERS

Antonio Varsori & Monika Poettinger (eds.)

Euroclio
No.84

Financial Support for publication was granted by Foundation Cesifin Alberto Predieri.

This publication has been peer-reviewed.

Éditions scientifiques internationales
Brussels, 2014
1 avenue Maurice, B-1050 Brussels, Belgium
pie@peterlang.com; www.peterlang.com

ISSN 0944-2294
ISBN 978-2-87574-193-6
eISBN 978-3-0352-6472-2
D/2014/5678/71

CIP available from the British Library, UK and from the Library of Congress, USA.

"Die Deutsche National Bibliothek" lists this publication in the "Deutsche Nationalbibliografie"; detailed bibliographic data is available on the Internet at <http://dnb.de>.

Table of Contents

Preface

Italy and Germany: a "Marriage" Destined to Last?

Ginevra Cerrina FERONI

I am pleased that Fondazione Cesifin Alberto Predieri welcomed with enthusiasm the project of the conference titled "Economic Crisis and New Nationalisms: German Economic Policy as perceived by European Partners".

The relationship between Italy and Germany is a sensitive subject. A relation that has developed over the years in very different areas such as: politics, literature, sport, arts, economic relations and law. A long partnership that someone (G.E Rusconi) called "marriage" and, as every marriage lasting over the years, had its ups and downs, its lights and shadows.

Truth to be told the comparison with the German world has always been very important for Italy. For instance, it is paramount to recall that the connection with the German experience within the legal field is an obvious point of reference for Italian jurists, at least starting from Vittorio Emanuele Orlando's work. Indeed, the historical studies on his works as well as on the events of Italian public law highlighted well the influence of German legal dogmatics on Italian legal science. Likewise, the influences of the Weimar's constitution (1919) in Italy are well known, in the period between the two wars and afterwards particularly during the years of the Constituent Assembly. However, even during the sixty years or more of the German Basic Law's enforcement, the so called "German model" has been recalled many times in the debates on Constitutional reforms to be introduced in Italy. I am thinking about the most well known subjects such as: the federal system of the State and form of government. Hence, Italian politico-cultural *élites* have always shown a great interest towards the German institutional system (certainly greater than the specular one displayed by German politico-cultural *élites* towards our Country). During a period of economic crisis as the one Italy is facing, the forced comparison with the German model certainly becomes troubling. It says a lot the fact that our economic trustworthiness on the markets is measured daily according to the parameters established by German stability and productivity.

Nevertheless, Italy and Germany shared a similar historic past: they are both relatively young nations (born respectively in 1861 and 1871); the unification of both Countries was achieved thanks to the role played by leader-States which triggered progressive processes of annexation (Reign of Sardinia and Prussia), and their respective Prime Ministers (Cavour, the Reign of Sardinia's Prime Minister and von Bismarck, Chancellor of Prussia) played a decisive role in both events.

Other analogies can be found in the Countries' common authoritarian/ totalitarian experiences and in the fact that the advent of authoritarian/ totalitarian regimes both in Italy and Germany was caused by the crisis of the liberal State and a weak parliamentarianism.

Furthermore, Italy and Germany came out of the war heavily defeated and with limitations on their sovereignty and national feeling: the reason why the connection to establish a European perspective represented a great opportunity of political identity for both Countries.

Finally, they experienced a real economic miracle in the second Post-war period.

Nonetheless, nowadays the distances between the two Countries are huge. What happened? Why did Germany shift from being "Europe's big patient" to become its driving force, especially since the Two Thousands, while Italy seems to be destined to a relentless decline? Indeed, there are many differences concerning the state of health of their respective public finances, levels of employment, and productivity, competitiveness on international markets, levels of innovation, research and political stability.

History repeats itself. The Reunification Treaty, enabled Germany to become also a political giant drawing the analysts' attention and, I would add, a certain level of concern. Once again we face an unquestioned German hegemony.

This could explain why mistrust, nationalism, a spirit of revenge against who is held directly or indirectly responsible for all evils tend to be stirred within the context of a serious crisis. Trite stereotypes are exhumed, disapproving attitudes towards Europe are heightened, a withdrawal from the Euro is proposed and Germany which after a long period of purification from its faults deceived itself in thinking of having made peace with the world, has been hit by a new wave of resentment.

Moreover, the idea, provocative in its essence as much as dangerous for its effects, according to which it is perfectly legitimate to deny help to European Countries that are experiencing some difficulties, as they are guiltily indebted and thusly unworthy, has been supported by Germany as well. This idea is based on the principle that German people have the right (and the duty) to be led by their own reasonable interest with regards to international financial relationships without fearing moral reprimands (T. Sarrazin).

Refined analyses carried out by economists and political scientists highlighted that the problem is largely ascribable to the birth of the Euro and to the many incoherences of the Eurosystem (G. Guarino). Moreover, they showed that Germany's hegemony, far from being limited to the single currency, has further increased considering that the new currency was new only in name, since it was actually a replacement for the German Mark (E. Galli della Loggia). Hence, we face a paradox: the currency which was meant to unite European people caused a seemingly unbridgeable division.

Likewise, it is unquestionable that the survival of the European Union cannot but be linked with the solution of the European constitutional issue. Under the current circumstances, politics cannot be considered as an option for Europe to manage either the currency or the entire system: it is a necessity. The path is hard and full of traps, but there are no other ways left.

Likewise, it is unthinkable to go towards a united Europe without establishing a European schooling standard or choosing an official language (P. Savona).

However, "to bang one's fists on Europe", according to a widespread vulgate, will become a feasible prospect only if we are credible in Europe (L. Bini Smaghi). The task is to better employ the huge sources coming from tax levy which cannot be further increased without causing the Italian system to collapse. This is the issue. The problem of Italian economy is essentially about growth. However, within an economy where public spending is worth more than the half of the national product, no growth acceleration will be possible unless public spending will be more effective and efficient. Hence, there is a need for politics, a brave one, but political consensus hinders brave actions which could tackle that network of specific, strengthened and stratified interests that weigh on our Country's institutions, economy and society. The history of many missed reforms in the past is exemplary. This is why I cannot be fully optimistic. Behind numbers there are human beings with their history and character, for better and for worse.

As it happens in every marriage, we ought to learn from our partner and we can learn the following from our German friends: the culture of rigour, not so much (or not only) the one applied to public accounts, but the one to adopt as a lifestyle. A culture of rigour which, in my opinion, stands for: compliance with rules, awareness of the common good, meritocracy in every field without discounts, exceptions or do-goodism. Being aware that this is the winning solution would mean to have the tools to appear before Europe having what it takes to excel in global competitiveness.

However, Germany's political and economic hegemony is not under discussion. That is why it is not a matter of asking *whether* Europe should be led by Germany or not, but *how* this leadership should be exerted, i.e. how Germany should organise its *auctoritas.* The real issue lies in the fact that Germany – perhaps the least anti-European Country of the Union – has to take on its responsibilities before Europe, abandoning its tendency to disengagement, and playing an active role in establishing a European constitutional framework (A. Bolaffi).

The European elections held on May 25, 2014 seem to have highlighted new equilibria. On the one hand, they registered a numerically significant affirmation of Euro-sceptical parties (first among them Le Pen's right-wing party); on the other hand, they witnessed the end of the Franco-German axis in leading Europe, considering the fall of Hollande's left-wing party in France as opposed to the undisputed victory of Renzi's left-wing party in Italy.

Will an Italo-German axis henceforth lead Europe? It is too early to say. Certainly, starting from today the role played by Italy will be reflected in its relationship with Germany and thus with Europe.

In other words, Italy and Germany: a "marriage" destined to last?

Introduction

Monika POETTINGER

This volume hosts the proceedings of the international colloquium on "Economic crisis and new nationalisms: German economic policy as perceived by European partners", organized by the Foundation Cesifin Alberto Predieri and held in Florence, November the 15th, 2012. In this regard particular thanks are due to Prof. Ginevra Cerrina Feroni and Dr. Monica Degli Innocenti of Cesifin, and Prof. Piero Roggi, University of Florence, for their continuous support and the impeccable organization.

In consequence of the ongoing economic crisis, in 2010 the deterioration of cross-border relations between Italy and Germany was undeniable. In both countries the press hosted articles openly blaming present hardships on the squandering attitude of southerners or egoistic and mercantilist policies of northerners. "The double life of Chancellor Merkel, Prussian and European without remorse" titled for example Danilo Taino on *Corriere della Sera* in December 2010[1]. He was one of the kindest. In Germany, *Frankfurter Allgemeine Zeitung* noted in November 2010: "Italians count differently"[2]. Again one of the mildest.

At the end of 2011 Pierluigi Battista resumed the situation thusly: "Today, on balance, with the euro caught in a storm and Germany in the crossfire, considered too greedy towards weaker and more indebted European partners, the rumor makes the round that the euro has been colonized by the mark. Or that the euro is only a façade for a resurrected mark. In any case the result of these tales is the image of a diabolical Germany sacrificing to its egoistic national interest the interests of all European partners, with Angela Merkel in the foreground, tightening the grip on the purse and strangling European poor, while they plead for mercy, asking to be relieved from an oppressive debt. But no, the nefarious German begs off, pretends, conditions, appearing less than generous. Not for a political calculus, potentially wrong, but for an hegemonic assessment that ignores allies as if they were nothing worth"[3]. Battista

1 D. TAINO, "La doppia vita del cancelliere Merkel. Prussiana ed europea, senza complessi", *Corriere della Sera*, December 17 2010.

2 "Die Italiener rechnen anders", *Frankfurter Allgemeine Zeitung*, November 2010.

3 P. BATTISTA, "I fantasmi dell'egemonia tedesca", *Corriere della Sera*, December 3 2011.

clearly unveils how this representation of Germany and of its chancellor had the ultimate aim of blaming on them the hardship of the euro in the eyes of the public opinion. The fault for a crumbling Europe would so sit on the "obtuse" controller, stereotyped image of a German disciplined to obstinacy and governed by an ideal of steadfastness to which sacrifice poor and rebellious associates. "The demonization of Germany – concludes Battista – goes so far as to affirm that with different German politics the Euro would be saved and Europe would almost thrive, protected from its historical collapse". An illusion, obviously, with the terrible consequence of destroying the peaceful and cooperative ideal of Europe[4].

The reigning confusion among economists, split between pro-and anti-Euro positions in both countries, could not dissolve this growing wave of populist nationalisms[5]. Hence the idea of a conference with the aim of discussing the theoretical issues implied by recent economic policy debates, purging them of ideological and nationalistic tones. On both sides, economists readily accepted the confrontation and in due time the conference took form and content. In this regard I owe particular gratitude to all participants, facing harsh opposition and even open hostility with the disarming coherence of their theoretical background.

In the following I will concisely introduce the conceptual and methodological background of the conference and the contributions of participants to the present volume. I will also analyze the representation that two Italian and one German newspaper gave of the economic crisis from 2008 to 2013, underlining the different relevance accorded to single theories and economic ideologies, with reference to the political affiliation or nationality of the newspaper and also to the temporal evolution of the crisis. Divergences and convergences across-borders will so emerge and tentatively be explained. A brief sketch will also be drawn of the relationship between the two countries and of the two countries in respect to the European Union and the Euro, as derived from the press. The results of the analysis highlight how economic theories, in the long run, are transformed in general culture, in form of a prejudiced vulgate, and as such can become a populist instrument of politics. They also show how contemporary economists act, through the press, as critical voice toward governments' measures of political economy or directly participate in

---

4 *Ivi.*

5 A precocious analysis of the diffusion of "Euroscetticism" and "populism" in European countries during the crisis is to be found in E. Galli Della Loggia, "Europa, la fine di un ciclo", *Corriere della Sera,* June 11 2009. A more recent analysis of the complex phenomena of literary narratives of the crisis and the figure of the "populist economist" is in M. Gotor, "Il romanzo dell'economia", *La Repubblica*, October 7 2012.

the political process. Finally the study clarifies how the economic cycle influences both these aspects of the popularizing of economic theories, with the aim of purifying the current debate from nationalist and populist elements.

1. From Theory to Culture: Economics at the Test of Time

As hinted, the problem of Italo-German cross-border relations had many layers. Nationalistic sentiments were only the bottom end of the question. Such sentiments were the reflection of a widespread interpretation of economic processes based on deeply ingrained ideas, unconsciously absorbed by individuals through socialization processes. Many political decisions, too, are taken in the wake of such long term cultural traits: Walt Whitman Rostow named them broad collective decisions, underlining their unconscious origin[6].

The representation of Chancellor Merkel as "an obstinate egoist wielding a currency with the same cruelty shown once by those maneuvering tanks"[7], speaks of prejudices profoundly grounded in the historical past. These diverging long term cultural influences in the two countries can be understood only looking at the history of the international relations between Italy and Germany, as aptly done by Antonio Varsori in the present volume. Varsori clearly epitomizes the central theme of Germany's relation toward other European countries as the hegemonic threat represented by its extraordinary economic growth and expansionary goals after Unification in the 19th century. Many of the quoted prejudices, attached to the present Chancellor by foreign newspapers, can easily be traced back to the fame of Prussian military or the successive iconography flourished around Nazis (Image 1). This preconception of the German will of power is so ingrained in the public opinion, that it transcends political coloring, and finds expression both in foreign right- and left-wing journals and newspapers (Image 2).

The arena may have changed, from the battlefield to the market, but the perception of Germany remains, even today, that of a country prone on hegemonic control. The lecture given by Paolo Savona of German economic policy during the debt crisis of European partners, in his contribution to this volume, is based mainly on this assumption. "Your recent collective behavior – Savona reproaches Germans – seems to show that, at economic level, you are going again towards the direction

6 W. W. Rostow, *The Stages of Economic Growth: A Non-Communist Manifesto*, Cambridge, Cambridge University Press, 1990, 15.

7 P. Battista, "I fantasmi dell'egemonia tedesca", *Corriere della Sera*, December 3 2011.

suggested by the Funk Plan of 1936. The economic policy you are proposing lays the foundation for a break-up of the European dream of peace and common civil progress. The Funk Plan provided for Germany to become the country that would put order in Europe. This is what you now suggest".

Clearly the noun "order" in connection with Germany evokes in Europeans and in the world at large the specter of authoritarianism and imperialism. A particularly erroneous lecture of Germany's and Merkel's recent politics, because in Germany, on the contrary, "order", in connection to economic matters, just hints to ordo-liberalism, the economic school of thought that defended the ideal of economic free trade against Keynesian interventionism after the Second World War.

This kind of incomprehension generated, in the midst of the crisis, a dualist interpretation of the Chancellor's attitude toward Europe. While partners at risk of default viewed her as a cruel stepmother, in Germany Merkel had even been cartooned, in Berlin's newspaper *Der Tagesspiegel*, as dictatorial in favor of Europe, rescuing southern countries against the interests of Germany (Image 3). An ironic consequence of the persistence of old prejudices.

Image 1: Cartoon from the article Quanto a lungo (*Dagospia.com*, May 14 2012)

Image 2: Front page of the newspaper *Il Giornale* (August 3 2012); cover of *The Economist* (September 14 2013)

il Giornale

Spread tra Btp e Bund 510 Piazza Affari -4,64% Consumi italiani -2,8%

QUARTO REICH

I no della Merkel e della Germania rimettono in ginocchio noi e l'Europa
Borse a picco e Monti fa il finto tonto: «Non hanno capito Draghi»

I tedeschi salvatori dell'euro? Macché, l'Italia spende di più

Mediobanca blinda Nagel

Dio salvi la Juve da questa giustizia sportiva

Le regine di spade vincono odiandosi

Image 3: Cartoon from *Tagesspiegel*, August 17 2012. Merkel is guiding the tank against the Constitutional Court in Karlsruhe to convince the judges to vote in favor of fiscal compact and ESM

The current recrudescence of nationalisms depends on old rivalries and prejudices concerning the character of Germans, grounded in their historical past, but also on the influence and diffusion, in the long run, of economic schools in Germany and Italy. For if it is true that in the long run we are all dead[8], it is long dead economists' and philosophers' ideas that direct, in the words of John Maynard Keynes, the actions of individuals in the present[9] and in consequence also their interpretation of economic facts. Economic theories, so, can become part of that generic culture that imbibes, through socialization, the judgment and in consequence the decisions of individuals.

The easiest example is Karl Marx. Although the 1980s witnessed the crumbling of Communism in Eastern Europe, wiping out the political realization of his utopia, and his economic theory has long vanished from universities' programs, Marx remains the most quoted economist in all newspapers considered in this research, with no regard for nationality or political orientation. The advantage of Marx over fellow economists is outstanding. In Italy the research, including the *Corriere della Sera* and *La Repubblica*, considered Adam Smith, Karl Marx, John M. Keynes, Luigi Einaudi and Piero Sraffa (Table 1). In Germany, the *Frankfurter Allgemeine Zeitung* was searched for quotations of Adam Smith, Karl Marx, John M. Keynes, Ludwig Erhard and Piero Sraffa (Table 2). Marx's quota, on the total of articles naming the above mentioned economists, persistently remains above 50% with few exceptions, peaking at almost 70% on *La Repubblica* in 2010 (Table 3). In Germany Marx seems also to enjoy the advantage of a national champion, because, although *Frankfurter Allgemeine Zeitung* is a right-wing newspaper, Marx is not only the most quoted economist among the chosen ones, but shows an advantage over the second placed only comparable with the one of the Italian left wing *La Repubblica*, sometimes even higher (Graphs 1-2). *Corriere della Sera*, instead, appears more equilibrated: in 2013 Marx's quotations almost converge with those of Luigi Einaudi, Italy's most renown liberal economist (Graph 3).

Clearly Karl Marx has firmly entered the realm of culture. As Keynes noted, the long term effect of theoreticians is not to directly inspire individual, social or political decisions, but to determine how people at large categorize the world they live in, through concepts and relations that are not questioned but accepted as axioms. This way long dead economists define the conceptual language that people learn from cradle, without questioning it. Although the direct influence of Marx' theories

---

8 J. M. Keynes, *A Tract on Monetary Reform*, London, MacMillan, 1971, 65.

9 J. M. Keynes, *The General Theory of Employment, Interest and Money*, London, MacMillan, 1936, 383.

on politics and economics has almost vanished, his name has become something as a "brand" in which people can recognize themselves and as such worth of continuous quotation. It could easily be said that, at least in Germany and Italy, we all live in a "Marxian" world. Such profound and pervasive impact has not escaped historians and critical studies on Marx's writings have been flourishing in the years analyzed.

A more recent example is German ordo-liberalism. As in the case of Marxism, the ordo-liberal school, although academically dead already in the 1970s, kept a lasting impact on German economic culture up to today[10] and still exerts a strong influence on present politics, as recognized in recent studies[11]. Gerhard Wegner discusses in depth the legacy of this school of thought in the essay collected in this volume. Wegner precisely relates how ordo-liberalism conditioned entire generations of journalists, bankers and politicians: Germany's elite. Its principles are still diffused by the *Frankfurter Allgemeine Zeitung*, as shown by this research (Table 1). Ordo-liberalism, as a noun, hardly finds expression in the columns of the newspaper, although showing a significant peak during the first years of the American financial crisis. Ludwig Erhard, instead, one of the main offshoots of ordo-liberal thinking, successfully contends to J.M. Keynes, in four out of six years, the second place in the frequency of quotations in articles. The same can be said for political programs of German parties regarding the European economic crisis. A recent study analyzes these programs in respect to ordo-liberal normative indications, demonstrating that, although never referring to the originating school of thought, their content constantly refers, in positive or negative, to it[12].

Ordo-liberalism is a tradition of thought bound to Germany and, till recently, hardly known outside its frontiers, if not in narrow circles[13]. When such a national thought suddenly crosses frontiers, having caught the attention of foreign politicians or media, curious things happen. In the first years of the crisis, for example, ordo-liberalism, considered in Germany a liberal economic philosophy and as such championed by a newspaper like *Frankfurter Allgemeine Zeitung*, would be particularly appreciated in Italy by left wing *La Repubblica*, because assumed synonymous with state intervention.

---

10 G. Braunberger, "Das verwaiste Erbe der Freiburger Schule", *Frankfurter Allgemeine Zeitung*, June 19 2008.

11 S. Dullien, U. Guérot, "The long shadow of ordo-liberalism: Germany's approach to the euro crisis", *ECFR*, 49, 2012, 2.

12 *Ibid.*, 9.

13 In Italy a recent publication on Ordo-liberalism, not accidentaly dates to the first year of the economic crisis: F. Felice, *L'economia sociale di mercato*, Soveria Mannelli, Rubbettino, 2008.

As economic theories gradually become intellectual domain of elites, guiding politics and dominating academia, and then transform into widespread culture, their influence is delimited to the precise space where they have taken roots. In the case of ordo-liberalism such space overlapped with the national boundaries of Germany. Outside such space theories are ignored except for their political and cultural consequences. Past ideas rule the present in this form of broad culture, but, having lost in time the originating theoretical background, they easily become object and subject to prejudices and therefore reduced to nationalistic tendencies. The originating theory must undergo a process of interpretation and adaptation to be correctly received by foreign traditions, otherwise, as seen in the case of Merkel' s advocated "order", it can be profoundly misunderstood and cause a recrudescence of nationalism.

Not all interpretation of economic facts, though, is based on socialized tradition. Political maneuvers and social interplay deliberately influence mass media and ignite public opinion, which in turn determine the political decision process with uneconomic rationales. Rostow labels the resulting policies social decisions, differing from the broad collective ones because consciously taken by the collectivity[14]. In this case dead economists have less an influence than living ones, in particular those writing on newspapers and journals, or lending their voice to political parties or other social actors. The role of economists as intellectuals is in this case called into question[15]. Should economists represent the voice of reason, criticizing the instrumental use of economics made by political parties, or should they intervene directly in the political scene, advising politicians and even taking part in governments?

Economic theories can so be used as a means to a political end, often refuting real theoretical confrontation, inside a single country and across-borders. In his analysis of Europe's economic crisis, contributed to the present volume, Bertram Schefold clearly describes such risk. "Which solutions, if any, can economists offer under such circumstances? – writes Schefold – Before making proposals, their task is to identify the theoretical conception, which guide actual policies and underlie, as determinants of the policies in the past, the present state in which each country is found. The policies turn out to have been ambiguous and can often be justified or criticized from different points of view, hence there is much ideology in what claims to be analysis".

---

14 W. W. Rostow, *The Stages of Economic Growth. A Non-Communist Manifesto*, Cambridge, Cambridge University Press, 1990, 15.

15 See F. Caffè, *Politica economica. Sistematica e tecniche di analisi*, Torino, Bollati Boringhieri, 1966, 18-24.

To defuse the growing incommunicability between Italy and Germany, general economic culture as expressed in media and by the public opinion had to be brought back to its originating theories, past or present, and opened to confrontation. To understand different political stances on questions as the role of the state in the economy, the management of public debt and default, the use of monetary policy as a form of public financing, labor policies and development measures, traditions of thought, represented by politicians, journalists and national elites at large, had to be led back to schools of thought and their philosophical foundations[16]. In synthesis: the process of vulgarization of economic theories had to be reversed: from culture back to theory.

Table 1: Articles containing sample words on *La Repubblica* (white rows) and *Corriere della Sera* (grey rows) in 2008-2013

Articles containing the words	2008	2009	2010	2011	2012	2013
Capitalism and Crisis	251	265	145	145	173	132
	699	490	363	427	447	249
Europe and Crisis	1,469	1,737	1,603	2,119	2,348	1,104
	4,778	3,865	4,274	6,382	5,862	3,614
Financial Crisis	785	612	423	464	360	288
	3,780	1,093	1,011	3,085	691	386
European Union	1,026	1,020	1,003	1,121	867	115
	4,036	2,321	3,331	3,926	3,185	2,342
Monetary Union	15	13	79	103	150	10
	99	32	232	268	297	105
Merkel	462	604	598	1,033	1,394	734
	793	866	998	2,424	2,497	1,059
Statalism	60	32	18	40	48	33
	84	55	33	48	47	17
Marx	140	156	131	131	128	76
	595	380	458	499	347	207
Keynes	54	64	42	45	43	31
	155	126	87	152	143	71
Sraffa	6	0	3	2	6	5
	3	3	2	0	10	6

16 In the years of the economic crisis, some discussion on philosophy and economy was dealt with also on newspapers: E. Severino, "La decadenza del capitalismo ridotto come una foglia secca", *Corriere della Sera*, February 18 2012; A. Gnoli, "Ciò che i greci nell'antichità avevano capito della crisi", *La Repubblica*, April 22 2012; G. Rossi, "Il mercato che uccide la democrazia è il nuovo Leviatano degli egoisti", *Corriere della Sera*, August 9 2013; E. Severino, "Oltre il profitto: il capitalismo domain", *Corriere della Sera*, August 20 2013; F. Gambaro, "La fine della Società. Alain Touraine: 'Siamo tutti soli come attori in un teatro vuoto'", *La Repubblica*, October 31 2013.

Articles containing the words	2008	2009	2010	2011	2012	2013
Liberism	127	60	43	74	90	48
	268	120	134	171	239	90
Adam Smith	19	24	25	17	25	14
	76	27	26	18	53	28
Luigi Einaudi	50	31	42	87	100	70
	97	91	94	182	115	73

Table 2: Articles containing sample words on *Frankfurter Allgemeine Zeitung* in 2008-2013

Articles containing the words:	2008	2009	2010	2011	2012	2013
Capitalism and Crisis	181	290	98	139	162	130
Europe and Crisis	1,279	1,566	1,444	2,173	2,704	1,766
Financial Crisis	5,552	5,221	3,466	3,167	2,784	2,683
European Union	4,887	4,374	4,706	7,679	9,478	8,211
Monetary Union	175	198	868	1,214	1,719	899
Merkel	2,702	3,614	3,430	3,915	4,201	4,499
Social market economy	349	390	179	237	229	262
Ordo-liberalism	7	18	9	8	7	13
Liberalism	118	103	110	192	142	211
Marx	485	449	423	405	455	463
Keynes	88	159	117	113	131	162
Sraffa	1	2	1	0	0	2
Adam Smith	57	107	57	44	67	77
Ludwig Erhard	199	218	142	109	102	177

Table 3: Weight of Marx in respect to other economists quoted in articles of *La Repubblica, Corriere della Sera* and *Frankfurter Allgemeine Zeitung* in 2008-2013

Quoted economist	2008	2009	2010	2011	2012	2013
Corriere della Sera						
Marx	52%	56.7%	53.9%	46.4%	42.3%	38.7%
Einaudi	18.5%	11.2%	17.2%	30.8%	33.1%	35.7%
Keynes	20%	23.2%	17.2%	15.9%	14.2%	15.8%
La Repubblica						
Marx	64.2%	60.6%	68.6%	58.6%	51.9%	53.7%
Keynes	16.7%	20%	13%	17.8%	21.4%	18.4%
Einaudi	10.4%	14.5%	14%	21.3%	17.2%	18.9%
Frankfurter Allgemeine Zeitung						
Marx	58.4%	48%	57.1%	60.3%	60.2%	52.5%
Erhard	23.9%	23.3%	19.1%	16.2%	13.5%	20%
Keynes	10.6%	17%	15.8%	16.8%	17.3%	18.3%

Graph 1: Number of articles quoting relevant economists in the *Frankfurter Allgemeine Zeitung* during the years of crisis

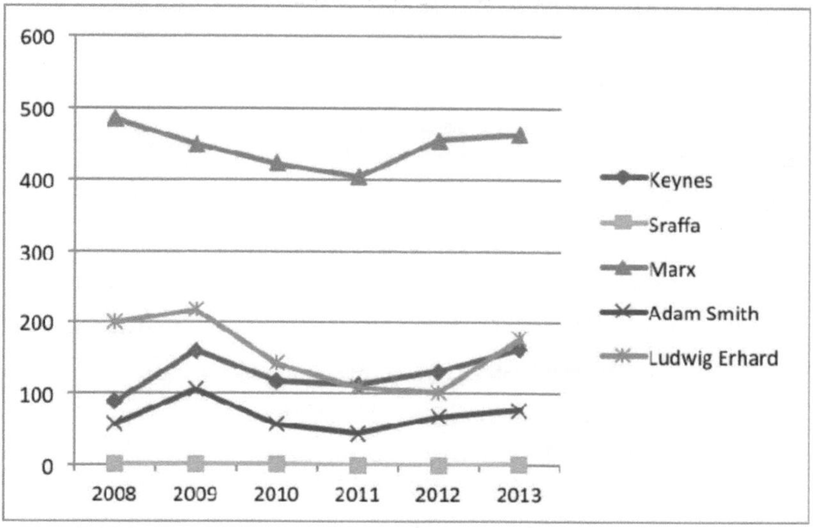

Graph 2: Number of articles quoting relevant economists in *La Repubblica* during the years of crisis

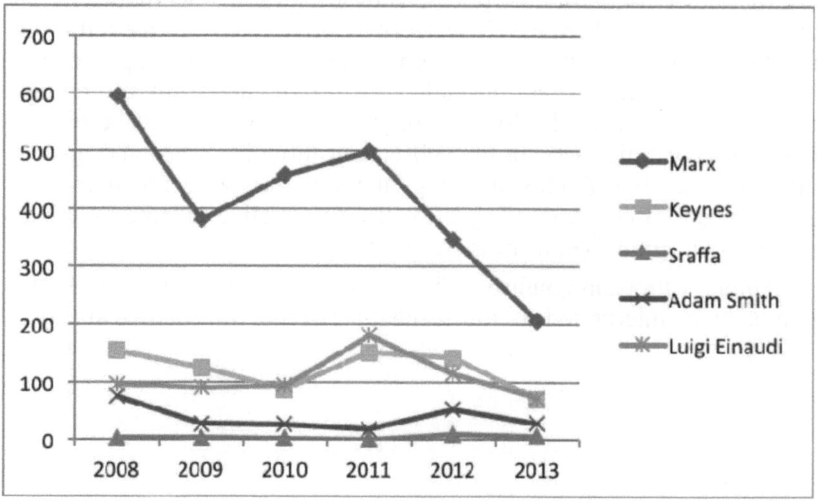

Graph 3: Number of articles quoting relevant economists in the *Corriere della Sera* during the years of crisis

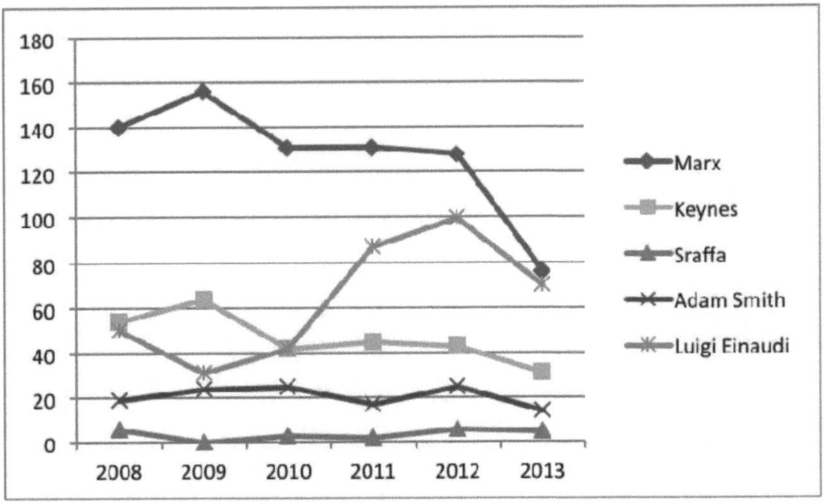

2. From Culture to Theory: Economics in Time of Crisis

From 2008 onward, obviously, the economic question occupying the attention of German and Italian public opinion has been the understanding of the economic crisis. Crises usually represent a period of creative destruction not only for enterprises, as in Joseph Alois Schumpeter[17], but also for economic theories. Crises defy theories centered on equilibrium or growth, fostering alternative interpretations. Past theories, particularly those blaming the inherent unstable structure of capitalism, are brought back to life, often in the form of prejudicial knowledge to be used to interpret economic facts. In the subsequent turmoil of past and present, orthodox and unorthodox thinking, the intrinsic scientific dignity of economics is often menaced by the call for normative judgments, ethical and religious guidance, institutional primacy.

Among European countries, the external financial crisis of 2008 was immediately interpreted as the result of extreme speculative practices

[17] J. A. SCHUMPETER, *Capitalism, Socialism and Democracy*, London, Routledge, 1994, 82-3.

in the US[18]: Gatsby's green light having bewitched America again[19]. After all the financial sector has historically been the first and preferred scapegoat on which the miseries of economic crises were blamed[20], and bankers always had, in the imagination of the public, a eviler reputation than entrepreneurs: an easy target of prejudice. The crisis of the new millennium was no exception. "The crisis has a name and surname: banks and rating agencies" titled *La Repubblica*[21], while the at the time Italian minister for the economy, Giulio Tremonti, even called entrepreneurs and labor unions to watch over banks and their practices[22]. The devil of speculation had been evoked around the ultimate bonfire of vanities[23] and economists had to confront it. Liberalists couldn't do otherwise than defend the freedom of markets. Francesco Giavazzi, remarking on the presumed speculation on oil prices in 2008, immediately recalled how Alessandro Manzoni described in his *I Promessi Sposi* the terrible famine of 1628-29 and the consequent human chase on imaginary speculators[24]. History seemed to continuously repeat itself, and all the while people found it easier to mistake the scarcity of goods as the cause of a crisis and not as a consequence. Likely voices those of Angelo Panebianco and Piero Ostellino[25], all writing on *Corriere della Sera*.

The majority of economists, though, called for some form of regulation in financial markets. As one of the earliest, Marcello de Cecco, on the columns of *La Repubblica*, blamed American monetary policies and absence of controls for the collapse of the US economy[26]. The bailout of Freddie Mac and Fannie Mae and the spectacular maneuver of 700

---

18 J. Stiglitz, "La follia dei mercati e il sonno delle autorità", *La Repubblica*, May 6 2008; V. Zucconi, "L'America e il falso mito dell'identità tra due libertà", *La Repubblica*, May 25 2008; G. Rossi, "Così il supercapitalismo uccide la democrazia", *La Repubblica*, May 30 2008; M. Calabresi, "La finanza americana tra intrighi ed eccessi", *La Repubblica*, February 20 2009; L. Villari, "Quando la finanza divora l'economia", *La Repubblica*, June 6 2009; S. Bragantini, "Se la finanza (incontrollata) scommette contro gli Stati", *Corriere della Sera*, July 8 2011.

19 F. Rampini, "L'America della crisi e lo specchio buio del '29", *La Repubblica*, January 25 2009.

20 S. Bocconi, "'Speculazione peste del secolo'. Duello Tremonti-Guido Rossi", *Corriere della Sera*, July 15 2008.

21 A. Bonafede, "La crisi ha nome e cognome: banche e società di rating", *La Repubblica*, December 15 2008.

22 C. Lopapa, "Sindacati e aziende vigileranno sulle banche", *La Repubblica*, December 11 2008.

23 M. Giannini, "Capitalismo al gran falò delle vanità", *La Repubblica*, June 30 2008.

24 F. Giavazzi, "La vera origine della crisi. Il nuovo shock petrolifero", *Corriere della Sera*, July 4 2008.

25 P. Ostellino, "Il capitalismo e la politica", *Corriere della Sera*, September 19 2008.

26 M. de Cecco, "Il mondo affondato dal dollaro", *La Repubblica*, March 10 2008.

billion dollars in September 2008 to save the American financial sector where then greeted as "The revenge of Keynes"[27]. Supply-side economic policy had been abruptly substituted by measures that to Italian observers easily recalled the experience of IRI[28]. Ugo Marani on *La Repubblica* even glorified the economic crisis as the cause for the anti-liberal change in American economic policy[29].

Angela Merkel herself, at the World Economic Forum at Davos, January 2009, boasted of the virtues of extending the German ordo-liberal model to Europe, with guidelines to dampen the excesses of speculation, comparing them to the catastrophic consequences of the absence of regulation in Anglo-Saxon capitalism. Merkel even invoked the creation of a UN Economic Council to lay down a charter for a global economic order and transpose the German model to the entire world economy[30]. In Italy, on the columns of *La Repubblica*, the speech was praised as "The revenge of Europe" over liberalist America[31].

The recurring desire for revenge, shown by the Italian left-wing newspaper, in the name of Keynes or a European way to the regulation of the economy, is a telltale sign of the frustration of interventionists over the past diffusion of liberalist theories and policies at national and international level[32]. "Yes. This is the moment to defend the market from all who demonize it and want to get rid of it. – Tommaso Padoa Schioppa observed in an interview to *La Repubblica* – But a market that does not dominate political economy. Because the market is not a value, nor an idol to be sacrificed to; the market is a useful instrument if regulated and used well"[33]. Sergio Bocconi, on *Corriere della Sera*, relating the works of a congress titled: "Liberals taking capitalism on trial", likewise contended that capitalism could be absolved from all charges, but needed new rules[34].

Data collected on the three analyzed newspapers confirm that, in this early phase, the crisis was generally perceived as a financial disaster

27 V. Zucconi, "La rivincita di Keynes", *La Repubblica*, September 20 2008.

28 A. Zampaglione, "Finanza americana, i giorni dell'Iri", *La Repubblica*, September 22 2008.

29 U. Marani, "Le virtù della spesa pubblica", *La Repubblica*, October 16 2008.

30 C. Dougherty, "Merkel, at Davos, calls for a global economic charter", *The New York Times*, January 30 2009.

31 F. Rampini, "La rivincita Europea", *La Repubblica*, January 31 2009.

32 G. Rossi, "Come combattere il liberismo globale", *La Repubblica*, January 10 2008.

33 M. Giannini, "Padoa-Schioppa: 'Ora si muova l'UE. Bisogna difendere il libero mercato'", *La Repubblica*, October 6 2008.

34 S. Bocconi, "Processo al capitalismo: assolto, ma ora nuove regole", *Corriere della Sera*, December 1 2009.

due to a lack of control over speculation (Tab. 1). The exact phrase "financial crisis" is most frequently quoted in 2008 in all newspapers and subsequently steadily declines. The same evolution is shown by the number of articles mentioning "capitalism" and "crisis" together (Graphs 4-6). At the time, the historian and linguist Massimo Arcangeli even counted, for *La Repubblica*, the thirteen times that the Italian President, Giorgio Napolitano, quoted the word "crisis" – financial, global or profound – in his new year's address of 2009, a frequency never reached before, in all the years the speech had been held[35].

As in the wake of 1929, the spectacular failing of US liberalism provoked in all newspapers a lively debate over the possible end of capitalism[36]. "Statalism" and "liberalism" confronted with a virulence unseen in previous or later years (Tab. 1). Marx, as seen, held the center of the stage. Articles referring to the German economist peaked in 2008 on *La Repubblica* and *Frankfurter Allgemeine Zeitung*, in 2009 on *Corriere della Sera.* Keynes showed a similar pattern on Italian newspapers, with a maximum of quotations in 2008 on *La Repubblica* and in 2009 on *Corriere della Sera.* Germany had its own ordo-liberal bias and instead of Keynes it was Erhard that reached the highest number of citations in 2008 and 2009. All possible alternatives to capitalism, or, as Padoa Schioppa suggests because better to define, to free market economy[37], were at some point proposed to discussion: statalism, ordo-liberalism, keynesianism and even, if rarely, protectionism[38].

If Marx, Keynes, Erhard and List would not be enough, also the Pope readily attacked the deteriorating market economy. "Money vanishes, only God's word is eternal" titled *La Repubblica* in 2008, citing the head of the catholic church[39]. A call for the return to more values that continued

---

35 M. Arcangeli, "Un 'linguaggio della verità' dominato dalla parola 'crisi'", *La Repubblica*, January 1 2009.

36 For example Eugenio Scalfari, director of *La Repubblica*, cited the economists Joseph Stiglitz and Luigi Einaudi, forecasting the end of a capitalism based on consumption (E. Scalfari, "Campane d'allarme e trombe stonate", *La Repubblica*, December 7 2008). Other examples are G. Ruffolo, "Le promesse tradite", *La Repubblica*, November 24 2011; M. Giannini, "La fine della civiltà capitalista", *La Repubblica*, February 27 2012. A critical appraisal of such early interpretations of the economic crisis can be read in W. Weimer, "Schuld an der Krise ist der Supernanny-Staat", *Handelsblatt*, February 22 2013.

37 M. Giannini, "Padoa-Schioppa: 'Ora si muova l'Ue. Bisogna difendere il libero mercato'", *La Repubblica*, October 6 2008.

38 "Smith oder List: Wer gewinnt? Lists 'Nationales System' in neuer Auflage", *Frankfurter Allgemeine Zeitung*, December 15 2008; V. Zucconi, "Protezionismo. Quando la paura fa alzare le barriere", *La Repubblica*, February 10 2009.

39 "Mutui, Papa: 'I soldi scompaiono; solo la parola di Dio è solida'", *La Repubblica*, October 6 2008.

for all the duration of the crisis[40]. The same can be said for the laical demand for more ethics in the economy. *Frankfurter Allgemeine Zeitung* openly denounced the crisis of an economy without values in New Year's Eve 2008[41], while *La Repubblica* hosted in 2009 many articles pleading for a return to morals, among them those by Jean-Paul Fitoussi and Giorgio Ruffolo[42]. In the same year, on the columns of *Corriere della Sera* Antonio Marzano discussed at length about the ethical crisis of the economy[43].

With the subprime crisis, the adventure of capitalism seemed so at its end[44], at least in its liberalist form, as institutions reclaimed their role in the economy[45]. Not everyone agreed. In Germany Werner Plumpe maintained that "were a functioning market economy existed, capitalism transformed 'egoism' into society's interest". "Only someone ignoring Europe's historical past – concluded Plumpe – could affirm the contrary"[46]. The already quoted Italian liberalists repeatedly warned that speculation was the result of erroneous state policies, not absence of regulation, and *Corriere della Sera* remained detached toward the new economic order advocated by the German chancellor at Davos at the beginning of 2009[47]. German newspapers, too, were doubtful of the Chancellor's idea, as the forecasts for the world economy continuously worsened[48].

---

40 "Il Papa: 'La crisi alimentare è causata dalla speculazione'", *La Repubblica*, December 11 2008; G. G. Vecchi, "Etica e crisi. L'appello del Papa ai politici", *Corriere della Sera*, January 13 2009; *Id.*, "Giustizia sociale e rendite tassate. La ricetta anticrisi del Vaticano", *Corriere della Sera*, October 25 2011; M. Ventura, "Primato della Politica sulla Finanza. La visione economica del Vaticano", *Corriere della Sera*, November 4 2011; E. Livini, "Il Papa contro la finanza selvaggia: 'Il denaro serve, non governa'", *La Repubblica*, November 27 2013; R. Hank, "Ethik in der Wirtschaft. Kirchen wettern gegen Gier und Maßlosigkeit auf den Finanzmärkten", *Frankfurter Allgemeine Zeitung*, February 22 2014.

41 "Wertlose Ökonomie Die Krise", *Frankfurter Allgemeine Zeitung*, December 31 2008.

42 J.-P. Fitoussi, "Se torna l'etica nel capitalismo", *La Repubblica*, February 23 2009; G. Ruffolo, "L'economia e il ritorno alla morale", *La Repubblica*, March 9 2009.

43 A. Marzano, "La crisi etica dell'economia", *Corriere della Sera*, July 8 2009.

44 F.-X. Kaufmann, "'Der Kapitalismus ist ein großes Abenteuer'. Wehe, wenn es schiefgeht!", *Frankfurter Allgemeine Sonntagszeitung*, December 21 2008.

45 D. Taino, "Le istituzioni, non la geografia creano la fortuna delle nazioni", *Corriere della Sera*, June 4 2013.

46 W. Plumpe, "Eigennutz macht alle reich", *Frankfurter Allgemeine Zeitung*, December 7 2009.

47 D. Taino, "Per fermare la crisi la Merkel vuole un'Onu dell'economia", *Corriere della Sera*, January 31 2009.

48 J. Ward, "The World from Berlin: 'Davos Health Spas Won't Heal the Global Economy'", *Spiegel Online International*, February 2 2009.

The subsequent profound crisis of the Mediterranean countries inside the European Union[49], the "Greek Tragedy"[50], could not so easily be attributed to extra-UE countries or some devilish speculative monster. The resurgence of the pejorative acronym PIGS, in 2010[51], clearly indicated that the once external shock had become an internal issue of the European Union.

Europe's newspapers ratify how, in 2010, the attention of the public in economic matters had shifted from the US, speculation and finance, toward Europe and its institutional construction (Tab. 1). In the *Frankfurter Allgemeine Zeitung*, in the course of 2009, the primacy of citations switches from "financial crisis" to "European Union" and the couple "Europe" and "crisis" and "Monetary Union" start a climb that will peak in 2012 (Graph 4). In Italy's newspapers the evolution of quotations is similar, ignoring political coloring. The only difference toward Germany is the primacy of the pair "Europe" and "crisis" over "European Union" and "Monetary Union" (Graphs 5-6). A confirmation that in Italy, in respect to Germany, Europe was perceived much more in relation to the hardships of a deepening crisis than in itself. Otherwise the tendency of the citations is the same, growing from 2009 to 2012.

While at this point European media started the afore mentioned blaming game[52], recurring to whatever old prejudices could be useful to ignite public opinion, many German and Italian economists begun charging the institutional construction of the Monetary Union and of the Economic Union for those continued imbalances that had transformed the American financial crisis into a European affair of gigantic proportions[53]. Bertram Schefold, writing on *Frankfurter Allgemeine Zeitung* in 2011[54], clearly unveiled that the greatest obstacle on the way of Europe toward

---

49 "Banken zittern mit den schwachen Euro-Staaten", *Frankfurter Allgemeine Zeitung*, February 5 2010.

50 E. Livini, "Tragedia Greca", *La Repubblica*, February 12 2009.

51 D. Gros, "Greek burdens ensure some Pigs won't fly", *Financial Times*, January 28 2010.

52 To quote just a few examples on both sides: R. Hank, W. von Petersdorff, "Die Deutschen werden gepiesackt", *Frankfurter Allgemeine Zeitung*, February 28 2010; "Angriff auf die deutschen Steuerzahler", *Handelsblatt*, June 22 2012; S. Montefiori, "'Merkel egoista'. Vacilla l'asse tra Parigi e Berlino", *Corriere della Sera*, April 28 2013; F. Debenedetti, "Fare la morale non cancella i debiti. L'Europa si cura con il realismo", *Corriere della Sera*, July 29 2013.

53 Some economists, like Paul Krugman and Lorenzo Bini Smaghi had begun early to question the positive effects of the Monetary Union (see F. Fubini, "Dieci anni di euro: il costo di un successo", *Corriere della Sera*, September 14 2008; P. Krugman, "La recessione e le colpe della Merkel", *La Repubblica*, December 16 2008).

54 B. Schefold, "Die Engländer sind schuld", *Frankfurter Allgemeine Zeitung*, November 25 2011.

integration was the discrepancy between the European Union, including Great Britain, and the Monetary Union, excluding it. This hiatus impeded to use EU's representative institutions to manage a coordinated fiscal policy that could constitute the missing fundament for the euro.

In his essay in the present volume, Charles B. Blankart, instead, clarifies, that one of the major causes of the economic crisis has been building a common currency among countries with different fiscal systems: a dangerous mixture of oil and vinegar. While Germany's system is based on the economic and hence political responsibility of the institutions spending the taxpayers' money, the French system, as the Italian one, centralizes public income and at the same time decentralizes public expenses. The absence of economic responsibility, in these cases, constrains the central state to guarantee the debts of local institutions. Incentives implied by such fiscal system create in the long run a deficit bomb, that can be defused only recurring to inflationary monetary policy or devaluation of the currency. At present, every partner state expects Europe to replicate its own fiscal system at Union level, generating a decisional impasse that impedes the needed establishment of a common European fiscal policy.

Clearly the hypothesis underlying these interpretations of the European debt crisis is that, given no such institutional constraints, the crisis would have had a much lesser impact, because the inherent equilibrating forces of markets or the intervention of the single states would have quickly resolved the question. In such a view, be it based on Keynesian or liberalist assumptions, a national state with its economic construction and its monetary and fiscal sovereignty represents the ideal framework for a well-functioning market economy and also the ideal regulating agency if a market economy does not function so well. The only efficient way to govern the Union, then, would be to replicate the institutional framework of the national state at European level[55]. An idea that had commonly circulated among economists during the advent of the euro. Padoa Schioppa, for example, in the afore mentioned interview in 2008 reaffirmed: "I warned at the beginning of the Euro, against the perils of a 'money without a State'. It is clear that more European State was necessary, not less European money: without the euro, Europe today would experience a catastrophe"[56].

---

55 J. Habermas, P. Bofinger, J. Nida-Ruemelin, "Il passo decisivo per salvare l'Europa", *La Repubblica*, August 4 2012; G. Ruffolo, S. Sylos Labini, "Una federazione contro la crisi", *La Repubblica*, October 5 2012; S. Montefiori, "Lo sconforto di Delors: 'Avremmo fatto meglio a lasciare fuori gli inglesi'", *Corriere della Sera*, November 25 2012; S. Ravaschio, "Dalla crisi la spinta verso un'Europa che non sia solo euro", *Corriere della Sera*, January 20 2013; A. Carioti, "Europeismo rivoluzionario", *Corriere della Sera*, February 8 2013.

56 M. Giannini, "Padoa-Schioppa: 'Ora si muova l'Ue. Bisogna difendere il libero

Aside from breaking up the Monetary Union[57], possible solutions of the crisis could so be to transfer fiscal sovereignty at European level, to empower the democratically elected European Parliament with real legislative and governing power, or similar measures[58]. The imbalances and the restructuring of production along comparative advantages, caused by different factor endowments and factor prices in European regions, could then be overcome by direct transfers and development policies, as would easily be done inside a single national body. What could not be achieved through interaction and cooperation among national states, having different institutional settings and different economic and political philosophy of reference[59], could so be obtained by transferring power to a supra-national body and its bureaucracy, legitimized by democratic election.

A different way to look at the problem was to consider the Monetary Union and/or the European Union in the light of game theories, as Giacomo Vaciago suggested in 2012 on the journal *Il Mulino*[60]. Europe is so seen as a constraining environment with good guys watching over bad guys, and rules inciting the spendthrift countries to cheat, while making parsimonious countries incapable to accept the partner's bankruptcy. A continuously worsening scenario, leading the Union to an inevitable bad end. Similar to this, with a more optimistic outcome, the idea that the Monetary Union created a competitive arena for differing institutional settings, so that virtuous states would emerge and vicious ones would be constrained by disastrous economic results to adopt better institutions. An interpretation proposed in the present volume by Gerhard Wegner. Such theory, however, presumes a positivistic attitude according to which the evolutionary selection of national institutions would automatically lead to the rise of the best one: a matter of faith.

Both these last interpretations, moreover, equate European States to individuals, playing a game or competing in a neoclassical environment. But there is more to a state than a community of private interests as

---

mercato'", *La Repubblica*, October 6 2008. See also T. Padoa Schioppa, *Regulating finance. Balancing freedom and risk*, Oxford-New York, Oxford University Press, 2004.

57 "Die Griechen und der Euro 'Ein Austritt wäre langfristig besser'", *Frankfurter Allgemeine Zeitung*, October 12 2010.

58 J. Habermas, "Un'altra Europa è possibile quattro mosse per costruirla", *La Repubblica*, February 7 2014.

59 S. Romano, "Le dimensioni dell'UE troppi cuochi in cucina", *Corriere della Sera*, December 21 2011; A. Tajani, "L'unità di intenti che serve all'Europa", *Corriere della Sera*, November 21 2012; E. Galli Della Loggia, "Un'antica diversità. Europa tedesca e mediterranea", *Corriere della Sera*, July 25 2012.

60 G. Vaciago, "A che gioco giochiamo?", *Il Mulino*, October 23 2012.

the *Frankfurter Allgemeine Zeitung* underlined in 2010, remembering Wilhelm Röpke, one of the founding fathers of the social market economy[61], and Europe needed more than just additional bureaucracy, as Alberto Quadrio Curzio wrote on *Corriere della Sera* in the same year[62]. Opposed to such liberal and ordo-liberal views were the renewed calls for Keynesian policies, this time not in contrast to ruinous American deregulation as in the beginning of the crisis, but with the aim of reducing the deflationary effects of Europe's recession[63]. Newspapers testimony how, between 2010 and 2012, the number of articles quoting Keynes form a peak, with no difference in regard to nationality or political stance of the newspaper considered (Graphs 1-3). The same can be said for citations of Adam Smith[64], in Italy also of Luigi Einaudi, having a relative maximum in 2011.

As the American financial crisis had called for a lively discussion on capitalism, the ensuing European recession and its disastrous consequences on the debt/GDP ratio of Mediterranean countries[65] sparked a profound debate opposing Keynesianism to liberalism not only in reference to European policies but also to national traditions of thought and national economic policies. Particularly in 2011 and the beginning of 2012, during the brief government led by the liberal economist Mario Monti, *Corriere della Sera* came so to discuss at length Italian liberalism, while *La Repubblica* championed with polemical vigor the opposite Keynesian view.

Writing on *Corriere della Sera* in 2011, two weeks before Monti's assignment, Giuseppe Galasso, renowned historian, revived the historical debate between Benedetto Croce and Luigi Einaudi distinguishing *liberalismo* and *liberismo*, liberalism as a political philosophy the first, liberalism in the economy the second[66]. A debate, not incidentally, raging when the effects of the crash of '29 had reached Italy. While Croce affirmed that liberalism as an end could be achieved, under given circumstances, even through the means of an illiberal economic policy, Einaudi harshly

61 M. Spieker, "Der Staat ist mehr als eine Aktiengesellschaft", *Frankfurter Allgemeine Zeitung*, December 23 2010.

62 A. Quadrio Curzio, "All'economia dell'Europa servono rigore e crescita, non burocrazia", *Corriere della Sera*, October 7 2010.

63 A. Baccaro, "Draghi: lavoro e debito, i nuovi problemi all'orizzonte", *Corriere della Sera*, October 23 2009.

64 M. Gaggi, "La 'mano invisibile' di Adam Smith, precettore del mercato. Il filosofo conteso tra destra e progressisti", *Corriere della Sera*, December 15 2010.

65 M. Ferraris, "L'illusione economica. Come lo spread è diventato il reale", *La Repubblica*, January 12 2013.

66 G. Galasso, "Le ragioni del liberalismo alle radici dell'Occidente", *Corriere della Sera*, November 2 2011.

dissented, sustaining the non-neutrality of means like economic policy toward the chosen end of liberty. Easy comparisons to the situation of Italy in 2011 were absolutely not coincidental. Massimo L. Salvadori, likewise a famed historian, of left wing sympathies, analyzed, in a book reviewed by Paolo Mieli only days after Monti's assignment[67], the biggest failure of Italian liberalism: the incapacity to generate a real democratic alternation of governments. Reference could obviously be made to the extraordinary situation of Monti's "technical" prime ministry, delaying the possible democratic election of a political government led by the left.

The greatest contradiction of Italian liberalism, though, concluded Ernesto Galli della Loggia in 2012[68], again on *Corriere della Sera*, had been its obstinate refusal of economic liberalism, in the wake of Croce's lesson. None of the Italian generations of liberals since Unity in 1861 had ever really believed in free trade and its normative expressions, except for a bunch of isolated academics. According to the analysis of *Corriere della Sera*, then, the recession needed a liberal solution like it had never really been adopted in Italy and was hoped for by the newly assigned Prime Minister Monti. Giuseppe Bedeschi[69] and Alberto Alesina[70], in 2011 and 2012, conscious of the eumenical support needed by Monti from right- and left-oriented parliamentarians, even went so far as to propose, through the columns of the newspaper, such extreme liberal agenda to Italian left-wing parties. Answers were trenchant[71]. Although accused of offering no solution to the contemporary economic crisis[72], left wing parties stuck to their Keynesian credo, while social democratic Giorgio La Malfa counter proposed the German social market economy as the best solution to present hardships[73].

In the last tormented months of the government Monti in 2013, *La Repubblica* started so a campaign in favor of Keynesian policies, citing

67 P. Mieli, "Liberalismo all'italiana: l'alternanza impossibile", *Corriere della Sera*, November 29 2011.

68 E. Galli Della Loggia, "Il vestito fuori misura dei liberali italiani. La cultura liberale in Italia rimane un fantasma senza eredi", *Corriere della Sera*, December 10 2012.

69 G. Bedeschi, "Una sinistra davvero moderna deve farsi carico delle battaglie liberali", *Corriere della Sera*, October 6 2011.

70 A. Alesina, "Gli antichi pregiudizi economici della sinistra. Welfare, tasse e flessibilità: la sinistra abbatta i tabù", *Corriere della Sera*, December 13 2012.

71 G. La Malfa, "Le frontiere del liberalismo tra mercato e intervento pubblico", *Corriere della Sera*, October 16 2011; M. Mucchetti, "La strana pretesa dei liberisti Chiedere alla sinistra di fare la destra", *Corriere della Sera*, December 4 2012.

72 P. Franchi, "Le (non) terapie della sinistra europea", *Corriere della Sera*, November 4 2011.

73 G. Bedeschi, "La terza via liberale di Einaudi e Roepke", *Corriere della Sera*, May 31 2012.

the positive results of expansionary measures adopted in the United States. In January Federico Rampini titled "Europe tries the American recipe: 'Enough austerity, it's time of growth'"[74], comforted by positive economic data arriving from the other side of the Ocean. As austerity, though, remained on the agenda of the Italian government, even if by then led by the leftist Enrico Letta, in December 2013 Giorgio Ruffolo and Stefano Sylos Labini indignantly wrote: "It is time to close the season of rigor and launch a grand plan of investments in order to reverse the atrocious policy of "delay" that is driving Europe to disaster. That Germany is again responsible for Europe's tragedy is a circumstance that defies the belief according to which history cannot repeat itself"[75].

At the end of the period considered by this research, seemingly, a perfect circle had been drawn, as *La Repubblica* proposed to its readers a prejudiced image of Germany, based on the historical past of the third Reich, as a country devoted to economic imperialism. In reality the analysis of national newspapers contradicts such conclusion. The effort of *La Repubblica* to demonize Chancellor Merkel in 2013 must be considered a rather rare offshoot of a permanent electoral campaign, devoid of any general significance. It might suffice to remembered how enthusiastically *La Repubblica* celebrated in 2009 Merkel's call for a worldwide ordo-liberalism to prove it, but looking at the data on the frequency of citations, a renewal of populist nationalism in Italy can definitively be ruled out. All indicators for *La Repubblica* and *Corriere della Sera*, be they relative to articles referring to Europe, crisis, or single economists, significantly diminish in the course of 2013 (Graphs 1-6).

In effect, due to its better economic performance, Germany slowly became, in the consideration of Italians, an example to be followed[76]. The crisis, instead, was increasingly interpreted as a structural one, caused by internal problems and calling for a local solution[77]. Piero

---

74 F. Tessitore, "La miope Italia del rigore finanziario", *La Repubblica*, January 5 2013; F. Rampini, "L'Europa prova la ricetta americana: 'Basta austerity, è l'ora dello sviluppo'", *La Repubblica*, January 11 2013.

75 G. Ruffolo, S. Sylos Labini, "L'ideale che manca nell'Europa in crisi", *La Repubblica*, December 15 2013.

76 I. Angeloni, "A lezione di tedesco", *Corriere Economia*, March 29 2010; D. Di Vico, "Imbroglio liberista e modello renano", *Corriere della Sera*, September 10 2010; G. Bedeschi, "La Terza via liberale di Einaudi e Roepke", *Corriere della Sera*, May 31 2012.

77 C. Magris, "Il primato tedesco. Solidarietà, efficienza, comunità e modernità senza indulgenze pop", *Corriere della Sera*, February 13 2011; A. Alesina, "I virtuosi tedeschi non hanno colpe", *Corriere della Sera*, July 6 2011; L. Reichlin, "La malattia italiana nasce prima dell'euro", *Corriere della Sera*, May 17 2012; S. Romano, "Per la terapia della crisi non sbagliare la diagnosi", *Corriere della Sera*, May 7 2013.

Bini, in his contribution to this present volume, precisely depicts the different stances assumed by Italian economists in respect to the crisis, including this last one. Economists adhering to it describe Italy's bad performance, in comparison to other European partners and OCSE countries in general, as the result of institutional problems, regarding taxation, economic responsibility, and diffused corruption, but also of economic issues like insufficient investments, private and public, infrastructural deficiencies, collapsing productivity and scarce competition. All these questions, unresolved since the 1980s, slowly eroded Italy's competitiveness, greatly accelerating the collapse of the economy after the external shock of the American financial crisis[78]. Surely the easiest solution would be to conquer back the possibility to discretionally use the monetary policy, exiting from the Monetary Union. In the long run, however, the best answer to Italy's structural crisis would be to politically tackle the cited questions, guaranteeing the institutional environment and the functioning markets needed for a stable economic growth.

One last notation emerges from studying how Italian and German newspapers represented the economic crisis in the years 2008-2013, and it concerns Germany. In 2013, in contrast to Italy, indicators about single economists (graphs 1 and 3) and economic schools (tab. 1) increase significantly. In this case, nonetheless, the debate had less to do with the economic crisis – articles quoting crisis significantly diminish – as with Germany's role inside Europe. The renewed discussion, in fact, concerned the economic order that, in the eyes of Germans, Europe should adopt, liberal, ordo-liberal or Keynesian, and in consequence Germany's involvement in a future Union with fiscal competences. Germany so appears, in the end, to take seriously a leadership inside Europe, assuming a proposing role. A fact significantly demonstrated by the continuously growing number of articles quoting Merkel during the whole crisis (graphs 1-6). The German chancellor, notwithstanding all prejudiced, chauvinist and even sexist representations on Europe's newspapers, emerges from the analyzed troubled years as an undisputed leader, a veritable point of reference for European partners, particularly in times of crisis.

---

78 To cite just one influential example of this interpretation of the Italian crisis, see P. Ciocca, "Se la BCE aiuta i 'Paesi illiquidi'", *Sole 24 Ore*, January 25 2012; *Id.*, *Ricchi per sempre? Una storia economica d'Italia (1796-2005)*, Torino, Bollati Boringhieri, 2007.

Graph 4: Number of articles quoting relevant concepts in the *Frankfurter Allgemeine Zeitung* during the years of crisis

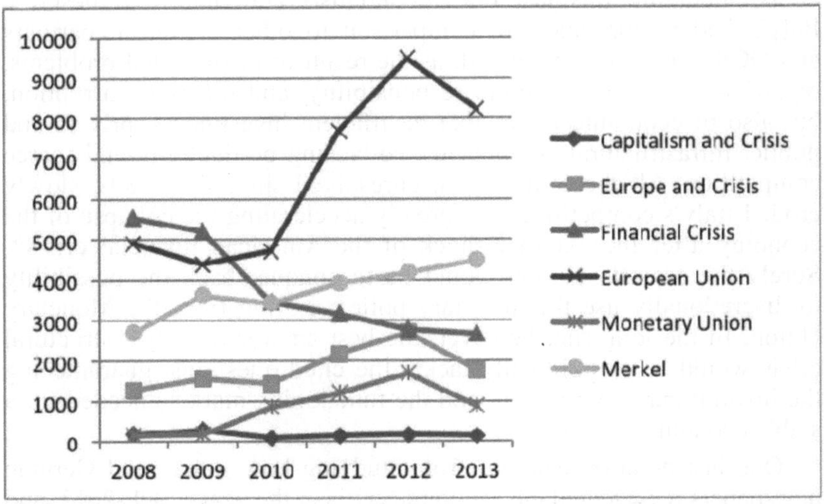

Graph 5: Number of articles quoting relevant concepts in *Corriere della Sera* during the years of crisis

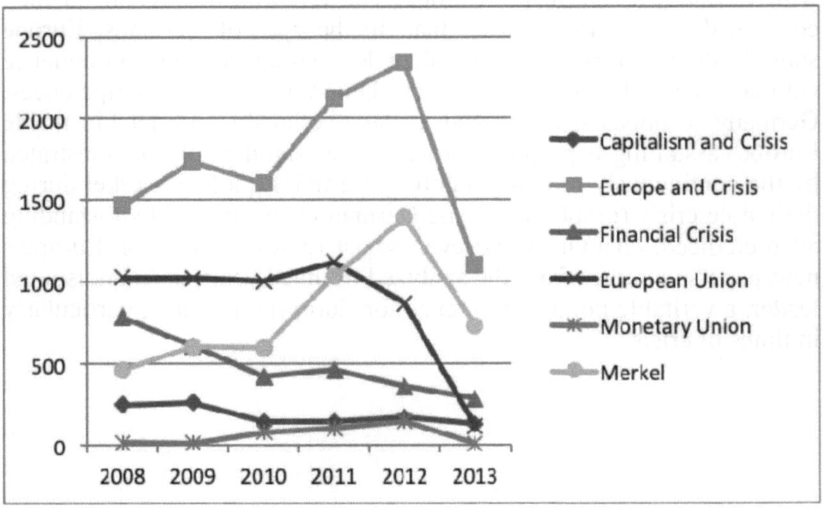

Graph 6: Number of articles quoting relevant concepts in *La Repubblica* during the years of crisis

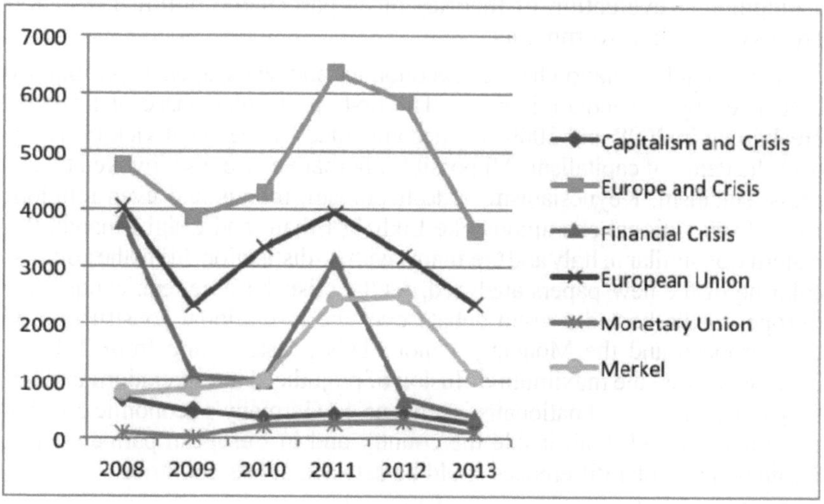

3. Conclusions

The recrudescence of nationalism in Europe, during the economic crisis started in 2008, called for a more in depth understanding of how economic theories are popularized into general culture and hence influence public opinion. Defusing the prejudices poisoning international relations between Italy and Germany, required then to bring theories back in the foreground, allowing a confrontation purified from ideological and political biases. Aspiring to contribute to this end, this volume hosts essays of German and Italian economists, historians of economic thought and political scientists. These contributions clarify how the historical past and the permanent influence of long dead economists still determine present interpretation of economic facts, allowing a better understanding of the most diffused explanations, proposed by German and Italian economists, of the causes and consequences of the crisis.

Further the research presented in this article analyzes one German and two Italian newspapers over the period 2008-2013, exemplifying how prejudiced categorizations, past economic thought, political interference and theories of contemporary economists have been mingled and filtered by media to inform public opinion about the economic crisis. The study confirms the relevance of economists long dead and of the historical past in the structuring of present categories of thought and symbolic imagining. It also unveils how economic theories are used in relation to the political cycle and to ignite nationalism. Lastly it testifies how economists interact with media and politics, as a critical voice against a judgmental evaluation of theories or as part of the political decision process, even in governments.

This complex relation between economics and newspapers is profoundly influenced by the economic cycle. The first spectacular phase of financial breakdown in 2008 and 2009 was accompanied by the usual victorious cry over the death of capitalism. All possible alternatives were so invoked by the press: statalism, Keynesianism, ordo-liberalism, morals and even religion. Apart from national champions like Ludwig Erhard and Luigi Einaudi, the pattern was similar in Italy and Germany, with no distinction due to the political coloring of the newspapers analyzed. As the crisis became real, conquering Europe, media hosted a vivid debate over the institutional construction of the European and the Monetary Union. This phase, lasting from 2010 to 2012, witnessed the maximum diffusion of prejudiced interpretations and the frequent insurgence of nationalistic tendencies. Germany's economic policies came under attack both inside the country and in European partner states. Again no particular differences could be detected across countries.

In 2013 the lessening of the debt crisis and the contemporary good economic results in the US and Germany sobered the economic debate on Italian newspapers. Italian economists concentrated on the structural crisis of the country, proposing alternative Keynesian and liberalist solutions to its loss of competitiveness. On the contrary Germany, having conquered a leading position in Europe, continued discussing at length, in the media as in political circles, the future institutional structure of Europe and the related economic order. Only at this point did indicators really differ between the two countries.

In synthesis the study uncovered more similarities than divergences between the German and Italian interpretations of the economic crisis lasting from 2008 and 2013. A common economic culture, the "Marxian" world we live in, and the widespread diffusion of the same economic thought, based on the alternative between Keynesianism and liberalism, granted a similar language and a common ground of discussion. The crisis also acted as a potent agent of diffusion for those theories, like ordo-liberalism, that had till then mainly remained rooted inside a single country. Nationalistic and chauvinistic interpretations of Europe's problems, based on prejudiced images of its historical past, were brought back to memory by the growing influence of German politics inside the European Union and mostly diffused by newspapers as part of political campaigning. By clearing the economic debate from such disturbances, though, it is possible to reconstruct a useful dialog between Italian and German economists on theoretical issues, allowing the adoption of coordinated national and European policies conductive to long term economic growth.

Germany and Europe: Between Co-operation and Suspicion

Antonio VARSORI

It is not an easy task for an historian dealing with to-day's relationship between Germany and Europe in a period which is characterized by a serious and widespread economic and social crisis, as well as by resurging nationalisms, if not jingoist tensions. Such a task, however, if we do not want to limit ourselves to simplistic explanations must take into consideration long-term processes and the influence exerted by deep historical roots.

At first it must be pointed out that Europe's history between the mid-Nineteenth century and the Second World War has been marked by a fundamental issue: Germany's emergence as the major economic, industrial and military power in the "Old Continent", closely tied to Berlin's aspiration at being recognized an hegemonic role[1]. As an almost obvious reaction the other European great powers' policies aimed at impeding the achievement by Germany of such goals in the international scenario. Besides the relevant ideological differences – there is a clear and deep difference between Imperial Germany and the Nazi régime – both the First and the Second World Wars can be interpreted as the opposition by Britain, France and Russia to Germany's economic, political and military expansionism[2]. In both cases it was the intervention by an external non-European actor, by far economically and industrially stronger, as well as the standard-bearer of more modern and global political views – the United States – to decide the fate of both world wars and to impose a new international political and economic order, in which Germany could become

---

1 On the emergence of Germany as a great power during the Nineteenth Century see for example H. BOEMHE, *L'ascesa della Germania a grande potenza. Economia e politica nella formazione del Reich 1848-1881*, Milano-Napoli, Ricciardi, 1970; on Bismarck's role see for example L. GALL, *Bismarck*, Milano, Rizzoli, 1982. The Italian translations at our disposal are quoted here.

2 There has been a well-known debate on the military leaders' role in German history and in their part in the outbreak of the First World War; in this context see G. RITTER, *I militari e la politica nella Germania moderna*, 3 Vols., Torino, Einaudi, 1967-1973 and F. FISCHER, *Assalto al potere mondiale. La Germania nella guerra 1914-1918*, Torino, Einaudi, 1965; see also G. A. CRAIG, *Il potere delle armi. Storia e politica dell'esercito prussiano 1640-1945*, Bologna, Il Mulino, 1984.

an element of stabilization instead of a factor of international instability. It is not the author's intention to adhere to a deterministic interpretation following which since the creation of the German Empire "through blood and iron", as Bismarck put it, till Hitler's aggression against Poland in September 1939, Germany was destined to develop an aggressive foreign policy, but it is impossible to deny that during the first half of the Twentieth century those elements shaped Germany's international role and that such a process, as a consequence of decades of harsh conflicts and dramatic wars, deeply influenced the image, the policies and the perceptions of both decision-makers and public opinions in all the nations that have maintained close relations with Germany since 1945[3].

The outcome of the Second World War and the tragic defeat suffered by Germany in 1945 appeared to put forever an end to the problem of Germany's aggressiveness and its hegemonic ambitions. The appearance of two world super-powers and the ensuing ideological conflict between East and West could be interpreted as phenomena which were destined to create a radical change in Germany's international position, a nation and a people which, owing to the dramatic revolution which had occurred in the international system, would be destined to be divided into two openly conflicting entities. Nevertheless, even in the post-war period, dominated by the cold war, there have been episodes both of a political and a psychological and cultural nature that, although two decades have passed since the fall of the Berlin Wall, may help us in understanding today's European attitudes towards Germany.

Although the Second World War can be regarded as a "total", global war and the outcome of the conflict was mainly decided by America's intervention, the "Big Three" were convinced that Germany had been the main enemy, not only for military, but also for ideological and political reasons. If such an assumption can be regarded almost obvious for both Britain and the Soviet Union, it could be less obvious for the United States, which in December 1941 had been involved in the war as a consequence of Japan's aggression and whose attention might mainly focus on the Pacific theatre of operations. Since December 1941, however, President Roosevelt decided that US "grand strategy" had to be based on the "Germany First" concept, that is Germany, not Japan, would be the main enemy to be defeated, so pointing out the ideological character of the war, a conflict between "evil" and "good", moreover so laying the foundations of Washington's direct involvement in Europe's future destiny[4]. It is true

3 See A. Hillgruber, *La distruzione dell'Europa. La Germania e l'epoca delle due guerre mondiali (1914-1945)*, Bologna, Il Mulino, 1991.

4 On Roosevelt and Germany see for example S. Casey, *Cautious Crusade: Franklin D. Roosevelt, American Public Opinion and the War against Nazi Germany*, Oxford,

that Germany was not subject to Japan's tragic experience to be the first and the only one nation which suffered a nuclear bombing, but of the three Axis powers only Germany was subject to a complete "debellatio", to the end of a German state and the transformation of the German soil into a sort of "res nullius", whose fate would be the outcome of the victorious powers' will. Only the German ruling élite was called to respond in so an evident manner for its moral responsibilities and guilt in front an allied tribunal, on the occasion of the Nurnberg trial to the Nazi war criminals. Germany and the German people were called to respond for the outbreak of the war and for the brutalities and the atrocities related to Hitler's war, moreover it was thought that for decades in the minds of world opinion it would be impossible both to forget and to forgive the Nazi holocaust, as well as the savage occupation policies pursued by the German authorities against civilian populations, especially in East-Central Europe and in the Soviet Union. In 1945 it appeared that such episodes would have tarnished Germany's image forever[5].

Nevertheless in a few years the Cold War appeared to soften the tragic heritage the Second World War and the Nazi régime had impressed on the German people, at least in the eyes of US decision-makers: very early in Washington the Soviet threat substituted the memories of the previous Nazi danger. In 1948 a well-known picture appears to sum up the quick evolution in the western attitude towards both Germany and the German people's future: the group of Berlin boys looking with a mixture of hope and admiration to the US cargo planes bringing vital goods to the citizens of West Berlin on the occasion of the air-lift which was destined to save the western part of the former German capital from the Soviet blockade: the former enemies were already becoming potential allies[6]. In these same moths US, British and French leaders had already decided to favor the rebirth of a new German state, definitely smaller than the Third Reich, without its Prussian core, transformed into a Federal, fully democratic republic, which would be closely integrated into a western system under the American steady and benevolent leadership. In that same period the core of German industrial and economic power – the Ruhr area – became a vital element in the Marshall Plan and the US decision-makers were

Oxford University Press, 2001. See also in general P. Calvocoressi, G. Wint, *Total War. Causes and Courses of the Second World War*, London, Pelican Books, 1974, 185-207; R. Overy, *La strada della vittoria. Perché gli Alleati hanno vinto la seconda Guerra mondiale*, Bologna, Il Mulino, 2002.

5 On Germany's, as well as the Soviet Union's responsibilities see the recent contribution by T. Snyder, *Bloodlands Europe between Hitler and Stalin*, London, Vintage Books, 2010.

6 On the relevant role played by Berlin in the Cold War see for example A. Tusa, *The Last Division. Berlin and the Wall*, London, Hodder and Stoughton, 1996.

fully aware that Germany's economy would be the cornerstone of Western Europe's economic and social reconstruction[7]. Although not without difficulties and obstacles, in a few years, through the Paris agreements signed in October 1954, the German Federal Republic, under Konrad Adenauer's able leadership, would recover its full sovereignty, with the obvious exception of West Berlin, it would possess a national army, the Bundeswehr, and it would become a full and influential member of the Atlantic Alliance[8]. Actually since 1950 West Germany had been invited to join the first European project based on the functionalist approach, the Schuman Plan, which would lead to the creation of the European Coal and Steel Community (ECSC). In 1957 West Germany was among the founding members of both the EURATOM and the EEC; moreover in collaboration with France the West German government became the most active promoter of the integration process. If the nation's partition was still an open and unresolved question – since 1961 the Berlin wall would become the most evident symbol of a division which would be destined to last "forever" – West Germany began to be perceived as the symbol of a sound and stable democratic system, as well as the most important factor in Western Europe's booming economic growth[9]. The statement following which the Federal Republic was "an economic giant and a political dwarf" might perhaps be valid till the early 1950s, but it became void of any real meaning during the following decades, not only if we take into consideration the political influence exerted in the international scenario by leading statesmen such as Adenauer, Brandt, Schmidt and, last but not least, Kohl; but Bonn's increasing international influence was confirmed by the role West Germany played both in the integration process and in the détente policy, through Brandt's and Schmidt's "Ostpolitik".

Such a positive image of West Germany as a peaceful, positive and influential actor in the western system during the Cold War era did not avoid the survival of ambiguities and "dark spots" which concur in explaining today's situation and perceptions. The Cold War and

---

7 On the reconstruction of the Western European economy see A. S. MILWARD, *The Reconstruction of Western Europe 1945-51*, London, Methuen, 1984. On the part played by Germany see C. MAIER, *The Marshall Plan and Germany*, Oxford, Oxford University Press, 1990.

8 On the relationship between the US and West Germany in the context of the European economic recovery see for example T. A. SCHWARTZ, *America's Germany. John J. McCloy and the Federal Republic of Germany*, Cambridge (Ma)-London, Harvard University Press, 1991. For a stimulating analysis of the German question since the immediate post-war period till the fall of the Berlin wall see P. GUILLEN, *La question allemande 1945 à nos jours*, Paris, Imprimerie Nationale, 1996.

9 On Konrad Adenauer's central role see H.-P. SCHWARZ, *Adenauer*, 2 Vols., Munchen, Deutsche Taschenbuch Verlag, 1994.

the emergence of two super-powers, the US and the USSR, the former a non-European nation, the latter a euro-asian reality, which regarded the whole world as the arena of their contrasts, must not make us forget that the East-West conflict, a process which characterized the international system for more than forty years, was mainly a confrontation for the control of the European continent, which had its origins in 1947/1948 on the thorny issue of Germany's fate and ended in the Europe in 1989 owing to the fall of the Berlin wall and the German reunification[10]. Only as a consequence of the fear of a nuclear holocaust and of the complex and dangerous European balance based on two conflicting military alliances the two super-powers preferred to move their conflict outside Europe. A vital factor in such a complex and delicate European balance was Germany's partition, a situation which was implicitly accepted by both the US and the Soviet Union since the Geneva summit conference held in July 1955 and would be sanctioned with the building-up of the Berlin Wall in August 1961. It is of much significance that the Kennedy administration did not react, with the exception of some vague and ineffective condemnations, to the decision taken by Moscow and Pankow. Only a few weeks before the building up of the Wall the influential US Senator Fulbright had openly stated that he did not understand the reason why the Soviets did not impede the flow of refugees towards West Berlin through closing the accesses to the western zones of the former German capital[11]. On this aspect of the European balance the US and the Soviet Union shared a similar attitude: in order to avoid a nuclear war Germany had to be divided. The potential danger inherent in a German unified state had been implicitly recognized also in the context of the Atlantic Alliance, it suffices to remember here the well-known definition of NATO's main goal by the Alliance's first General Secretary, who stated that the Atlantic Pact had been created in order to have "the Americans in, the Russians out, and the Germans down". Moreover it is impossible to forget the lasting and heated debate on West Germany being recognized the role of a nuclear power and the fears about such a possibility which shaped the attitude of most US political and military leaders, perhaps with the exception of General Lauris Norstad. If the concern about West Germany's role as a nuclear power influenced the attitude of most US decision-makers, at least till the late 1960s when Brandt complied with the non-proliferation treaty, Western European's fears about West Germany's international role were, if possible, even stronger and they were not limited to the

10 F. Romero, *Storia della guerra fredda. L'ultimo conflitto per l'Europa*, Torino, Einaudi, 2009.

11 See for example F. Kempe, *Berlin 1961. Kennedy, Khrushchev, and the Most Dangerous Place on Earth*, New York, Berkley Books, 2011.

military context[12]. Only the worsening of the Cold War contrasts and its implications of domestic nature convinced the French leaders in 1948 to accept the creation of a West German state, although at that time it was characterized by a sort of "limited sovereignty". Till the Moscow Four Foreign Ministers Conference held in March/April 1947 the French authorities dreamt of a special agreement with Moscow which could envisage the end of the German unity and the creation of several German states[13]. Even Schuman and Monnet, the founding fathers of the European integration and the authors of the French-German rapprochement, hoped that the supranational European construction would offer to France the opportunity to achieve West Europe's leadership and to maintain the control over West Germany's economic and political recovery[14]. If we take into consideration Britain's position it may suffice to quote the secret memorandum which in 1952 Harold Macmillan, at that time an influential member of the Conservative Churchill cabinet and a future Prime Minister, circulated among his colleagues; in this document he openly stated his fears about the ECSC and the plan for a European Defense Community, which, in his opinion, if created, would lead to an economic and political German hegemony on the Western half of the continent, so creating the situation which Britain had firmly opposed in 1914 and in 1939. Even in the mid-1950s in the major Western European capitals there was a widespread concern about the possibility that West Germany could work out a compromise with Moscow through which Germany would be reunited and become a neutral state. Besides such a compromise everybody feared the possibility of a renewed Rapallo agreement and the partition of continental Europe into two spheres of influence, a German one and a Russian one. De Gaulle's policy that aimed at the creation of a French-German couple and appeared to be sanctioned on the occasion of the signature of the Elysée treaty in January 1963, was launched as a consequence of the failed attempt by de Gaulle in the immediate previous years to create a three-power directorate – the US, Britain and France – in the Atlantic Alliance, but such a solution would mark West Germany's minor role in comparison not only with the two Anglo-Saxon powers, but also, and above all, with France. When between 1962 and 1963 General

---

12 On the nuclear issue and on the Federal Republic's position see B. Heuser, *Nuclear Mentalities? Strategies and Beliefs in Britain, France and the FRG*, Basingstoke, Macmillan, 1997; as well as *Id.*, *NATO, Britain, France and the FRG. Nuclear Strategies and Forces for Europe, 1949-2000*, Basingstoke, Macmillan, 1997.

13 On France's early policy towards the German question see C. Buffet, *Mourir pour Berlin. La France et l'Allemagne 1945-1949*, Paris, Armand Colin, 1991.

14 On Monnet's and Schuman's position see G. Bossuat, A. Wilkens (eds.), *Jean Monnet, l'Europe et les chemins de la paix*, Paris, Publications de la Sorbonne, 1999; R. Poidevin, *Robert Schumann homme d'état*, Paris, Imprimerie Nationale, 1986.

de Gaulle began to pin his hopes on a French-German rapprochement, he also aimed at confirming France's political and military leadership, as well as the possibility to exert some control on West Germany's recovery of a leading international role. In 1963 while Adenauer hoped that de Gaulle could favor Bonn's nuclear ambitions, the French General opined that West Germany could substitute NATO's nuclear umbrella with the atomic guarantee of the future French "force de frappe"[15].

The undeclared concerns about Germany were not limited to political élites but they deeply affected public opinions too. The memoirs of the Second World War were too near to wipe out in a few years the deep rooted suspicions about the German people and their "obvious" aggressive tendencies. Such feelings can explain the success, which went by far beyond the Communist rank and file, of the peace campaigns developed in France and in Italy against the EDC and the creation of a European Army; those campaigns were based on the need to impede the creation of a new "Wehrmacht" and the possibility to see once again German soldiers in France and in Italy, although as a part of a European integrated army[16]. If we focus our attention on the Italian case, it would be possible to point out the hostility towards Adenauer which characterized most of the leading politicians of the center-left in the early 1960s: the West German Chancellors was perceived as a conservative, if not a reactionary, and warmongering leader, a "Cold Warrior" who was hostile to both the "turn to the left" in Italy and to the Détente process. Such a negative attitude appeared to be confirmed by the suspicions about the sympathetic feelings nurtured by the Bavarian CSU towards the South Tyrolese secessionist groups, as well as the fears about the supposed militarist ambitions by the CSU leader Franz-Josef Strauss. On the other hand it was not easy to forget the negative image of Germany as occupying power and supporter of the Fascist régime between 1943 and 1945[17]. Once again the Italian attitude, which will be dealt with in detail

15 On Gaullist France's policy towards West Germany see J. Binoche, *De Gaulle et les allemands*, Bruxelles, Complexe, 1990; G.-H. Soutou, *L'alliance incertaine. Les rapports politico-stratégiques franco-allemands 1954-1996*, Paris, Fayard, 1996; C. Defrance, U. Pfeil (eds.), *La France, l'Allemagne et le traité de l'Elysée*, Paris, CNRS Editions, 2012.

16 R. Brunori, I partigiani della Pace e la CED: il caso italiano (1950-1954), *Storia delle relazioni internazionali*, 2, 1992.

17 See in particular F. Niglia, *Fattore Bonn. La diplomazia italiana e la Germania di Adenauer (1945-1963)*, Pisa, Le Lettere, 2010 and the recent special issue of the journal *Res Publica*, (January-April 2013), edited by T. Di Maio. For an analysis of a general character of the relations between Italy and Germany see M. Gehler, M. Guiotto (eds.), *Italian Oesterreich unde die Bundesrepublik Deutschland in Europa*, Wien, Boehlau, 2012. For an interesting analysis of the role played by stereotypes in the mutual relations and understanding between Italians and Germans see D. Brogelli Hafer, C.

by Federico Niglia, is an interesting case study, especially if we take into consideration the image of the "bad German" to be opposed to the image of the "good Italian", an image which was created by both Italian politicians and intellectuals since the immediate postwar period and developed deep roots in both political milieu and the public opinion[18]. The recurrent negative image of Germany and its potential threat marked the feelings of several public opinions in the European continent; in Britain, for example, England's victory over West Germany on the occasion of the World football championship in 1966 had psychological implications which went beyond the one of a mere football match[19]. The European press carefully watched every episode which could be regarded as the rebirth of Nazi tendencies in the German society and political milieu. Till the late 1960s war films, especially the ones produced in the US or in Britain, went on proposing episodes from the Second World War which opposed the "good", that is the Anglo-American allies, to the "evil", Germany, although those cinematographic products usually draw a line between on one hand the "good German guys" belonging to the regular Army and on the other hand the "bad guys" of the SS and the Gestapo[20]. Moreover it is not possible to forget the spy fiction which very often proposed the fight of courageous agents against the revival of dangerous resurgent Nazi movements. One of the most interesting case is perhaps the well-known novel "The Odessa File" written in 1972 by Frederick Forsyth, on the basis of whose plot a popular film was produced; both the novel and the film showed a Federal Republic whose political and economic establishment was deeply influenced by former Nazi leaders, now enjoying important responsibilities and powerful roles in the West German democratic system[21].

There is no need to go on with further examples of how in numerous European milieu till the late 1960s fears about the resurgence of German aggressive tendencies, mainly based on the Nazi past, were largely widespread. Such feelings appeared to experience a sharp decline during the second half of the 1970s and the 1980s, not only owing to

---

Gengaroli-Bauer, *Italiani e tedeschi. Aspetti di comunicazione interculturale*, Roma, Carocci, 2011.

18 On the image of the "bad German" opposed to the image of the "good Italian" see F. Focardi, *Il cattivo tedesco e il bravo italiano. La rimozione delle colpe della seconda guerra mondiale*, Roma-Bari, Laterza, 2013.

19 On Britain's attitude see J. Ramsden, *Don't Mention the War. The British and the Germans since 1890*, London, Abacus, 2007.

20 A significant example is the movie *The Guns of Navarone*, a great hit filmed in 1961, directed by J. Lee Thomson and based on the novel by Alistair Maclean.

21 F. Forsyth, *The Odessa File*, 1972. The movie appeared in 1974 and has been directed by Ronald Neame.

the fact that the memoirs of the Second World War began to fade, but also as a consequence of some relevant policies pursued by the Federal Republic, especially during the long period of Social Democratic rule: from the decision to adhere to the non-proliferation treaty with the obvious choice to give up any ambition at becoming a military nuclear power, to some symbolic episodes such as Brandt's official visit to Poland and his kneeling in front of the monument of the Warsaw ghetto uprising, to the important role played by both Brandt and Schmidt in the European integration process in cooperation with Pompidou and Giscard d'Estaing[22]. Another element which appeared as a firm guarantee against any resurgence of German expansionist ambitions was the deep rooted belief following which Germany's division had become a permanent pattern of the European scenario and such a condition would contribute to reduce Germany's potentialities and aspirations. It was now possible to concede to the Germans the role of "economic giant", an "economic giant" whose room for diplomatic manoeuver would be seriously limited by the Cold War, as well as by its membership in both NATO and the European Community. Germany's division had become a positive element for both the West and the East and in both camps it was hoped that also the German people had become assuaged to such a situation which was the most powerful guarantee of Europe's stability. In this context it is of some significance an episode which took place in 1984 and of which the Italian Foreign Minister Giulio Andreotti was the protagonist. On the occasion of a public debate the Christian Democrat leader stated his support of Germany's division and he expressed his hostility to any pan-German tendency. Such a statement provoked a diplomatic storm in Bonn, but in a private letter to the President of the Republic, Pertini, Andreotti argued that his statement was not the consequence of a personal hostility towards Germany rather than the obvious concern that any radical change to the European borders born out of the Cold War in the postwar period and ratified through the Helsinki agreements would threaten the stability and peace of the whole continent[23].

The fall of the Berlin Wall, the end of the Cold War and the perspective of a quick German reunification with the creation of powerful state of about 80 million people in the middle of the European continent and with the most powerful economy provoked the reappearance of long-time

---

22 See for example the evaluation written in the mid-1970s in J. K. Snowden, *The German Question 1945-1973. Continuity and Change*, London, Granada, 1975. See the interesting interpretations in G. Bernardini, *Nuova Germania, antichi timori. Stati Uniti. Ostpolitik e sicurezza europea*, Bologna, Il Mulino, 2013.

23 A. Varsori, *L'Italia e la fine della guerra fredda. La politica estera dei governi Andreotti 1989-1992*, Bologna, Il Mulino, 2013, 23-6.

forgotten suspicions and fears about Germany's international ambitions[24]. Nevertheless such concerns seemed to characterize mainly the positions and attitudes of the major western European leaders rather than European public opinions. Statesmen such as François Mitterrand, Margaret Thatcher and Giulio Andreotti had had direct experience of the Second World War and they had personal memories of German aggressiveness and expansionism. So it is not surprising that at least in an early stage the British, French and Italian decision-makers appeared to be not too happy about the perspective of a rapid German reunification[25]. Obviously very few, if any, appeared to fear the resurgence of a Nazi Germany, but some opinion-makers were concerned about the possibility that a unified Germany could choose a "sonderweg" in its foreign policy, so transforming Germany once again in a central European power, whose ties with the West would be destined to fade. In this context it would be possible to remember the reactions by the international media and some diplomatic milieu to the Stavropol agreement on the German reunification reached in summer 1990 by Gorbachev and Kohl, which was perceived as a new "Rapallo". Western European leaders however could not disregard that their public opinions were in favor of the German reunification which was mainly perceived as the symbol of both the end of the Cold War and of an anachronistic partition of the European continent[26]. The joyous images of East and West Berliners in the fateful days of November 1989 could reassure the Europeans about Germany's future international role. In order to limit new hegemonic tendencies it would suffice to safeguard the US presence in Europe through the survival of the Atlantic Alliance and the strengthening of the political and economic integration; especially the creation of an Economic and Monetary Union would compel the Germans to abandon the symbol of the economic predominance, the "Deutschmark"[27]. Such an optimistic outlook ended up in influencing also Britain, especially after Thatcher's resignation from power. Margaret Thatcher was perhaps the only European leader who till the last aimed at impeding a rapid reunification to the point to envisage an alliance with the Soviet Union. It is not surprising that on

24 On the collapse of the German Democratic Republic see for example C. Maier, *Il crollo. La crisi del comunismo e la fine della Germania Est*, Bologna, Il Mulino, 1999.

25 On Mitterrand's position see F. Bozo, *Mitterand, la fin de la guerre froide et la réunification allemande*, Paris, Odile Jacob, 2005; on Margaret Thatcher's position see M. Thatcher, *The Downing Street Years*, London, Harper Collins, 1995. On Andreotti's attitude see A. Varsori, cit., passim.

26 For some stimulating remarks see E. Rusconi, *Germania, Italia, Europa. Dallo stato di potenza alla "potenza civile"*, Torino, Einaudi, 2003.

27 In general see K. Dyson, K. Featherstone, *The Road to Maastricht. Negotiating Economic and Monetary Union*, Oxford, Oxford University Press, 1999.

the occasion of a private conversation with Andreotti, to the Italian leader who showed an optimistic mood especially as far as the positive influence the integration process would exert on the reunified German state, the British Prime Minister retorted that Andreotti's hopes were mere illusions and that in a not too distant future the continent would be characterized by German domination rather than by a European Germany[28]. Thatcher's fears appeared to be confirmed by Germany's policy towards Slovenia's and Croatia's aspirations at a full independence in the early stages of the Yugoslav crisis[29]. But those German ambitions at spreading its influence to the Balkans appeared to be short-lived. On the other hand during the 1990s and the early 2000s Germany was compelled to focus its attention and energies on the cost of the reunification and Germany's international ambitions appeared to be limited to the achievement of a permanent seat at the UNO Security Council.

In spite of those reassuring developments very few commentators seemed to understand that Germany's role in the integration process was going to change radically. Among the consequences of the German reunification there was the fading of the "French-German couple" concept. For a few months the war against Iraq decided in 2003 by the Bush administration led to a close rapprochement between Paris and Berlin. But very quickly it appeared evident that Germany was the most powerful actor and that the German authorities could resort to a close cooperation with France when they thought it coherent with German interests and goals[30]. Another relevant development was the German people's emancipation from their past guilt. The new century and the disappearance of the older generations which had a direct experience of the Second World War were going to wipe out the concerns and worries about German expansionist tendencies, that were tied to the events which had taken place in the first half of the past century. Such a change does not imply the danger of a reevaluation of the Nazi past, on the contrary, Germany is one of the most stable democracy of the continent, but the Nazi past cannot be exploited any longer in order to condemn or to create obstacles to Germany's foreign policy decisions. Another emerging pattern is the growing interest showed by Berlin towards Germany's economic ties with Central Europe, a development which has been further strengthened owing to the adhesion to the EU between 2004 and 2007 of twelve new member states, most of them former members of the

28 A. Varsori, cit., 38.

29 See for example M. Libal, The Road to Recognition: Germany, the EC and the Disintegration of Yugoslavia, *Journal of European Integration History*, i, 1, 2004: 75-96.

30 A. Varsori, L'Europa e gli Stati Uniti dopo l'11 settembre, *Ventunesimo Secolo*, x, 25, June 2011.

Communist bloc[31]. Such a "big bang" is provoking a growing projection by the EU northwards and eastwards to the detriment of countries such as France and Italy, whose interests are tied also to the Mediterranean area and the Middle East.

Nevertheless it has been the recent economic and financial crisis to reveal new divisions and cleavages in the EU and to favor the resurgence of concerns, fears and stereotypes which appeared to be almost completely forgotten. Not every member of the EU shares a critical view of Germany's economic policy choices: some Northern nations, which are members of the group of the "good guys" of the EU agree with Germany's position, while Britain seems to be a bit detached from the European problem and some central European states have to remember that their economic systems are dependent on Berlin's goodwill; as for France is concerned, France is so economically weak that she appears unable to oppose Germany or to work out a common front with Spain and Italy. It is mainly in Southern Europe that the opposition to Germany's economic policy is stronger and Berlin's patronizing attitude is often perceived in a negative way with the resurgence of long-forgotten stereotypes which had their roots in World War II tragic experience. Sometimes it is easy to disregard that the recent official visit in Greece by Angela Merkel has been something new and dangerous in the history of post-war Europe since the end of the Second World War. The mission by the German Chancellor has provoked violent manifestations and feelings of deep hostility which Europe has experimented only on the occasion of visit by US presidents during the Vietnam War[32]. As I already stated, the Italian case will be dealt with in detail by Federico Niglia, but I would point out the public statements by some influential leaders and important political parties or it would suffice to read the comments by thousands of average readers on the websites of some Italian newspapers to realize how some sectors of the Italian public opinion are largely influenced by rabid anti-German feelings[33]. If it is an easy task to reject most of those evaluations, we must not disregard that the exploitation of negative stereotypes about southern

---

31 On the enlargement process see L. Mattina, *La sfida dell'allargamento. L'Unione Europea e la democratizzazione dell'Europa centro-orientale*, Bologna, Il Mulino, 2004; A. Varsori, Europe after 1989. The Strategy of Enlargement, in V. Dujardin, P. Tilly (eds.), *Hommes et réseaux: Belgique, Europe et Outre-Mers*, Brussels, PIE-Peter Lang, 2013, 377-88.

32 See for example Thousands Protesting Greece at Angela Merkel's Visit, *BBC News Europe*, October 9 2012.

33 In this context it suffices to point out the position by the newspaper *Il Giornale*; see for example A. Sallusti, Quarto Reich, *Il Giornale*, August 3 2012.

Europe and its peoples or patronizing attitudes are not so uncommon in the German press or in German political discourse[34].

Can we regard those phenomena as the resurgence of nationalist and jingoist feelings which are destined to threaten the cohesion of the European Union? Can we hope that those phenomena are limited to some consequences of the economic crisis and they would quickly disappear if the economic situation improves? As an historian I have no definite answers as far as the future is concerned, but it is evident that the heritage of a dramatic past is still deeply influencing the feelings of large sectors of the European public opinion: if some Southern European countries have to think about the economic mistakes of a recent past and it would be a wrong and counter-productive choice to justify through the past such mistakes, it would be another serious mistake on the part of the German leaders and opinion to limit themselves to give lessons to those who are perceived as "naughty children": it is true that Germany's international role, especially in the EU, is the consequence of its economic power as well as of the sound management of its economic system, but the German economy is part of a closely interdependent system which is largely based on mutual cooperation among all the partners of the EU, also the ones which are members of the "Club Med" or of the group of the so-called "PIGS". The only alternative is the creation of two conflicting groups and such a development may have ominous consequences for the whole European continent as it had in the past.

[34] In this connection it suffices to remember some comments on both Italy and the Italians which appeared in the magazine *Der Spiegel* on the occasion of the sinking of the boat Costa Concordia.

Letter to German and Italian Friends
How the European Economic Mechanism Works

Paolo SAVONA

1. Letter to German Friends

Rome, 1 October 2012

Dear German Friends,

No one can deny that you belong to a great nation. Your philosophers, jurists, musicians, scholars and scientists have contributed to shape civilisation on the entire planet. You have made some mistakes. However, who has not made them? The history of extermination carried out by each country in the world has been described in the extensive work by Matthew White on the atrocities committed by mankind during our millenary history. There is something for everyone! Karl Popper was right: humans are the worst beasts on Earth because, as compared to animals, they consciously put their intelligence to the service of evil.

Let's stay out of this issue by preventing that the roots of violence, including economic violence, become stronger. Therefore, I would like to urge you to show greater commitment to prevent another tragedy in Europe – that of some nations returning to poverty with the resulting hatred and conflicts – by acting in such a way as to guarantee continued growth in your country as well as in all the other countries through a collaborative effort. We need to go back and pursue the objective that the civil advancement of European national societies had led us to believe as irreversibly attained: "The greatest possible happiness for the highest possible number of people", a principle whose best theoretical expression is shown by our British friends and the founding Fathers of our civilisation and theirs. This being said, we find ourselves with the irreversibility of the Euro, obviously the current Euro and not the Euro we had dreamed of. Its forms prevent the fulfilment of the hopes that had led to its launch: a tool to grow and spread peace and wealth to everyone. A myth from the past is coming back with a vengeance: that of a balanced budget, which has now become a constitutional value and which we had thought to have rejected due to the gains in terms of knowledge of the economic science.

However, and this is even more serious, conflicting competition has come back. Fortunately, it is not of a military nature, like the ones that caused dramatic wars and imposed a strong desire for peace and guided, even though with problems, the process of European unification. It is more underhand. Your recent collective behaviour seems to show that, at economic level, you are going again towards the direction suggested by the Funk Plan of 1936.

The economic policy you are proposing lays the foundation for a break-up of the European dream of peace and common civil progress. The Funk Plan provided for Germany to become the country that would put order in Europe. This is what you now suggest. The Funk Plan provided for national currencies "to converge into the Mark's area" and this is what you would like and have partially achieved. It also envisaged that industrial development only pertained to yourselves and that you would only be accompanied by France, your "historical" ally, a solution now caused by the common European market and the single currency. The Plan wanted other countries to devote themselves to agriculture and tourist services, something that will happen out of necessity or because of a natural "calling" and they will lend skilled labour to your leadership project. I am on the side of those who believe that someone's or some country's leadership is indispensable not only for geo-political stability but also for the healthy meritocratic principle that, for the good of everyone, the best must win. However, leadership, particularly at supranational level, entails duties in terms of security and wealth, something that, for instance, the US have performed rather well during the post-war period. Therefore, if your policy is not nationalistic by nature, because it would then be outdated and would also not take into account your interests in terms of exporting country, your ambition to be European leaders misses these two fundamental principles to support it.

National interests must be balanced with those of the communities that make up Europe. In turn, these interests must be balanced with those of the international community. In foreign policy, this is called cooperative strategy. I was taught that whoever looks after his (her) own interests – and the success of Adam Smith is due to the fact that he clearly highlighted this in a famous passage of his, just as famous as the book *The Wealth of Nations* – serves the interests of each of us. However, as the theory of social classes specified, he becomes a member of the leading classes if he manages to balance his interests with the general ones. In order to avoid the reactions caused by the transfer of the Funk Plan to a different political habitat, the mechanism created in Maastricht and subsequently integrated on various occasions needs to be used, but with stability as the prerequisite of development. Economic knowledge, however, suggests that it needs to be on the same level as political commitment. This is what the United States is doing. However, their central bank has free rein on the three channels of creation of monetary base (Treasury, banks and foreign trade) and plays a useful role that includes development with commitment to stability. A Government can act on its public deficit to fight unemployment. This is feasible because the dollar is said to be the currency of international reserves. However, the Euro too was becoming the currency of international reserves until hesitation in defending it stopped its ascent.

One of our illustrious jurists, Giuseppe Guarino, explained that institutional set-ups, once created, become bio-juridical organisms, i.e., they have a life of their own and move autonomously until others are created to avoid unpleasant consequences. The way bio-juridical organisms like the Euro and European fiscal policies function revitalises the substance of the Funk Plan, perhaps without your actually wanting it. However, we beg you to clarify your ideas and explain to us what you really want, so that we can decide what to do, too.

I have attached my interpretation of how the European economic bio-juridical mechanism works and the dangers that it poses to good, as well as bad, governments, to the lucky rich as well as the disadvantaged poor.

Therefore, let's focus on this important aspect of the problem in order to carry on in the direction of political unification, without which we cannot rely on the definition of geo-policies to guide European countries. Do not delude yourselves into believing that you are able to make it on your own or with a handful of countries. You need a united Europe as much as we do.

I do not reject the idea that Germany is the country that can put Europe in order, but I ask that, at the end of this process, the term takes on a different meaning. If sufficient policies to make up for asymmetric shocks and if a true free movement of input and output lacked, the Euro's exchange rate would, for you, be undervalued and for others overvalued, and it would tend to absorb international capital flows and industrial growth in your economy (and that, it goes without saying, thanks to your own merits, too). This, however, would mean that French development would be in serious difficulties and that Italy and Spain would be de-industrialised and their energies redirected towards agriculture and tourism. Consequently, this would lead to emigration in those countries facing difficulties. However, this time round emigration would have to face fierce competition from economically backward countries. All these implications of the bio-juridical mechanism are similar to those envisaged by the Funk Plan. European fiscal policies accelerate this process and, given current institutional conditions, remove any room for independent development by European countries in difficulty. Monetary policy, that needs to comply with fiscal commitment, prevents the crisis of the Euro, but it does not remedy the perverse effects of the mechanism itself.

If, as we believe, you do not want that relationships between our people become sour, corrections to the pacts that govern the EU must be seriously re-discussed irrespective of what many consider to be the indispensable condition to be able to matter in this world: political unification. We do not ask you to pay other people's debts because it is not technically possible and it is also unthinkable. We ask you to allow everyone to pay their own debts by rationalising their economies so that they can carry on along the path of development. This is what the Americans did for Europe when they launched the Marshall Plan.

Ideally, intellectuals of European countries should come together for a serious discussion of this issue in the utmost respect of respective ideas and traditions, but with general objectives that coincide again.

Paolo Savona, independent economist

2. Letter to Italian Friends

Rome, 1 October 2012

Dear Italian friends,

It is my fear that no one realizes the full gravity of the situation which, day by day, is propelling Italy down the road toward underdevelopment and social crisis. To the world context of increasing competitivity are added the effects of the far from optimal monetary nature of the euro, and of an ever more rigid fiscal policy imposed upon us by the EU and accepted by us under the alarms of the emergency, but now made justifiable as a solution, if not ideal, at least a plausible one, for the ills of Europe. All this leads toward the deindustrialization of Italy and ever higher unemployment. The alimentary and tourist services sectors are not sufficient to compensate for the loss of the two prime motors driving our development, industrial exports and construction. The decision on the part of Draghi to defend the euro but on the condition that the fiscal compact and other European initiatives are respected, periodically renegotiated, allows us time to act, but it does not resolve the basic problems at the root of the European institutional order requiring urgent resolution.

In my letter to our German friends, which I pray you read, I asked them if they are conscious of the fact that they are in substance putting into practice the economic Plan advanced in 1936 by Nazi economic minister Walther Funk, who foresaw Germany's role as that of becoming the "Sergeant at arms" of Europe, so that its development be prevalently industrial with some concessions made for its historical ally, France, while the other nations of Europe concentrate on agricultural production and serve as labor pool, to the end that European currencies flow into the Deutsch Mark zone in observation of its rules.

Is this what we wish to see happen?

Since the entrepreneurial capacities of Italy are capable of finding an outlet in foreign investment besides in further exportation, the consequences of the current situation of European relations are not then of an economic nature, but prevalently of a socio-political one. The solution for the problems of adapting the economy to the new geo-political conditions inside Europe as desired by Germany, jointly with those which the global market imposes on us, proceeds in fact by tossing the hot potato of unemployment and the redimensioning of the social protection net to the hands of politics, which is not in a condition to cool it, lacking as it does instruments adequate to this end. It will certainly not be the anti-corruption and anti-tax evasion campaign, however necessary, to reverse the process of de-development now under way which remains heterodirected and given to unpredictable social meltdown. Nor is the inheritance tax so dear to the Left a solution, as it would only speed up economic decline and capital flight, on which the international Monetary Fund has already informed us. It is a source of worry to see the scarce attention devoted to problems of unemployment.

Yet it is true that we are at war, as even Mario Monti has reminded us, a war altogether economical and "systemic", and, as the generals know all too well, to win it they must accept losing a percentage of soldiers on the field of battle; in times of peace these victims come from the ranks of the unemployed. No one can remain impassive in the face of these losses, which touch not only the ranks of workers but the companies themselves; the disappearance of these companies, moreover, is the equivalent of a purification of the market on the part of incapable entrepreneurs: what the neo-classicists refer to as "creative destruction" which is invalid for the unemployed of the work force. The Italian economy will know how to adjust itself by rationalizing the nation from within and investing outside of it. Society at large does not possess the possibility of an outlet short of emigration. But is the rest of the world ready to accept us, given that it was we who pursued that path? For this reason the last solution to the problem of unemployment is not limited to the economic developments, but rather to the capacity for sacrifice on the part of society in the face of a decline in well being. My evaluation is that social resilience is elevated in Italy but, on the one hand, it represents a danger, because it leads to adapting to decline without fighting back, and on the other, it causes uncertainties concerning the future which are registered by the BTP-BUND spread, because the explosion of the market is forever unpredictable and the outcome traumatic. The real problem as I see it does not lie only in supply and demand, but mainly in the institutional order between which we operate. The solution to our ills passes from a redefinition of the international monetary architecture, shifting the reference of exchanges on a currency of international significance, as would likewise be the special reformed rights of withdrawal, and adding to the clause of the WTO the obligation of the same rate of exchange. On the European level renegotiating the pacts in order to transform the bio-juridical organism that kicked in after Maastricht into a creator of opportunity and not merely of pathways that lead to deflation. The fixed exchange outside the seventeen nations of the euro zone with the possibility of another nine member nations of the EU, and of the rest of the world, to be able to adjust the rapport and the certitude that the dollar remain thereby comparatively weak, holding the euro over-valued for others; together with the confusion (perhaps a consequence) of our political climate, the off-balance rapport of exchange causes a slow transfer of industrial development toward Germany and the few other strong industrial areas. The European policies of compensation, which would be indispensable to confront the monetary non-optimality of the Eurozone, goes on transforming into national policy of pathways by the use of fiscal instruments and limitations obvious or occult on the movement of input and output. All this accelerates the process of transferment of development from the areas in difficulty to those which are not. Surely some lessons should be gleaned from the case of Greece. It is a pure illusion, perhaps even utter folly, to believe that the rigorous respect of European regulations now in place will lead us out of the situation in which we find ourselves.

The much awaited "replacement" of private demand following the reduction of public demand and the ensuing effects of the reforms (principally liberalizations and modifications of the labor market) are not certain, nor quantifiable, and even while wishing to consider them possible they manifest themselves with great slowness as the effects of the crisis come swiftly and cause irremediable losses to productive capacity and market share. When the wagons come unhooked from a moving locomotive it is difficult to connect them back again.

The proposals of the traditional parties and those of the new political formations are disconnected from the real conditions to be confronted, which consist of the search for a new geo-political arrangement in the European sphere, if there is opened the space for a more serious reform of institutional order, or in the international sphere, if the European space, as seems likely, remains irremediably closed to alternative solutions. The markets ask us to guarantee the contamination of the policy of the Monti Government, because they feel discontinuity in the management of the reformation which the Left in power would decide, but the choice is the decline between the possible effects of discontinuity and those of the economic policy in place. One can be in agreement as to the necessity of blocking discontinuity that brings about flight of capital, the lost investments and the transferment of taxation from earnings to inheritance, which would still function in the same way, or else would cut into wages and savings. In the absence of a plan for development the market also fears a fall in national product which would augment or sharpen the growth of the rapport public debt/GNP. The necessary and sought-after continuity is of a seriousness demonstrated by the very persons who make up the technical government, beginning with President Monti, but it is necessary to ask that it be passed to the electorate. Continuity on the other hand cannot be in European policy and in its internal counterpart; in the former to avoid the "Funk effect", and in the latter to avoid retaining that, with the campaign against evasion which increases the fiscal pressure and the campaign against corruption carried out forces of order (operators in the field and judges), it result in a successful outcome from the crisis. We are informed that the campaign against evasion has permitted the recovery of approximately thirteen billions of Euros; if the increase of the fiscal yield has caused to lower the GNP by one mere percentage point, it would seem to me that no great gain has been made! The crisis lies in the economic policy consequent to the nature of the international and European accords and to the sharing of their deflationary and redistributory address on our part. Since there is lacking a political force to embrace objectives of seriousness and development, we would end up with a prevalence of forces who call themselves anti-political, which is in and of itself a form of politics, but one of the lowest order. This is the discontinuity to avoid without falling into the continuity of an economical policy that does not respond to the needs of the nation. As I explain in my analysis of the situation herewith attached, which I pray you read, it is necessary to work on two fronts: to reverse the condescending attitude on the part of European policy gone wrong, and to prepare ourselves for an extraordinary operation with regard to the public debt and the patrimony of the State, along the lines I have laid out with my colleagues Michele Fratianni and Antonio Rinaldi. A consolidation of the State debt to seven years, paying a fixed rate comparable to inflation and at 20% of the development which will be obtained, plus a warrant on public patrimony. This operation would immediately free up approximately forty billion derived from the reduction of the financial burden currently paid by the State, offering space to provide either a second wind to demand, in my opinion detaxing and not spending more, or time for the policies of supply to take effect. But let us not delude ourselves, recovery won't be spontaneous, a phenomenon known only to occur to unemployment!

Paolo Savona, independent economist

3. How the European Economic Mechanism Works

As is well known, the European Union was built on two institutional pillars: the exercise of monetary sovereignty entrusted to the European Central Bank and the regulating of the various aspects of the functioning of the common market entrusted to communitarian consensus. Fiscal sovereignty has remained in the hands of the member states, initially in the form of parametric ties on the deficits of public balance on the entity of the public debt/GNP, thereafter in the rapport of more restrictive normatives decided upon by treaty (as in the case of the fiscal compact) or negotiable bilaterally to obtain financial assistance on the part of the Central Bank or the ESM.

From this institutional order of bio-juridical nature, which once set in motion acts automatically, there emerged a peculiar economic policy with which the current Italian Government agrees: it can be taken up once more if it guarantees, immediately and on a permanent basis, the stability of public finance while also preserving on a long term basis, monetary stability: to the action of these two classical instruments there are added structural reforms in the use of labor and, more generally, in the conditions of competition that are coherent with the ties of the global market. Monetary and fiscal stability and the adaptability of supply is therefore the presupposition for arriving at the recovery of demand and of employment; these would be in any case prevalently endogenous in nature, to the degree it issues from the effect of crowding in of the private demand and, more generally, of the State in the economy and from the minor ties to competition. Since nevertheless the aforementioned President of the Consiglio Mario Monti has admitted that, to avoid "a fall into the abyss" it has been necessary to increase fiscal pressure, the choices effectuated added to the deflation already underway and, consequently the positive effects of his policies will be late in manifesting themselves, but a long waiting period is not necessary, insofar as he sustains seeing a recovery by the end of 2013. The recent law for a re-launch of development, not by accident called "of stability", proceeds on the road of increased fiscal pressure, nonetheless with the redistributive effects of the burden.

This policy comes tacitly accompanied by a moralistic conviction, by which nations in difficulty for reason of not having preserved fiscal stability must pay a cost in terms of a decrease of the GNP and of employment to prevent a repeat in the future of behavior of moral hazard whether public or private. The approach is similar to that which brought to the dramatic error of the Bush administration with its decision to let Lehman Brothers fail in order to "teach a lesson" to those who had been gambling on derivatives.

The briefly described political address finds thin basis in known economic paradigms, above all because it should take into account at least three aspects of the problem to resolve: 1.) the "path dependence", that is to say the dependence of development on a variety of conditions of departure inherited from the past; 2.) the diversity in existing productive and institutional structures on the national level that urge differentiated interventions instead of forcing a single solution for all; 3.) the role played by aggregated demand in the process of development.

An indiscriminate application of fiscal stability and of reforms, above all in a situation such as that inherited from the transmission of the grave financial crisis in America to the real economy, leads to those already well off being far better off, and to those already being bad off being worse off, undermining the stability of the euro area not only for the economic effects it causes but also for the social effects which it brings with it and which, apparently, are not a source of worry although they should well be so. The judgment of the international markets confirms this evaluation, as testified by the modest decline of the spread on sovereign debt in Spain and in Italy after the decision by Draghi to guarantee an intervention in the dimension necessary to confront speculation. Above and beyond the declared availability of intervening in a limited measure – bound to remain at a level of low inflation and therefore not easily evaluated in the long haul – the market discounts the deflationary effects of the "conditionality" which, through more stringent ties on fiscal and wage policies, render even more problematic and therefore risky the reimbursement of debts and the self-same banking stability, because of the fall in productivity and the consequential failures of private businesses. If we add to these deflationary effects, as is being seen, those deriving from the campaign against evasion without restitution of the proceeds to those who pay taxes, the situation can spiral downward or, in any case, admitting that crowding in functions can permit a recovery of sufficient scale and in the time frame necessary to reverse the drop in employment.

Limiting ourselves to the examination of existing conditions pertaining to the euro group to which Italy belongs, the institutional architecture has been lowered in the system abstracting from the not optimal monetary nature of the euro area, given that inside of it exist various structures of productivity born of cultural attitudes, of the diversity of the dimension of businesses, from composition according to sector of the internal product, from the degree of openness to the competition of the markets, from the general fiscal treatment and from the existent institutional picture both legal and de facto on the labor market. The unfounded assumption was that a common solution failing in the euro area, the economies that compose it would have demonstrated a spontaneous (endogenous) convergence. The European Commission and the Central Bank attempted again and again to demonstrate that this was not occurring, in spite of evidence to the contrary. Certain "strange" documents from official sources also have sustained that they are not as "non optimal" as some unthinking few believe. In the presence of the dualisms summarily indicated, to the point where the euro area does not produce this same interior distortion – in the international distribution of work and of capital, it should have counted on incisive compensative policies, of the asymmetrical shock besides the complete liberalization in the movement of input (capital and labor) and output (goods and services). On the subject of the free movement of input and of output there still exists rigid limitations that may be estimated in three-quarters of the European gross product and of the factors employed: agriculture is largely protected, services bound in respect to various wage levels of the particular nations where they come to be offered, and industrial production, although being the most competitive, is variously regulated; the work force struggles to achieve an inter-European mobility sufficient to compensate the degree of non-optimality of the euro area, while capital, which moves more freely, is placed under the constrains of de facto ties often of nationalistic inspiration (such as that of protecting the "national Champions"). The compensative policies on the part of the Union consist of a ridiculous dimension of perhaps 0.20% of the European GNP on a total of the communitarian balance which arrives at little more than %; beyond this limitation the political c.d.s regarding cohesion are not oriented to compensate asymmetrical shocks nor to remove the dualism of productivity, but pursue primarily social objectives. The rigidity imposed to the administration of national fiscal policies, which take into account the departure point conditions and other recollected important factors, prevents nations from carrying out substitutive functions with regard to those compensative one which should be tasks carried out by the European Community and the Central Bank.

In the functioning of the mechanism of the euro area is also erected the imperfect architecture of the international monetary system, caused by the dominance of the dollar and by the diversity of the regimes of exchange. The creation of dollars is decided on the basis of the international need of the American economy, the excess held in official reserve by nations that avail themselves of the faculty conceded by the WTO statute to choose the preferred regime of exchange. Only euphemistically can one say that there exists a "global" market because – since as Europeans we know a market is not such until there exist a variety of regimes of exchange – there cohabitate floating and fixed exchanges, the latter in a dirty form, that is to say with interventions on the part of the nations on behalf of various entities from one period to another.

The accumulated official reserves come to be inverted: 1.) in "pure" financial forms (mainly American state titles); 2.) in participation with companies, also strategic ones, increasingly through the sovereign Funds of wealth; 3.) or converted into euros passing however from the market, which favors strategically those nations which possess a non-corrigible surplus through variations of the exchange and make up a revaluation of the euro which is superimposed on the direct effects of the weakness of the dollar.

The financial market and the self-same real economy are therefore influenced by the excesses of the creation of dollars toward internal American ends, a consequence very clearly in the minds of the reformers at the act of signing Bretton Woods, while the quest for a solution has continued thereafter up to the birth of special rights of withdrawal.

Of this engagement all trace has vanished from current literature and in governmental valuations. There remain only a few traces of the religion of stability to be obtained with instruments of the market such as flexible exchange and not with transparent norms and occult comportments.

The effect of the conversions of dollars in euros carried out directly on the market has brought the exchange of the euro, before the crisis which broke out in 2008, to values close to 1.60 then falling to 1.20-1.30 with an oscillation independent of the conditions relative to the exchange between the euro area and the dollar area.

The combined effect of the "implicit" divarication, on the one hand, between the average value of exchange of the euro respective of the dollar and the national productive and competitive reality and on the other the rigidities of management of fiscal policies at whose carrying out monetary policy remains also "conditioned", does not consent the effectuation of manoeuvres on the demand and reduces the efficacy of manoeuvres on the supply, as with those on which the Monti Government have counted, also to wish to retain that the interventions be of such dimension so as to have the capacity to produce the anticipated positive effects.

In a situation in which previsions for 2013 announce a fall in growth rates of commerce worldwide which will be felt on our exports and that other motor of growth in the Italian economy, construction, in the absence of specific provisions, these remain at the post because of the difficulty of financing and for fear of further property tax hikes, so that one cannot perceive a push toward recovery until next year. The adaptability of the Italian people is high, as confirmed in the face of this current situation, also because they possess a high level of wealth and have the capacity to procure maintenance for themselves off the market by various means. In this historical moment, in any case, adaptability is not what we need, but rather to react in the face of these difficulties. If property tax rates were to be reinforced the acceleration of the plunge in productivity would be increased and the destruction of the capacity for productivity could turn out to be irreversible, neutralizing the possible effects derived from the contraction of public demand and from the modification of the conditions of supply. It is therefore imperative to work both on the external front and on the internal one. On the first, by limiting ourselves to the EU changing the condescending attitude of a European policy inappropriate when it comes to attenuating the negative effects of the productive dualism emerging from the appearance of the Euro area.

It is imperative furthermore to see to it that into the European agenda there comes to be inserted the extension of the American statute of the Federal Reserve to the Central Bank and the political reunification at least among the nations belonging to the Euro area.

On the internal front it is imperative to activate an extraordinary operation on combined public debt and State patrimony according to the guidelines already laid out with my colleagues Michele Fratianni and Antonio Rinaldi. A consolidating of the maturity of public titles at seven years, recognizing a revaluation of the value of the act of reimbursement equal to the rate of inflation, an annual coupon equal to 2% of the rate of real growth and an option (warrant) for acquiring on quota of the patrimony of the State, so as to free up at once resources amounting to approximately forty billions currently earmarked as interest payments by the State; this would give a second wind to both demand passing preferably from a de-taxation of income and in necessary time so that the policies of supply can have their positive effect.

At the same time an action of an external political nature is set in motion to propose in the agenda of the G20 the use of an international monetary standard different from that of a national currency and at least the inclusion into the statute of the WTO of the obligation to have this same regime of exchange if it is desired to participate in the benefits of world trade. Perhaps we will not find ourselves accommodated, but worthy proposals cannot be eliminated from the international round by faulty arguments, without those who advance them paying in terms of prestige. Such as they are, the world and European bio-juridical organisms do not produce well being and moreover run the risk of executing a step backwards in terms of the civility of world society.

4. Post datum

In light of the present day, the exercise of the profession of an economist is becoming more and more problematical. Immediately upon having finished putting down on paper one's reflections a breaking bulletin comes across the wires, not infrequently touching on the topic of policy choices. It has been my experience in the matter at hand to suggest that, if it is prevalently the market that counts, previsions have good probability of grasping what will occur in the future. If, however, it is politics that counts, such previsions lose almost all meaning. It is the old problem between economic rationality and political rationality.

When this text was (self-)delivered to the press, the Monti Government decided to anticipate the introduction of the Tobin Tax with respect to the time frame requested by the EU for introducing it, admitted and not conceded that it be carried out. For a long time Italy has gone on its way constructing the most irrational tributary system and it is astonishing that Monti, long having maintained the goal of harmonizing tax levels in Europe, proceeds to go on his own to disharmonizing it. If, as I have suggested to an expert on the matter, my friend Giulio Tremonti, one of the new coalitions would wish to propose to us a "serious" tributary reform, perhaps it would find those who would vote in favor of it: taxes, development and democracy are the triangle of a civil society, not the more notorious Bermuda Triangle of development!

Toward the conclusion of the 1970s of the last century, I had occasion to accompany Prof. Tobin by car from Fiumicino Airport in Rome for a conference organized (as I recall) by the industrial Union of Vicenza. We discussed, in the course of the four hours in the car, a vast range of topics. At that time the Italian problem centred around the effects on development by the oil crisis, inflation, and the petrol dollar. He agreed with me that it was necessary to compensate the fall in productivity resulting from the "tax of the sheiks" by recourse to the international financing of the dollars accumulated by the petrol producing nations. He cut me short, however, concerning the need to fight inflation, an instance that in me came out of the influence exerted by Karl Brunner rather than by Milton Friedman: he limited himself asking me if, with the struggle against inflation, one still could eat. He did not accept my further counter-arguments.

I ask myself whether he would offer the same answer today for that which was defined, without his gradiment, the Tobin tax. With it, does one still eat? This tax was proposed by Tobin to "pour sand in the gears of finance" in order to contrast the anomalous development which was being delineated. If it had been introduced at the right time for the derivative contrasts it would perhaps have limited the damage which these have caused the world economy. Now it comes to be introduced in Italy to procure resources by which to finance the detaxation of minimal income. I have already had occasion to state that fiscal imposition is by now a social pandemic. For pity's sake leave Tobin to rest in peace!

The Economic Crisis and the Euro

Theoretical and Political Reactions to a Singular Historical Experiment

Bertram Schefold

1. A Challenge to European Economists

As the discussions at this conference have shown, in particular in reaction to Paolo Savona's *Lettera agli amici tedeschi e italiani* (Savona 2012), not only the politicians but also the economists of Europe differ as to what should be done to overcome the impact of the global economic crisis. The European countries are reluctant to cede sovereignty. Nevertheless, they are committed to the use of a joint currency, administered by a common central bank, but, apart from the relatively modest common means for redistribution, such as the common agricultural policy or the measures to create a European knowledge society, the European Union is bereft of a common fiscal authority. This and the Treaty of Maastricht imply that each country must solve its problems by its own devices, although the instrument of monetary policy and the control of the exchange rate have been taken away from the national governments. The crisis has hit European countries in different degrees, pending on the initial conditions and the policies individually pursued. If the common monetary policy is good for some countries, it is inconvenient for others. Which solutions, if any, can economists offer under such circumstances? Before making proposals, their task is to identify the theoretical conception, which guide actual policies and underlie, as determinants of the policies in the past, the present state in which each country is found. The policies turn out to have been ambiguous and can often be justified or criticised from different points of view, hence there is much ideology in what claims to be analysis (Blankenburg *et al.* 2013). I here present my understanding of the situation and of the prospects for future policy.

2. The Actual Situation

The European crisis began with a largely parallel movement of the economies of the major regions of the world: United States, European Union, Japan and China. The growth rates of Japan were somewhat lower, a little higher those of the United States and of the European Union, significantly higher those of China. One recognises a moderate reduction of activity 2001 to 2002 in diagram 1. The sharp crisis 2007-09, implying negative rates of growth between three and five percent, was paralleled by a corresponding reduction of high growth in China. Growth and decline were less synchronised after 2010. Diagram 2 shows the real development of gross domestic product in the European Union in quarterly data, expressed as annual rates; these give a stronger impression of the oscillations. If one considers the index for the gross domestic product (right hand scale), the development appears as less dramatic. As one should expect, the movement of the rates of unemployment followed that of the gross domestic product. However, the European Union as a whole had a higher rate of unemployment prior to 2005, afterwards a lower one than Euroland – a first indication that the crisis hit Euroland more heavily (diagram 3).

The indebtedness of the states also followed the movement of gross domestic product. The United States managed to reduce the level of debt somewhat in the second half of the 1990s and to press it below sixty percent of gross domestic product, but debts increased again with the Dotcom-crisis, and debts exploded to more than one hundred percent of GDP in the course of the present crisis (diagram 4). A similar pattern resulted for Euroland and the European Union, the position of the latter being a little more favourable also in this regard.

Germany suffered from an increase of the level of debts which implied a doubling – or nearly – during the two decades since 1990 (diagram 5). Much of this increase had to do with the attempts to mitigate the consequences of the demographic transition in ways which reflect a profound transformation of the patterns of family life. There is wide disagreement as to whether such levels of debt are sustainable. They would be, if abstraction could be made from uncertainty – then, new debts could pay for old ones, indefinitely. But in the world, in which we live, trust in the debtor will collapse at an unknown date, borrowing becomes expensive and the debt cannot be serviced. A State can always repudiate its domestic debt at the expense of being unjust, of robbing part of the population of their savings, and printing money is another way out – much easier than paying back by running budget surpluses, as the British did after the Second World War. History shows that inflation has repeatedly been a way out, but inflation is not likely to occur soon because of competition from low-wage developing countries.

The situation is much more diversified within Europe than is generally known and is visible in the aggregate (diagram 6). The countries mainly hit by the crisis, Greece, Italy, Ireland, Spain and Portugal, were affected by the partial crises of production and employment, public and private indebtedness, foreign trade, bubbles of house prices, banking crises to quite different degrees. The differences have persisted and new ones appear. In the table, one measure is provided by the European average, the other by a comparison with Germany, as the largest country in Euroland in economic terms. We compare the years 2008 and 2011, and stress the following differences:

- It is not generally known that Irish income per head 2008 was the highest among the ones here to be compared; it fell all the more till 2011, whereas the German was the only one to grow somewhat after the onset of the crisis. Portuguese income per head is only about half as large as the German one.
- The rate of unemployment more than doubled in Greece and Ireland in the three years considered, and almost as big was the effect in Spain and Portugal, whereas unemployment diminished in Germany.
- The increase of the level of State indebtedness led to the highest level in Greece, but the change was most remarkable in Ireland, with a tripling of this index; in Spain it nearly doubled.
- Private indebtedness was and is colossal in Ireland; it seems to have been the price of the high initial income. Private indebtedness increased everywhere during the crisis, but it did not change as much as the other indices.
- A strong trade deficit is evidence of the weakness of the Greek economy. The trade balances in the countries most affected by the crisis improved except in the case of Italy. The trade surplus of Germany does not only reflect surpluses with regard to European countries, but also with regard to the rest of the world; nevertheless, it is often said that Germany should import more from the European South so as to reduce the imbalances.
- Greece and Ireland suffered from intense crises of the housing sectors and of banks, whereas these did not play an important role in Italy and Portugal.
- The indebtedness of the State in Ireland and Spain was quite modest in the beginning of the crisis, and only Italy had a large public deficit from the start. High State indebtedness therefore is, by and large, more a consequence than a cause of the crisis. As it developed, states had to support the failing private sector, in particular the banks, and this was the main single cause for the growth of the deficits.

Diagram 1: Growth of the regions

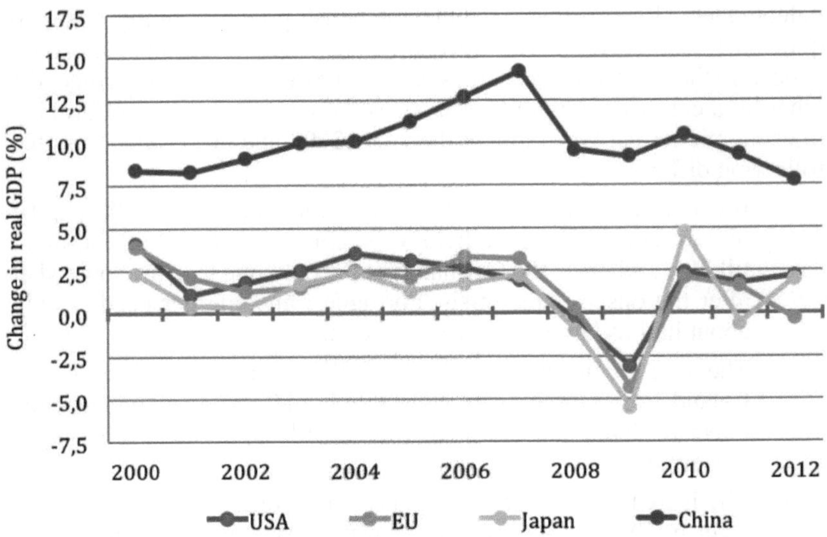

Source: Own illustration following IMF data, World Economic Outlook, April 2013

Diagram 2: Real GDP in the EU

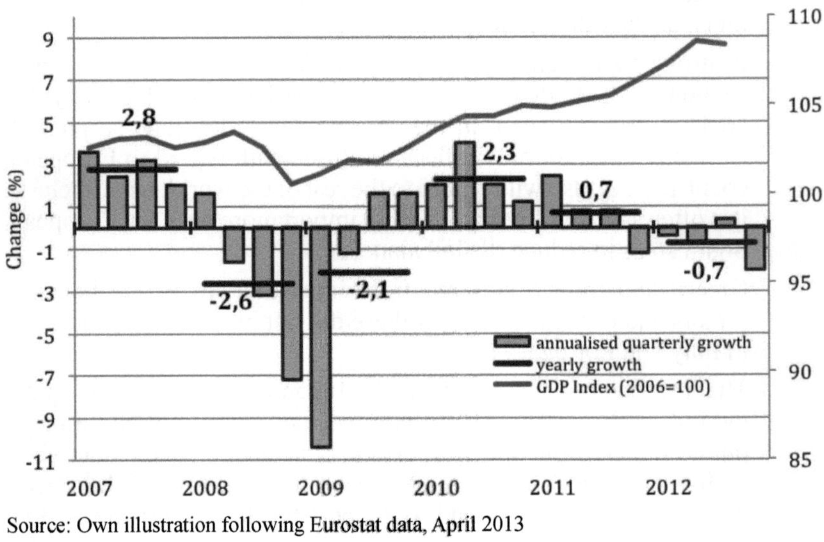

Source: Own illustration following Eurostat data, April 2013

Diagram 3: Unemployment rates in the EU and in Euroland

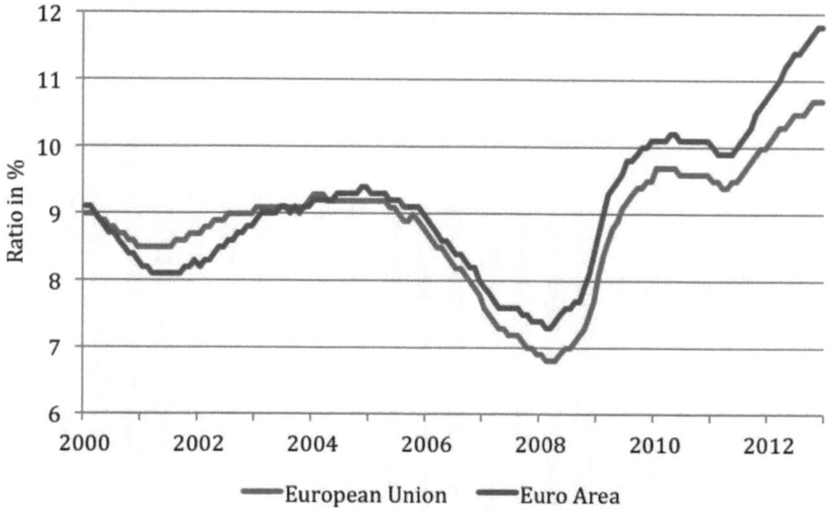

Source: Own illustration following Eurostat data, April 2013

Diagram 4: Debt evolution in the USA (Gross debt level as percentage of GDP)

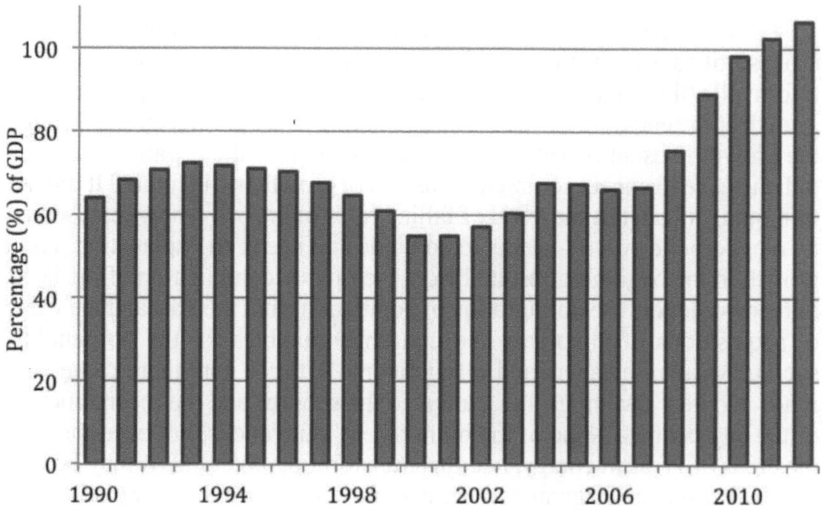

Source: Own illustration following IMF data, World Economic Outlook, April 2013

Diagram 5: Debt evolution in Germany (Gross debt level as percentage of GDP)

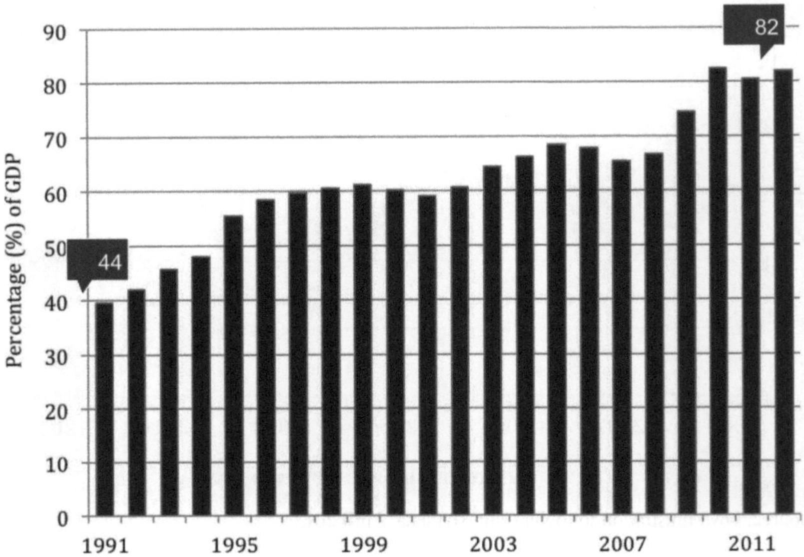

Source: Own illustration following IMF data, World Economic Outlook, April 2013

3. Different Dimensions of the Crisis

As far as Germany is concerned, the crisis seems to imply the end of a phase of first high, then continually weaker growth since the currency reform after the war (diagram 7). I recall how some tried to grasp the trend of growth at the end of the 1970s by intrapolating a straight line going through the growth rates since 1950. It pointed directly into the negative orthant – did one have to expect contraction instead of growth in the future? It did not turn out that bad, but the trend of falling rates of growth – now represented by a hyperbolic curve – seems to continue and needs an explanation. High growth in the beginning resulted from the unique combination of the tasks of reconstruction, the immigration of population from the East and the wave of acquisitions of motorcars and consumer durables for the households, such as vacuum cleaners and refrigerators. With the cars there came new roads and new dwellings, the exodus to the suburbs and the reconstruction of the city centres. None of the more recent innovations, not even those in the areas of IT or in energy, had this transforming potential. It may be that we shall approach stagnation more and more with an aging population and a lessened dynamic of technology, but it seems more probable that we shall live with positive, but low rates of growth, such as prevailed also in the late 19th and early 20th century on average.

Diagram 6: The current situation in 2008 and 2011 in comparison (Euro Area, Germany and the GIIPS countries)

		Euro Area	Germany	Greece	Italy	Ireland	Spain	Portugal
GDP per capita	2008	28.400	30.124	20.914	26.420	40.452	23.859	16.198
	2011	28.300	31.702	19.214	26.065	34.704	23.054	16.069
Unemployment rate		7,66%	7,60%	7,68%	6,78%	6,3%	11,30%	7,59%
		10,17%	5,98%	17,33%	8,43%	14,39%	21,65%	12,74%
Debt ratio (Gov., in % of GDP)		54,1%	50,2%	112,6%	88,8%	24,6%	30,8%	67,4%
		68,0%	55,3%	165,4%	99,6%	94,9%	57,5%	97,3%
Private debt ratio (in % of GDP)		177,9%	123,6%	119,3%	121,1%	279,0%	220,5%	240,3%
		193,0%	127,8%	125,0%	128,6%	309,5%	218,1%	249,3%
Trade balance (in % of GDP)		1,0%	6,3%	-14,5%	-0,8%	9,1%	-5,8%	-10,1%
		1,4%	5,1%	-8,1%	-1,5%	22,0%	-0,8%	-4,4%
Housing bubble			no	severe	no	severe	severe	no
Banking crisis			moderate	severe	no	severe	moderate	no

Source: Eurostat & IMF World Economic Outlook, April 2013

Germany, like all advanced countries, exhibits a close correlation between the growth of domestic product and the growth of the volume of employment known as Okun's law; this rule, based on experience, says that a growth of domestic product by two or three percent is required for a growth of the volume of employment by on percentage point (diagram 8). But the growth of employment has been a little more favourable in recent years and during the crisis in that the growth of gross domestic product in Germany from 2008 to 2013 was 4.3 percent, while employment rose by 2.7 percent over the same period. This is perhaps the most remarkable result of Germany's structural reforms, which preceded the crisis, and it stands in marked contrast to the loss of growth and employment in other countries where such reforms were not undertaken.

We only mention another aspect of crises which has not played a significant role so far in the present crisis, at least in Europe, the United States and Japan: inflation. The danger of inflation of prices of goods seems to be small at present, although the main central banks of the world are all accommodating in their monetary policy. The main reason seems to be the globalisation, which has increased the competition from East-Asian countries, still producing at low costs. Hence goods prices do not rise much, but the increased money supply repeatedly has led to an inflation of asset prices, of houses and shares, with the danger that the collapse of bubbles leads to a chain reaction for private persons, firms, and, in particular, banks, which then suffer from a contraction of credit. They then need to be rescued by the State, which increases its debts, possibly up to the point where bankruptcy seems a possibility.

Defaults of States have been frequent in history, but not among the advanced countries in the post war world. The problem is growing more acute not only because of the crisis, but also because of the generosity of governments in the modern welfare state who spend the money of taxpayers lavishly in order to get re-elected. True federalism is associated with the power of local governments, of provinces and cities, to collect some taxes on their own and to spend within the limits set by their budget. Their freedoms in this regard are measures of their autonomy; it is not real without the possibility of default of the local authorities. The European countries differ a great deal in this regard, and European unification cannot advance significantly without a consensus about the degree to which a future European State shall be federalist.

The German constitution is a mixture of federalism and centralism. The *Länder* are not free to collect their own taxes, but they are rivals in attracting population and firms through the conditions they create by spending. Hence a system of redistribution among the *Länder* became necessary (*Finanzausgleich*). Solidary help is called for, if a Land is in budgetary difficulties, and this induces them to let debts grow and to claim subsidies from the richer *Länder*. In consequence, more and more *Länder* are at the receiving end and the system of redistribution is in peril (Konrad and Zschäpitz 2012). According to the theory (there is a corresponding clause in the German constitution) the State should see to it that the conditions of life are the same everywhere, but true federalism is the art of letting different parts of the country live according to their own aims and possibilities, developing differentiated local cultures, and not to strive for homogeneity.

It is hardly necessary to recall that the present crisis was triggered by the crisis on the American real-estate market. The collapse of the bubble of house prices, caused by excessive loans to house-owners seemingly favoured by the growing values of their homes, led first to some insolvencies and then to many, as house prices fell and the banks and financial institutions also got into payment difficulties. It has been shown (Reinhart and Rogoff 2009: 217) that the coupling of bubbles in the estate markets and banking crises was a trigger for banking crises also in other cases (Finland 1991, Japan 1992, Norway 1987, Spain 1977, Sweden 1991), but it has by no means been a feature of all crises in the past. Rather, it seems characteristic for present arrangements of the financial system, where banking crises can spread rapidly because of the liberalisation of capital markets which, in itself, is favourable for growth in the upswing.

Diagram 7: Germany – decreasing GDP growth trend 1951-2012

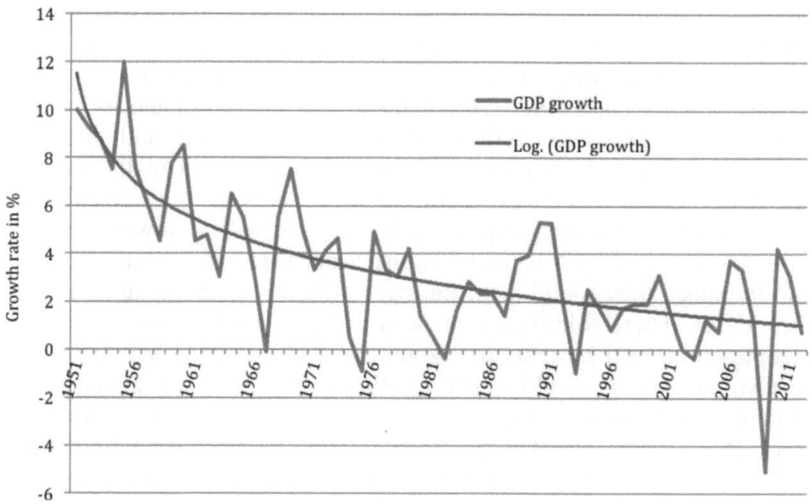

Source: Own illustration following Destatis data, April 2013

Diagram 8: Growth and Employment

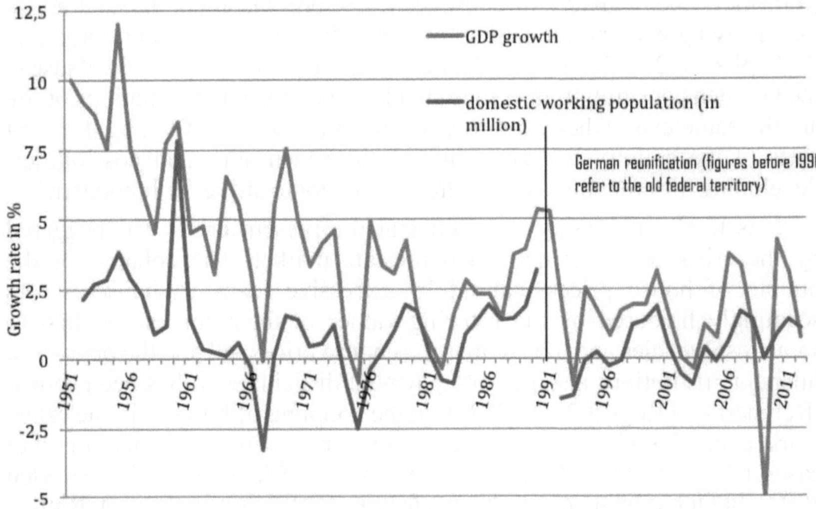

Source: Own illustration following Glasstetter (1991), Destatis und SVR data, April 2013

4. Peculiarities of Historical Crises

We now compare the present crisis with some of the past (Plumpe 2010). When, in the middle of the 19th century, the rhythm of production was not dominated anymore by the erratic sequence of good and bad harvests, the growth of industry resulted in endogenous cycles with a period of about ten years. The upswing would reach a new culminating point after about ten years, since each time future demand was overestimated in the heat of the boom. There was overinvestment to satisfy this demand, and debts increased to finance it. As the expectations of some firms were disappointed and they became cautious, reducing their acquisitions, the sales of other firms fell and the general expansion began to turn. The downward trend now was decisively accelerated, because firms were indebted to each other and to banks; they found it increasingly difficult to service and to repay their debts. There followed what was called a credit panic. It entailed a contraction, in the worst case down to a level dictated by the need of survival. The crisis would spread to other countries. Since solvency was in doubt, creditors increasingly demanded payment in gold, but the gold stock in existence was far too small relative to the outstanding debts, and the sudden scarcity of the only mean of payment, which was fully trusted, increased the general fear. Interest rates rose and the financing of production became more expensive. Production fell, prices fell, but demand did not tend to zero, since there was demand from recipients of fixed incomes; rich proprietors could even increase their demand at falling prices. One used savings in order to survive and when, after some years, it became necessary to replace used-up and obsolescent machinery, the demand for investment goods resumed and a new cycle could begin. This typical trade-cycle was described by Keynes in the last part of the *General Theory*, in a review of the phenomena of the 19th century by means of his new conceptual tools (Keynes 1967 [1936]: 313-32).

The cycles of the 20th century did not as clearly follow a regular pattern. The world crisis of 1929 seemed to be different. It began with the crash at the stock exchange in New York (Galbraith 1961), which was followed by a banking crisis. This rapidly became international and entailed a contraction of demand since the banks did not receive sufficient support from either central banks or governments. It is not really clear to this day whether this crisis was rooted in a malfunctioning of the real economy or whether it simply resulted from the mismanagement of a contracting financial sector. The growth cycles after the Second World War (diagrams 7 and 8) first resembled the business cycles of the 19th century, but the crises resulting from the sudden rises of oil prices had this very particular origin and resulted in pro-cyclical State intervention. For it was a question who should bear the real costs of these price rises. The trade unions were strong enough to resist so that inflation followed. In the subsequent constellation, governments could only get it wrong: if they stimulated demand, they accelerated inflation, if they contracted their demand, they contributed to further reductions of output.

Another peculiarity of the present situation is the possibly excessive growth of the financial system in consequence of the demographic transition: the proportion between the young, who pay for the rents of the old, and the recipients of rents becomes more and more unfavourable. Rents cannot be increased anymore at the same pace as wages, as in earlier years, and more and more strata of society are compelled to complement their rents and pensions by means of personal saving, and this must be channelled through the banking sector. Globalisation also contributed to a relative growth of the financial sector. Its power of acquisition has repeatedly being used for speculation in land values and other assets, with the consequent formation of bubbles and their collapse. These crises are therefore financial in origin. They have been analysed by Hyman Minsky (1986). He described in detail how the financing of investment during the upswing was first solid in that revenues were generated which were adequate both to service the debt and to repay it gradually, and how the upswing would lead to riskier forms of financing - up to Ponzi-games, when new debts are incurred in order to repay old ones. Ponzi-games must collapse sooner or later.

Yet another form of crises results from wages of innovation. Techniques are linked in many ways, in that one innovation, say the steam engine, calls for another, say, railway lines. Innovations and improvements made in one sector can often be used in others. New techniques thus appear in waves. They are initiated by true entrepreneurs, according to Schumpeter, and financed by banks. The upswing is slowed down, when the potential of a cluster of new techniques is exhausted, and a depressed phase results until a new upswing gets on the way.

I have tried in diagram 9 to characterise the crises with their accompanying characteristics, the institutional change they engender and the consequences for the development of economic theory.

Although fluctuations of industrial production were made responsible for the Ten-Year Cycles in Great Britain in the 19th century, practical and theoretical consequences did not, as one might have thought, looking at the matter from today, focus on a control of production and investment, as Keynes would postulate in 1936, but revolved around the reforms of monetary arrangements, since one did not aspire to avoid crises altogether, but their spreading through credit panics. The Bank of England was supposed to mitigate banking crises by lending to institutions of credit, which were exposed. The Bank of England therefore became the lender of last resort. It was also tried to limit the credits provided by the Bank of England in the upswing by prescribing that the money created should not exceed a certain multiple of the amount of gold available in the vaults of the bank. To this end, the creation of money (notes) was separated from the granting of credits (Peel's Bank Act), but, whenever the money market became tight, the act had to be suspended. These experiences were reflected in the monetary theories of the time (Currency School, Banking School). All the fundamental ideas of modern monetary theory were already being discussed, and in a very lively fashion, which contrasts with the rigid expositions of many modern textbooks.

The consequences of the crisis of the 1870s were similar in that one did not deal immediately with the first cause: it took some time before one attempted a better regulation of the stock exchange, but the efforts of the historical school to better the lot of workers were intensified, by introducing insurances for their protection (accidents, illnesses, unemployment). The historical school sought to transcend a merely material improvement, emphasised the importance of the system of education and hoped to raise the level of morality by means of schooling.

It is not surprising that the usual proposals to fight a crisis correspond to the historical facts most closely in the case of the world economic crisis after 1929, for the memory of this catastrophe is still fresh in our minds. Roosevelt introduced programs to improve infrastructure in the United States. The building of motorways and armament played an important role in the reduction of unemployment by the National Socialists in Germany.

Roosevelt had wages and prices controlled in order to avoid inflation – a necessarily temporary measure. The authoritarian governments in Europe were economically successful up to the beginning of the World War, because they had their ways to discipline the workers. In consequence, also insurance against unemployment and other measures of the welfare state in democracy were expanded; they helped to stabilise the business cycle by preventing sudden drops of demand from those who had lost their work. Theoreticians postulated that the level of State expenditure should vary anti-cyclically, but this proved possible only exceptionally. It was not only due to the lack of power or the incompetence of politicians, if expenditure was not reduced in the boom and expanded in the slump, but this followed also from the difficulty of diagnosing the actual position and to increase expenditure, before the crisis had grown really bad, and to begin to save, when an upswing was imminent. Economic theory was changed under Keynesian influence also for those who disliked State intervention. Some elements of this theory are generally recognised, such as the idea of the liquidity trap. Most importantly, Keynesianism led to the development of national accounting. Even if we are suspicious of gross domestic product as a measure of welfare, we are scarcely able to imagine a characterisation of the economic situation without it.

The fact that the Keynesian stabilisers have helped to mitigate the effects of the most recent crisis deserves more attention than it has received, given the historical experiences. The daring monetary policy by the ECB (sometimes difficult to distinguish from fiscal policy) undoubtedly has also helped, while programs for investment have not been mobilised on a significant scale, although one has asked times and again, how one could reduce unemployment especially in the Southern European countries. There is, however, one exception, the so-called "Energiewende" in Germany, that is, the attempted replacement of coal and nuclear energy by renewables. I feel uneasy about this program because of the deterioration of the landscape, which it implies, in order to erect windmills, to expand the grid and energy storage technologies, but there can be no doubt that the program leads to more employment in many industries, directly or indirectly linked with the energy sector. Moreover, the programme is popular, so that losses of economic efficiency and the inflationary pressure associated with any investment programme can perhaps be compensated to some extent by slower increases of wages.

One could regard the present crisis as a consequence of "overproduction" of the sectors of financial services and of the real-estate market – the share of financial services in GDP has grown fourfold since 1940 (Greenwood and Scharfstein 2013). It is obvious and in principle uncontroversial that the banking crisis requires new regulations for the entire financial system, but progress is slow, since no country wishes to put its own institutions at risk. Finally, the experiences of the recent and on-going crisis are a challenge for economic theory, especially in Germany. It cannot be disputed that Keynesian measures, in particular the automatic stabilisers, but also the policy of easy money, have prevented a more drastic collapse of the world economy. But all those concerned with economic policy will feel alarmed, because it becomes more and more difficult to recognise the direction of State interference. Thirty years ago, I wrote papers (Schefold 1981) postulating to integrate into Ordo-liberalism what is significant in Keynesian theory, and to create a new regulatory framework for intervention. This big task is nowhere closer to a solution. Ordo-liberals and Keynesians continue to fight each other; the former deliberately overlooking the not universal, but sometimes remarkable successes of demand policies, the latter disregarding the confusion associated with the economic, political and social consequences of arbitrary and erratic State intervention.

Diagram 9: Crises and their causes

Crisis	Trigger and Propagation	Institutional Consequences	Formation of Theories
The Ten Year-Crises in GB, 19th Century	Overproduction followed by credit panic	Bank of England becomes lender of last resort	Monetary debates: currency and banking schools
"Gründerkrach" Depression 1873-1896	War Reparations and Speculation in Shares	German Social Policy Weakening of Free Trade	Reinforcement of Historical School
Great Depression 1929-1939	Crash at the Stock-Exchange and Banking	Welfare State: Stabilisers	Keynesianism National Accounting
Today	US-Real Estate Market Banking Crisis	New Financial Order (especially in Europe)	Ordo-liberalism / Keynesian-ism: New Synthesis

5. Some Historical Lessons for European Integration

The ideas about the aims of European integration have always been vague. It is by no means generally accepted that a European State should be created within a foreseeable future, say within a generation. What is more, even those who advocate the creation of such a state are not clear as to its constitution and composition. But visions are important. Even practical politicians are – mostly unconsciously – dependent on ideas of a distant past which frame actual conceptions of nations and their characteristics, hence of the possibilities which exist or do not exist to integrate nations and thus to return to older, more universal conceptions of European unity. When Dante postulated an imperial reign for Europe in his book *De Monarchia* (Alighieri 1921: 305-80), he invoked a tradition which went back further over 1300 years to emperor Augustus whose rule was regarded as the model. Dante thus was of the party of the Ghibellines who preferred the governance of the emperor to that of the pope for the

Northern Italian cities, while the Guelfs were the party of the pope. In essence this vision of the Ghibellines of an ideal European universal empire has determined the image of a Europe united in peace for the subsequent centuries, but the real emperor was German, and the Holy Roman Empire one of German nations. Variants, however, existed already in Dante's time. Pierre Dubois, a French counsellor, wrote a book about a new crusade, *De recuperatione terre sancte* (Dubois 1977 [1307]), during the first decade of the 14th century, which was to follow from a close association between the French king and the pope. For Dubois, France was the country beloved by god, and peace was to be secured in Europe by extending French influence, in particular, by letting French princes ascend European thrones: the younger brother of the king was to become the emperor. An emperor of German descent, however, was preferred in German territories. The Holy Roman Empire was essentially a creation of Otto the Great. He had united it, including the provinces of Northern Italy, and he had extended his reign by means of federations and vassalage to neighbouring and even more distant countries, not in the form of a centralised government, but in a loose federation, corresponding to the essence of feudalism in the Middle Ages.

The relationship between France and imperial rule remained difficult. Charles V was elected emperor against François I, and Louis XIV declared his conquest of the Alsace as a re-conquest. And when, finally, under Napoleon, a French dominance arose over much of Europe and the old empire fell, German opinion was split. Nietzsche wrote, looking back in *Der Fall Wagner*:

> Die Deutschen haben endlich, als auf der Brücke zwischen zwei Décadence-Jahrhunderten eine force majeure von Genie und Wille sichtbar wurde, stark genug, aus Europa eine Einheit, eine politische und wirtschaftliche Einheit zum Zweck der Erdregierung zu schaffen, mit ihrem 'Freiheits-kriegen' Europa um den Sinn, um das Wunder von Sinn in der Existenz Napoleons gebracht, – sie haben damit alles, was kam, was heute da ist, auf dem Gewissen, diese kulturwidrigste Krankheit und Unvernunft, die es gibt, den Nationalismus, diese névrose nationale, an der Europa krank ist, diese Verewigung der Kleinstaaterei Europas, der kleinen Politik: sie haben Europa selbst um seinen Sinn, um seine Vernunft – sie haben es in eine Sackgasse gebracht (Nietzsche 1954: 394).

Nietzsche thus admired Napoleon as a genius, capable of creating European unity, and accused the German freedom fighters against Napoleon to have created German nationalism. Nationalism was an illness, a perpetuation of the division of Europe: for Nietzsche, the German liberation led to the loss of the very meaning of Europe. In fact, Napoleon seems to have understood, when on the summit of his power, that he could not submit all of Europe to a centralised government as he had created it in France, continuing the work of Louis XIV and Colbert. After the abdication of the Holy Roman Empire, he would study its institutions and began to imitate them. Perhaps he intended to become a kind of overlord of the European kings and princes. But, while Napoleon's envoys had diplomatic intercourse with the royal house of Prussia, the young Prussian officers would grind their sabres on the steps of stone leading to the French embassy in Berlin. There followed the fourth war of the coalition against Napoleon, which ended with a Prussian defeat. The French became occupants. When Napoleon had overreached himself in the conflict with Britain and Russia, the outrage of the European peoples annihilated his empire. However, not only Nietzsche saw a "wonder of meaning" in Napoleon's reign, but also Goethe as his contemporary admired his genius and accepted his rule, which seemed to guarantee the peace in central Europe and to permit an unprecedented flourishing of German culture.

It is true that it was the nationalism of the 19th century, which completed the splitting of the old European universal values and lead to the creation of national schemes. The reformation had destroyed the unity of the church, but humanism was a new unifying bond for the rising territorial States. The nobility and the upper bourgeoisie preserved their European ties. National, by contrast was the language, as regulated by national academies, leaving local idioms to the servants. National became the churches and the law, the military and the police, even education and universities, though to different degrees, and eventually nationalism culminated in the struggle for colonial empires. Merits of national movements in guaranteeing internal peace and mobilising the forces for growth and welfare cannot be denied, but if the European idea means anything at all, it means to transcend the national point of view, as it formed in the post-napoleonian century against the forces from below, against local self-determination, and against the forces from above: against the European universals. This nationalism was passionate, often bloody, often trite and mean, and this not only in the 20th century, but also before.

The modern European movement began with associations such as the Pan-European-Movement (count Coudenhove-Kalergi). Aristide Briand, as French foreign minister, proposed a European union with a federalist structure in 1929. The resistance movements during the Second World War – the German included – demanded a European collaboration. Churchill's speech in Zurich in 1946 helped to make such projects more concrete. There followed the Schuman Declaration in 1950, the European Coal and Steel Community (ECSC) and the European Union Customs Union (EUCU). The Roman Treaty for the foundation of the European

Economic Community and of the European Atomic Energy Community (EAEC or EURATOM) were signed in 1957: one had decided to achieve European integration by way of economic integration. The core of Europe consisted of Belgium, the Netherlands and Luxemburg, of Germany, France and Italy. The founding fathers pursued a pragmatic policy, but this was not all. They did not only want to overcome national enmities, but they acted from an awareness of European historical and cultural traditions, which was at that time still transmitted by schools with a program of classical education. It was visible in art and could be experienced in cultural exchanges.

The most interesting and critical phase in the process of integration came about in 1959 through the foundation of a second circle of European States, which wanted an integration of a different kind (Denmark, Great Britain, Norway, Portugal, Sweden, Austria and Switzerland; Bergmann 2012) The two concepts were essentially different. The European Free Trade Association (EFTA) identified with the goals of liberalism. Within the States concerned, nationalism was less of a problematic memory than, especially, in defeated Germany, as represented by the Federal Republic. The European Economic Community aimed to transcend the nation State. The agricultural policy was introduced to provide a basis for a unified economic area by levelling the natural and geographical differences and historical advantages and shortcomings in agricultural production. Processes of industrial concentration across the borders of the individual countries were encouraged to use advantages of scale. A common framework was to be created for the markets.

Looking back, the duality of these two conceptions of Europe seems well founded. Not only in Great Britain, but also in Scandinavia and in Switzerland, the Anglo-Saxon form of liberalism with the principle of free trade of confederated nations was stronger than the desire to integrate in a transnational construction, politically, economically and culturally. Moreover, it was well known that Great Britain oscillated between its interests on the continent and the Commonwealth. Charles de Gaulle therefore was opposed to an early entry of Great Britain to the EEC, but, in 1973, the accession of Denmark, Great Britain and Ireland meant the northern enlargement of the European Community and entailed a watering down of the old goals of integration in the core of Europe. The EFTA exists still today: however, it is a small and nearly insignificant apparatus. In view of the present debate between Great Britain and most of the members of the EU, which, today as before, aim at a political unity at least in principle – or pretend to aim at it – while Great Britain wants to avoid such integration today as before, one remembers the old conflict and asks oneself whether it would not have been better for both sides, if the peaceful rivalry between two different conceptions of European integration had been preserved.

Eight States of the European Community (the members of the EC at that time, without Great Britain) created a European monetary unit (ECU) in 1979, with the European Exchange Rate Mechanism, to keep exchange rates within narrow bands. The European Parliament in Strasbourg was elected for the first time in the same year. There followed further accessions: Greece in 1981, Spain and Portugal in 1986; Austria, Finland and Sweden in 1995 and, afterwards, the enlargement in the East. Euro and the creation of Euroland or the Eurozone followed upon the foundation of the Economic and Monetary Union (EMU) with the Maastricht Treaties (1991); its first stage began in 1993 with the free movement of capital between the member States. Close coordination of economic policies and cooperation between central banks was envisaged. The European Union (EU), a concept, which had appeared already in 1972 as a goal for the process of integration, is anchored in the Treaty of Maastricht and became a substitute for a proposed European constitution (which had not been ratified by all member States) in the Treaty of Lisbon in 2009. Its main institutions are the European Council (essentially the heads of State and of government), the European Parliament, the Council of the Union (the assembly of the ministers of each country in a given domain – e.g. the council of the foreign ministers, the council of the ministers of finance and so on in ten different compositions) and the European Commission.

The step decisive for the understanding of our present difficulties was, without doubt, the introduction of the Economic and Monetary Union or simply Monetary Union, for short, since the measures taken to ensure economic convergence and fiscal coordination are much less developed and hence of lesser significance than the introduction of a common currency. All earlier and all subsequent steps towards European integration had in common that it was possible to stand still, after the corresponding level of integration had been reached, without any need either to take back earlier steps of integration or to hasten it and to create new institutions in order to preserve stability. The Monetary Union, and only the Monetary Union, has proved to be dramatically unstable. It is the origin of fundamental disturbances, and further steps of integration have been taken in consequence, without being sufficient for a return to stability. I assert, with many others, that this stability will not be reached before Euroland will have been transformed into something like a State. Otherwise, Europe will fall back and the European Monetary Union will disintegrate.

Monetary unions have existed since antiquity: occasionally, different city-states would create a federation in order to maintain a common coin. Another interesting precedent is the monetary union, which existed in the early 15th century at the time of the reformation between the different Saxon countries, the Ernestines and the Albertines. The dynastic partitioning of Saxony, which became also a confessional partitioning in the reformation, had not prevented a common property of the Ernestine and Albertine dukes of the mines and the coinage, hence the monetary union. It was subject to explosive internal tensions when the Ernestine duke, who was the main supporter of Luther, lacked money and wished to increase his revenues by means of a deterioration of the coin, while the Albertine duke, the Catholic, insisted on keeping the good quality of the coin in circulation. Their dispute led to a famous controversy on economic policy, the first, which has been preserved in the form of printed pamphlets of 1530 and 1531. The Albertine pamphlets argued that Saxony prospered because of the export of silver, both in specie and in coins, while the Ernestine pamphlet denounced the mercantilist policy of England, Portugal and Venice, which robbed Saxony of her silver by exporting textiles, spices and other luxury items, thus competing with local agriculture and handicraft. Instead of proposing an alternative strategy of development, the Ernestine wished to close the country and to continue a simple life in accordance with early Protestant ideas (Schefold 2004). Another monetary union was that of the Latin countries, concluded in 1865 between France, Switzerland, Belgium and Italy. They had only certain coins in common, while each country printed its own banknotes and minted other coins used only in the country concerned. Notes and other coins therefore could appreciate or depreciate relatively to the common coins, which were issued within the curious system of bimetallism, but the cooperation which thus was necessary became problematic, when differences in economic development manifested themselves, and the union collapsed with the advent of the First World War.

Edgar Salin (1965) proposed that the European Community should also aspire to the creation of a coinage union, in which it is a matter of honour to maintain the parity between the own banknotes of the country and the common coins, as far as possible. Such a coinage union can be dissolved without grave consequences, if the discipline necessary to maintain the parity cannot be enforced. Euroland must live with the much more ambitious project of creating a full monetary union, therefore with a common system of central banks which controls the entire emission of money and the system of credit. This was reached via a long way, leading from the Werner Plan of 1970, which developed the idea of a European currency but foundered with the collapse of the system of Bretton Woods and the first oil-price shock. With the Basel-agreement of 1972, there followed the so-called "snake in the tunnel" as a bilateral system of intervention with regard to the US-Dollar, initially with nine countries, eventually with only the members Germany, Netherlands, Belgium, Luxemburg and Denmark, the "snake in the tunnel" was created as the exchange rates could not be fully stabilised. The European Monetary System was founded in 1978. It replaced the system of controlling the exchange rates. As mentioned above, an imaginary currency, the ECU, was defined by means of a grid of parities. The exchange rates could vary by 2.25 percent, from 1993 onwards by up to 15 percent, around the reference values, and if even that was not sufficient, a realignment of currencies was permitted. In consequence, a considerable revaluation of the German D-Mark took place with respect to other currencies in the system. For instance, the D-Mark re-valued with respect to the Italian Lira between 1979 and 1990 in total by 63.6 percent.

Other countries, especially France, did not like to have to orient their monetary policy according to the developments in the economically strongest country of the Union, the Federal Republic of Germany. Germany's reunification led to discussions about a future monetary system, which resulted in the Treaty of Maastricht. Hence the foundation of the European Monetary Institute in 1994, which was transmuted to the European Central Bank in 1999, when the exchange rates of the national currency with respect to the common Euro were fixed once and for all. It was a paradoxical procedure. The experiences with the previous systems had led to the insight that monetary policy was not adequate to keep exchange rates fixed. But why should then a currency union be able to function?

In effect, the Treaties of Maastricht and of Lisbon in combination led to close financial integration in the private sector, but the systems of public finance of each Member State were kept separate. The supervision of banks also remained national. The decision to create a European banking union after the crisis is only very slowly being executed. Despite migration labour markets have remained national. The Monetary Union thus can be compared to the gold standard system, with gold left out, and, internally, irrevocably fixed exchange rates (Bordo and James 2013).

6. The Crisis of Euroland and of the European Union: The Dilemma

Economists have long been discussing a so-called "uneasy triangle" (diagram 10). Of three goals, stability of the price level, stability of exchange rates and free circulation of capital, in general only two can be pursued simultaneously with success; the third goal will then usually be missed. If, for instance, there is stability of exchange rates and a free flow of capital between several States, the rates of inflation will usually be different. If one wants to realise the stability of prices and of exchange rates, it may be necessary to introduce capital controls. Germany was able to maintain the stability of prices and the free flow of capital after the downfall of the Bretton Woods system, but revaluations became necessary.

The introduction of the Euro, combined with the liberal principles of the integration of markets, really meant to pursue all three goals of the triangle simultaneously: instead of stable exchange rates, one had a unique currency, inflation was to be kept low and free movement of capital had become a matter of course.

The common economy required a common State, and if the hen (this common State) had been there, she had been able to breed the egg (the common currency), slowly and quietly. But now the egg had been laid, and who was to breed it? In this currency union, the differential development of prices, wages and productivity in the several States, which had been observed before, was still not only possible, but even probable. The economists among the politicians, who knew this, now spoke of the coronation theory: integration should eventually be crowned by the founding of a State. In order to minimise the risks on the way, the Treaty of Maastricht prescribed that only countries of the European Union with low rates of inflation and solid public finances could take part. Fiscal policy was to be kept separate, by prescribing that each State should stay within limits of indebtedness (maximum increase of debt of 3 percent per year, level of debts at most 60 percent of GDP). And lo and behold, the economy of Euroland developed fairly steadily during one decade. Issing wrote in 2008: "All in all, the criteria of convergence have fulfilled their task". However, he added: "The Treaty [of Maastricht] does not answer the question to what extent the catching-up process of the poorer countries [...] may create problems for a unified monetary policy" (my translation from Issing 2008: 13).

Two graphs may illustrate the relatively easy beginning. The governments were ambitious and wanted to participate in the common monetary system; hence they were able to let the rates of inflation converge at a low level (diagram 11). The participants in financial markets came to believe (and they were not altogether wrong, as things turned out) that the governments of the European Union would have to warrant their debts mutually, although the Treaty of Maastricht had excluded this explicitly with the so-called "no-bailout-clause". In consequence, the interest rates on the bonds of the several States also converged, as diagram 12 demonstrates. This convergence actually was dramatic some cases: the return on Greek bonds fell from almost 27 percent to only 5 percent, and the cost of indebtedness of Spain, Italy and Portugal also fell very considerably. If Italy had used this advantage to pay back the debts, the differential would have been large enough to reduce the total State debt of Italy to zero, as Hans Werner Sinn has shown (Sinn 2012). But another path was chosen. Diagram 13 shows how the rates of interests began to diverge again, as the weaker States in particular had to incur large debts in order to save the banks in the financial crisis.

The politicians had not made a wise use of the opportunity to raise finance at lower cost. Greece, for instance, had formerly solved its deficit problems by incurring new debts, by creating money and, in particular, by devaluation. It was clear that these three options would not continue to be available after the introduction of the Euro. Hence, the country should have improved fiscal discipline and it should have introduced an efficient system of taxation. But Greece multiplied its foreign debt in the ten years between 2000 and 2010 by a factor of 10 instead. The banks, which held the bonds, had to be rescued when interest rates rose and bond values fell, and this increased the debts of the States. To save all the banks meant to save too many; there are always some which continue to be in trouble. The European Central Bank interpreted monetary policy rather freely by buying State bonds and it thus calmed the markets. There is no room here to discus the European Stability Mechanism, which has since been introduced in order to lend to States (with conditions attached), based on capital in part given by the member States, but mostly borrowed with warrants provided by the members.

However significant the nexus between the crises of sovereign debt and of banks, as seen yesterday in Ireland and Greece or today, as I write this essay, in Cyprus, may be, endangering the economy of the country concerned and, via chain reactions, the economy of Europe and even of the world, the real problem of the Monetary Union is elsewhere. Behind the consequences of the economic crisis and the indebtedness of States there lurks the problem with the greatest explosive potential for the Monetary Union in the divergence of the rates of inflation, of wages and productivities. These magnitudes are described by so-called unit costs. Unit costs (on an hourly basis) relate the nominal wages, divided by the volume of employment, and gross value added, divided by the volume of the working population.

It is well known in Germany, but possibly less discussed in other countries, that these unit costs diverged significantly between 2000 and 2010. In this period, they rose very little in Germany, by about 20 percent on average in Euroland, but by about 35 percent in Italy, Greece, Spain, Portugal and Ireland. The difficulties encountered by the several countries of Euroland correspond on the whole to their ranking regarding the control of the unit costs. The austerity measures to limit State indebtedness have led to a fall of unit costs recently in Greece, Ireland and Portugal, while they begin to rise more in Germany, but convergence has not been reached by far. Measures to reduce sovereign debt depress the economy and are painful, and so are measures to reduce unit costs and, generally, deflation. But it is difficult to see how they could be avoided. The countries under pressure to pursue prosperity measures justifiably complain that it causes the economy to contract, they ask for relief in the form of demand policies and investment programs (Savona 2012). Such Keynesian measures are in fact likely to increase employment but, if the economy of the country concerned is not competitive, many, perhaps most of the employment effects will be created elsewhere. The danger is that, instead of improving employment, the trade balance will be deteriorated. The processes of cumulative causation run both ways. A good competitive position allows exports to increase. This expansion of demand permits to use advantages of scale in production and in the division of labour, which in turn imply more competitive power. The question is how a downward spiral can be interrupted in the opposite case. Unfortunately, Keynesian measures are likely to be counterproductive in an open economy in a weak competitive position.

Let us confront the situation in Germany and Italy paradigmatically. Wage costs in the private sector rose in the case of Germany between 2000 and 2010 nominally by 1.1 percent per year, in Italy by 1.9 percent. The larger increase of wages in Italy, however, was not justified by a larger increase of productivity, on the contrary: productivity over-all rose between 2000 and 2010 in Germany by 0.6 percent in real terms, in Italy it fell throughout the decade each year by 0.2 percent on average, according to the Eurostat figures. This loss of productivity represents the crucial fact about Italy, which grew very successfully in the 1950s and 1960s, continued to grow fairly well into the 1990s, but lost ground rapidly after 2000 (De Novellis, in Paolazzi and Sylos Labini 2013: 29-73).

It is not easy to see how the most direct remedy, an internal devaluation, a reduction of the levels of wages and prices, can be avoided in Italy. A successful internal devaluation means that the purchasing power of wages stays constant for domestically produced goods, but that it is diminished for foreign goods while exports become cheaper. A multitude of other reforms is also being discussed, many of them desirable, but they will only be useful if, in the end, the country reaches an above-average growth of productivity and lowers unit costs relative to its competitors. The austerity measures taken in Europe after the crisis to reduce deficits and lower costs were planned on the assumption that the fiscal multipliers would be smaller than they have turned out to be, according to Blanchard and Leigh (2013); incomes fell more than expected, yet the internal devaluations did not go far enough. What should Italy do?

It might be argued that the emphasis on unit costs is misplaced, to the extent, that it is comparative advantage, not absolute advantage, which matters in international exchange. However, the introduction of the Euro and the existing institutional framework imply in my opinion that it is absolute advantage, which rules the roost in this case. Another argument against the emphasis on unit costs is Keynesian. Keynesians focus on processes, rather than on static comparisons in terms of relative prices. But it is precisely a cumulative process by which Italy seems to lose competitive advantages, and I do not see how this process could be reversed without changing the price level. Keynes developed the theory of the multiplier for a closed country in his *General Theory* and the level of productivity was given. But there are different levels of productivity and wage costs in different countries. Prices can theoretically be explained as mark-up or normal prices. Italian economists who have worked a great deal on the post-Keynesian synthesis, combining mark-up prices (Kalecki) and normal prices (Sraffa) with the Keynesian theory of effective demand, should be the first to recognise that the theory of the multiplier must be modified profoundly, if it is to applied in an open economy, surrounded by countries with different levels of unit costs. In the present case, post-Keynesian and neoclassical theories lead to the same conclusion: internal devaluation is necessary, and direct means to achieve it (deflationary measures) can be avoided only if other methods exist which lead to the same outcome. This is where the real difficulties begin.

It is said that the rate of innovation should be increased to export more new goods, since existing goods are, on average, too expensive. This undoubtedly would help, but is it realistic to assume that this effect could, by itself, reverse the trend? Others also innovate and spend more on the development of the knowledge society. It is planned to facilitate economic growth in Italy by means of political reforms of the central State and in the regions and by intensifying the fight against corruption. This could have happened earlier, it should not happen much later, but it will not of much avail as a measure against the crisis quickly. Growth is to be accelerated by means of enhancing the credit of the State in order to improve infrastructure, to strengthen banks in trouble. But the State, which should shoulder the responsibility to finance these measures, is itself in difficulty. To avoid higher interest rates, forced borrowing has been proposed to finance investment (Savona 2012), but forced borrowing implies political risks. Other explanations of the specific difficulties of Italy have been sought; however, the main areas for national initiatives remain the reform of institutions, the functioning of markets and science and technology (Blake and Crotti in Paolazzi and Sylos Labini 2013: 93-137). At the international level, one observes that shifts in intraeuropean trade are connected with extraeuropean developments. Germany is exporting more to Eastern Europe and to China, so that the share of the European South in German exports has shrunk. This might justify Italian attempts to sell more goods in Germany, hence a more sophisticated strategy (Simonazzi, Ginzburg and Nocella 2013) considers influencing a more extended network of trade in the name of a coordinated European industrial policy, but the political bodies of Euroland are hardly up to the task of coordinating the remedies which would correspond to such a complex diagnosis.

In a more critical way, there has been talk of German mercantilism, and Germany has been asked to raise wages in the name of European solidarity. But the German competitive position is not all that good, if compared to a more glorious past of the German economy in the 1950s and 1960s or to the economic success of East Asia today, and the present advantages, which exist, have been bought at some cost. The Germans and their politicians will therefore not easily be persuaded to follow such a proposal. German wages rise little because of competition from Eastern Europe and in more distant countries. This competition demonstrates that development is not confined anymore to Western Europe and America, but that it has spread at last after long years, during which only a small number of developing countries had significant growth rates. All European countries will have to adapt to this new reality which should be accepted as evidence of the advent of long-sought progress elsewhere. The GDP of developing countries surpassed that of developed countries for the first time in 2012, and their share in world exports is nearly one-half (WTO, 2013: 14).

The Euro crisis has led to chauvinist reactions, to populist policies and to the immigration of able workers from the South who despair of the future of their country. Why does it seem to be impossible to have a more equilibrated growth in different areas of Euroland? We observe after all, that many States live with strong internal divergences between regions. Italy itself offers an example. The standard of life, measured in terms of gross domestic product per head, is about twice that of Sicily and Calabria in Lombardy and Piemont. There is some controversy as to the extent to which the difference can be traced to the conditions prior to the unification of Italy. It certainly has existed for more than a century (on policies for convergence and some continuing divergence see Felice 2012). It is clear that the central State has constantly been striving to reduce the differences; in effect, Italy was kept together. There are the common cultural elements and the language. The central State sometimes had to use force in order to keep down local separatist movements. The State itself was centralised, imposed unified law and used taxation, redistribution and expenditure to create more homogeneity, in a degree, which the EU is not able to attend, and be it only because its budget is much smaller in per capita terms than that of any national government. A State can in principle use every investment in infrastructure, the expenditures for defence, the subsidies to universities and schools to compensate differences in well-being between regions, much beyond the direct redistribution, which is more visible. Everybody agrees that mistakes have been made, in Italy as elsewhere, in that not all the public investment in the South has significantly contributed to the growth of local industry, but not everything went wrong, and where redistribution was successful, it was happily accepted. The sectionalism of the South has in recent years been complemented by a sectionalism of the North, but the idea of the nation State has not been defeated.

Diagram 10: The uneasy triangle

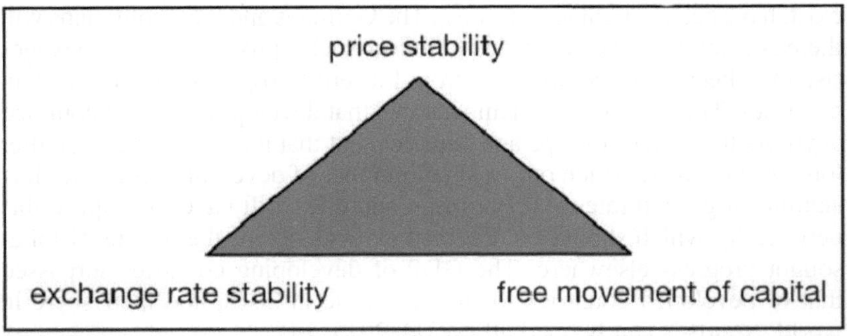

Diagram 11: Convergence of inflation rates, 1960-2012

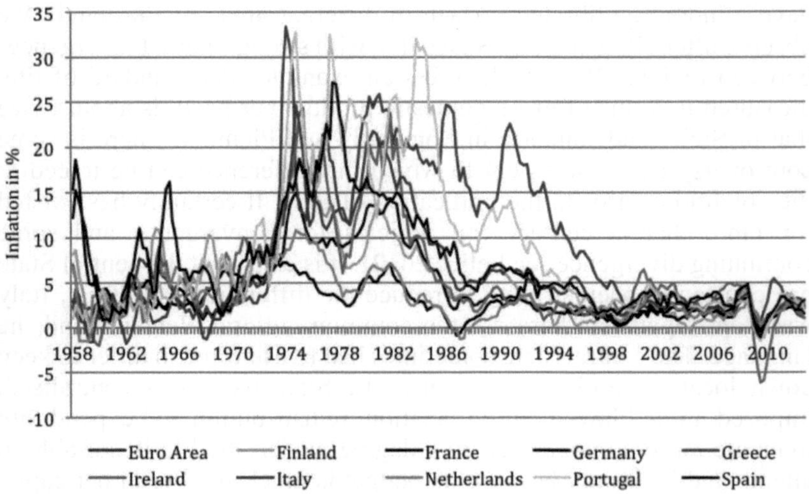

Source: Own illustration following IMF data, Statistical Yearbook, 2013

Diagram 12: Convergence of long-term returns on sovereign bonds

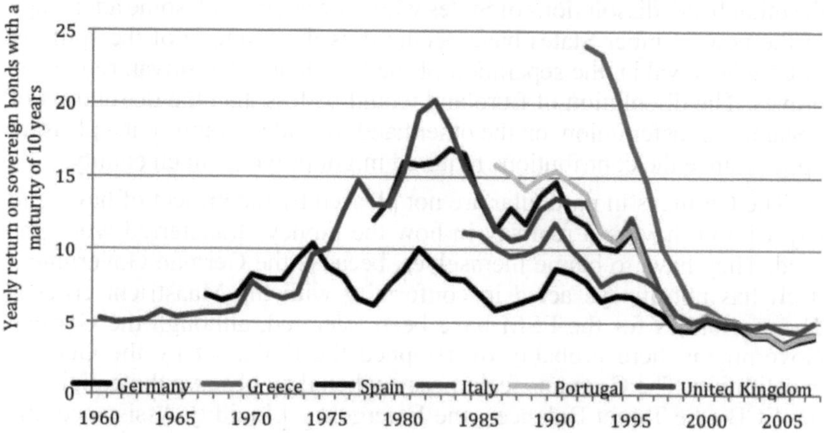

Source: Own illustration following Eurostat data, April 2013

Diagram 13 diagram: Divergence of long-term returns on sovereign bonds

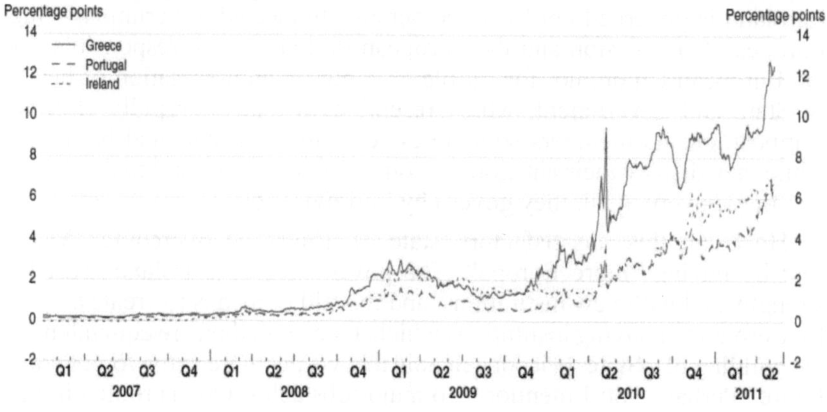

Source: OECD Economic Outlook 2011, p. 55

7. And Now?

We arrive at the decisive question: is Europe faced with the choice between the abandonment of the Monetary Union and the introduction of a system of transfers, administered by the governments of Euroland?

The abandonment of the Euro would be expensive. It would be associated with a terrific loss of prestige; it would also have a monetary cost. Germany would have to face a strong revaluation. The dissolution might not function orderly and could endanger other European institutions. On the other hand, dissolutions of States without war and with some advantage of the new member States have occurred as the example of the splitting of Czechoslovakia, the separation of the Czech and the Slovak republics, proves. The dissolution of Euroland would be less than the dissolution of a State. A transfer union, on the other hand, would not represent a pleasant option, since the contributions required might provoke much enmity.

The Germans in particular are not pleased by the project of having to pay without having a real say in how the moneys transferred would be used. They have to blame themselves, because the German Government itself has not always acted in conformity with the Maastricht criteria. The warranties for the ESM have been tolerated, although the German Government there probably overstepped the limits set by the German constitution. The Germans feel uneasy, when they observe the policies of the ECB (the Target Balances, the Emergency Liquidity Assistance, the Outright Monetary Transactions), although German exports have been favoured by the cheap interest rates and the consequent low exchange rate. Ordo-liberal principles are invoked, but one is dependent on Keynesian stabilisers. Euroland is in fact close to being a transfer union already. But Euroland is governed not by a democratically elected government – the European Commission and the European Parliament are responsible for the European Union, not for Euroland –, but by an association of heads of State and government, which resembles a club of rapidly shifting composition; its members sometimes seem to be in personal harmony, while they display their antagonisms on other occasions, and to the extent that they govern at all, they govern by improvisation.

How can this unsatisfactory state of affairs be overcome? Many say: by having “more Europe”. The governance of Euroland must be strengthened with new institutions, and this either means to create a State for Euroland or having institutions which, taken together, are equivalent to the building of a State. Is it conceivable that we get there in the foreseeable future? Perhaps not; I mention two major obstacles. One is rooted in the ambivalent position of Great Britain. They cannot abandon the European Union easily, since they are tied to Europe by strong economic interests and the desire not to lose all influence on the continent. Let us imagine nevertheless that they were not part of the European Union anymore. In consequence, the European Union and Euroland would largely coincide. The institutions created during sixty years for European integration would then, according to the logic of things, admittedly not automatically, certainly not without frictions, but more easily and rapidly than now, lead to the transmission of sovereignty to a government of the European Union which would emerge from a sequence of reforms of the European Commission. To obtain national consent would not be easy; not only one but probably several successive referenda would be necessary in most States. But it could be tried – what else do we want, when we talk about European integration?

But what do we really want? If we examine the parallel between European integration and the unification of nation States between the 17th and the 19th centuries, we note that the former provinces of the realms either had to be transformed – they even vanished in the case of France – or that imbalances resulted from the preservation of the old structures: Piemont was too strong for Sicily in the Italian case, Prussia too strong for Württemberg or Baden in the case of Germany. Could France, Germany and Italy be provinces of a future Europe, while other provinces had the size of one of the Baltic States, for example? Germany today is composed of the *Länder* such as Bavaria or Hassia. The *Länder* could remain the units for a future Europe as a federalist State, composed of regions with strong autonomous governments, own fiscal responsibility and considerable cultural diversity, for this is one of the main European assets. Not for nothing, the official motto of the EU is "United in diversity".

So the German Government would have to cede sovereignty not only to a European Parliament and Government, but also to its provinces or regions – in this case *Länder* – and the nation would eventually lose its form as a State and survive only as a language community. It is just conceivable that the Germans might be ready to continue to pursue this path, which seems to me to be the only logical continuation of the process of European integration, with its roots in the Middle Ages and the beginnings of its practical realisation after the Second World War. But we ask ourselves whether France and Italy, with their traditions of centralised government, would be prepared to undergo the same transformation. The French regions (21 in mainland France) have competences mainly in the field of education, but no fiscal autonomy and legislative powers. The Italian regions have some legislative powers and some fiscal autonomy; there is a process of decentralisation. A very long period of transition would be required to prepare the ground for such a shift of power from Paris and Rome to Brussels on the one hand and to these respective regions on the other. Meanwhile, Berlin, having a special responsibility because of the economic weight of Germany, should show more leadership to move forward (Savona 2012), but nobody dares to axe the nation State. There is the Committee of Regions, also created by the Treaty of Maastricht, the assembly of the regional and local representatives of the EU. It meets about six times a year, but it disposes only of powers of consultation to ensure subsidiarity – the initiative to create a federalist State for Euroland must come from elsewhere.

Hence the dilemma: we do not want to abandon the Euro and Euroland, but we cannot create the State required to preserve them, and the present constellation is unstable. Some believe (Otmar Issing is prominent among them) that we should return to a strict observance of the rules of Maastricht, but who is there to enforce the discipline, which that would entail, and would the system not fall apart anyway in consequence of the next crisis, once the present crisis is overcome after some more painful years? Unfortunately, there is not much time left to choose between moving forward and a retreat.

References

ALIGHIERI, D. (1921). *Dantis Alagherii Opera omnia*, II. Leipzig, Insel.

BERGMANN, J. (2012) (ed.). *Handlexion der europäischen Union*. Baden-Baden, Nomos.

BLANCHARD, O. J.; LEIGH, D. (2013). "Growth forecast errors and fiscal multipliers". *American Economic Review*, 103 (3): 117-20.

BLANKENBURG, S. *et al.* (2013). "Prospects for the Eurozone". *Cambridge Journal of Economics*, 37 (3): 463-77.

BORDO, M. D.; JONES, H. (2013)." The European crisis in the context of the history of previous financial crises". National Bureau of Economic Research W. P., No. 19111, June.

DUBOIS, P. (1977). *De recuperatione terre sancte. Dalla "Respublica christiana" ai primi nazionalismi e alla politica antimediterranea*, ed. by A. Diotti. Firenze, Olschki.

FELICE, E. (2012). "Regional convergence in Italy, 1891-2001: testing human and social capital". *Cliometrica*, 6: 267-306.

GALBRAITH, J. K. (1961 [1954]). *The Great Crash*. London, Pelican.

GREENWOOD, R.; SCHARFSTEIN, D. (2013). "The growth of finance". *Journal of Economic Perspectives*, 27 (2): 3-28.

ISSING, O. (2008). *Der Euro. Geburt – Erfolg – Zukunft*. München, Vahlen.

KEYNES, J. M. (1967 [1936]). *The General Theory of Employment, Interest and Money*. London, Macmillan.

KONRAD, K. A.; ZSCHÄPITZ, H. (2012). *Schulden ohne Sühne? Was Europas Krise uns Bürger kostet* (rev. ed.). München, C. H. Beck.

MINSKY, H. P. (2008 [1986]). *Stabilizing an Unstable Economy*. New York, McGraw-Hill.

NIETZSCHE, F. (1954). *Götzendämmerung. Der Antichrist. Ecce homo. Gedichte*. Stuttgart, Kröner.

PAOLAZZI, L.; SYLOS LABINI, M. (2013). *L'Italia al bivio*. Roma, Luiss.

PLUMPE, W. (2010). *Wirtschaftskrisen. Geschichte und Gegenwart*. München, C. H. Beck.

REINHART, C. M.; ROGOFF, K. S. (2009). *This Time is different. Eight Centuries of Financial Folly*. Princeton, Princeton University Press.

SALIN, E. (1965). "Für eine europäische Währung". In *Fundamentale Fragen künftiger Währungspolitik*. Tübingen, Mohr (Siebeck), 199-219.

SAVONA, P. (2012). *Lettera agli amici tedeschi e italiani*. Mimeo.

SCHEFOLD, B. (2004). *Beiträge zur ökonomischen Dogmengeschichte. Ausgewählt und hrsg. v. Volker Caspari*. Düsseldorf, Wirtschaft u. Finanzen.

SCHEFOLD, B. (1981). "Die Relevanz der Cambridge-Theorie für die ordnungspolitische Diskussion". In Issing, O. (ed.). *Zukunftsprobleme der Sozialen Marktwirtschaft*. Berlin, Duncker & Humblot, 689-715.

SINN, H. W. (2012). "Die europäische Fiskalunion. Gedanken zur Entwicklung der Eurozone". *Perspektiven der Wirtschaftspolitik*, 13 (3): 137-78.

SIMONAZZI, A.; GINZBURG, A.; NOCELLA, G. (2013). "Economic relations between Germany and Southern Europe". *Cambridge Journal of Economics*, 37: 653-7.

WTO (2013). *Annual Report*, Lausanne.

From Friends to Foes?

The Euro as a Cause of New Nationalism

Charles B. BLANKART[1]

I. Alarming Trends

The author is thankful to Monika Poettinger and Antonio Varsori for having organized the conference on "*Economic crisis and New Nationalisms*". It is indeed alarming to observe how national egoisms are growing in Europe, while old friendships seem to disappear. Will that be the future of the European peoples? Will yesterday's trust turn into today's distrust? Will yesterday's friends become tomorrow's enemies? The civil society is alarmed, but the public remains passive.

The concerns of the crisis are targeted to the euro. The European leaders – the Council, the Commission and the European Central Bank – have been trying to maintain the euro as a unifying tie around the European peoples for more than five years, but the euro makes no sign of becoming self-sustainable, instead, it depends on a permanent flow of fiscal and monetary transfers from the Northern to the Southern member states. The mixed evaluations of the euro policies by the press compiled by Monika Poettinger (2014) and the warnings of the historian Antonio Varsori (2014) both in this volume underline the worry which is widespread among all Europeans.

II. A Theory of the Euro Crisis

The new nationalisms are a riddle. But the public discussion does not contribute very much to solving the problem. The more the civil society condemns the new nationalisms, the more they grow in the underneath. Therefore it has to be asked: Does the civil society ask the right questions? Could it be that the problem perceived is upside down and has to be placed on its feet before an analysis can start? Are the new nationalisms a symptom rather than the cause of the crisis? In order to solve the riddle a theory is required explaining the new nationalisms endogenously. Why did the new nationalisms emerge now

1 The author is indebted to Konstantin KÖrner for helpful editorial suggestions.

and not earlier? The hypothesis proposed in this paper is that the euro is the cause of the crisis. New nationalisms are not growing despite of the euro, but because of the euro. This hypothesis may be uneasy for all those who believe in the common project of the euro. They may be disappointed that the goals in which they believe are evaporating. But after all, not the euro, but the friendship among the people of Europe is the goal. The euro is a means, not the end.

Figure 1 summarizes the history of the European Union since its beginning in 1958. It shows that the popularity of the European Union increased during the first half of its existence from 1958 to about 1992 and then declined constantly up to present.

The first period from 1958 to about 1992 may be characterized as the period of European *integration by trade in private goods.* It ended with the establishment of the free internal market for goods, services, labour and capital in different currencies in 1992.

Since 1992 the focus of the European Union has shifted from promoting gains of trade in private goods towards obtaining gains from *integration by jointly sharing public goods.* The Common Foreign and Security Policy (CFSP) and the Common Security and Defense Policy (CSDP) have been established. But above all, the euro has to be mentioned because it is the most important public good of the Union.

The euro needs two steps to work. First a set of common institutions (a central bank, a number of regulations on a common monetary policy, an enforcement system and a network for executing transactions) has to be established and then trade takes place within this institution. The institution of the euro is a public good shared by all individuals. Trade in the euro is a private good. The principle of self-interest applies only to the second step.

Establishing the public good is fundamentally different from trade in private goods. A public good needs a coordinated action. All participants have to join their efforts towards the same goal. This does not happen by the "invisible hand". For the more one individual contributes to the public good, the less has to be contributed by the other individuals. (With private goods, in comparison, trade is generated if individuals work in different directions, if they specialize and then proceed to market exchange.) A public good, however, needs a prior binding agreement among the participants on who contributes how much. If the partners are badly chosen or if they shirk on their contribution, the public good is not produced or it is badly produced and ends in a crisis. All participants are disappointed and quarrel on who is guilty. So the new nationalisms are generated. This is the central problem of the euro crisis.

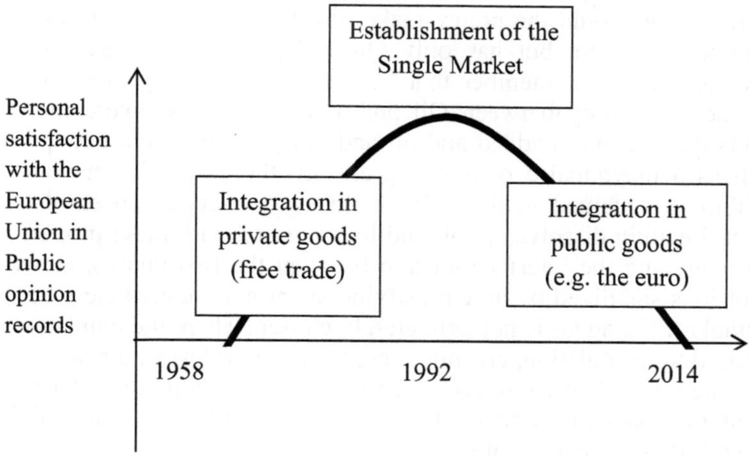

Source: Euractiv, several issues

III. Oil and Vinegar

A simple story may help to understand the problem of the euro as a public good. Since antiquity grocers have used Oil for canning olives and Vinegar for canning cucumbers. The grocers know that they may add Oil to Oil and Vinegar to Vinegar at constant returns to scale, but that they must not add Oil to Vinegar nor Vinegar to Oil because the resulting mix is useful neither for canning olives nor for canning cucumbers. The mix exhibits strongly decreasing returns to scale down to zero returns compared to Oil and Vinegar in separation. Therefore grocers carefully observe this rule, and so should policy makers when they plan to establish a monetary union. The success or failure of a monetary union depends on its founding members. Countries which are as Oil and Vinegar are not good partners for a monetary union.

This view has been, however, criticized by the adherents of the "Mutual-Stimulation-Thesis" who say that Oil and Vinegar should be deliberately mixed because their differences stimulate each other. So Oil and Vinegar are deliberately mixed to generate a salad dressing. But a closer observation reveals that Oil and Vinegar do not join to an inseparable solution such as salt and water which can only be separated by adding a substantial amount of energy. Oil and Vinegar remain inimical as if they were gladiators in a Roman arena to fight or if the crisis is the purpose of pouring Oil and Vinegar together. After a while the spectacle is over and Oil and Vinegar separate and cluster as useless substances at different places in bottom of the salad bowl. Therefore the Mutual-Stimulation-Thesis is not constructive unless one intends to generate a crisis.

But what should the policy maker do if he has the task to establish a monetary union, but has only Oil and Vinegar as ingredients? In this case he may remember that he learnt in chemistry in school that the incompatibility between Oil and Vinegar may be overcome if an emulsifying agent is added and oil and vinegar generate a new product such as a mayonnaise or a vinaigrette. In the case of a mayonnaise, lecithin – contained in the yolk of the egg – acts as an emulsifying agent. Lecithin dissolves in oil and in water and with these properties it can overcome the interface tension between the two phases. However, emulsions stabilized by an emulsifying agent may nevertheless become unstable if the agent is not deliberately chosen. Then, the emulsions are exposed to flocculation, creaming, coalescence, or Ostwald ripening that alter the internal structure and often worsen their properties.[2] Therefore, it cannot be taken for granted that Oil and Vinegar become compatible. It depends on the capacity of the emulsifying agent.

The European Monetary Union comes very close to a mix of Oil and Vinegar. Some of its participating governments are market oriented and some are redistributive. Therefore the latter exert negative externalities on the former, and the Monetary Union risks to end in a crisis unless the Maastricht Treaty appears as an emulsifying agent unifying Oil and Vinegar. The power of the emulsifying agent must be very strong. Its "lecithine" has to unite the market goals of the Oil country with redistribution goals in the Vinegar country. A Maastricht Treaty which is able to generate an emulsion out of allocation and redistribution has not yet been invented. Therefore a crisis seems unavoidable.

What can be learnt from this parable? Countries with heterogeneous political systems should not join to a monetary union. A redistributive (Vinegar) system is not compatible with a market oriented (Oil) system. A Treaty as the Maastricht Treaty is not a strong enough as an emulsifying agent to neutralize the externalities generated by Oil and Vinegar. For nobody has the power to enforce the Treaty.

Paolo Savona writes in his "letter to German friends" (Savona 2014 in this volume, p. 50): "I would like to urge you to show greater commitment to prevent another tragedy in Europe".

My answer is drawn from natural sciences, which teach us that the right setting at the start is necessary for a good outcome. A tragedy cannot be resolved by improving an undesired outcome ex post. Too much salt in a soup cannot be compensated by adding more sugar. It is too late. Preventing a tragedy means to set things right before the process starts.

---

2 From private correspondence with Prof. Rudolf Blankart.

The reader will ask: How could the founders of the euro overlook this basic condition? How was it possible to slip in this fallacy? The euro negotiators have discussed ten years (from the summit of Hanover in 1988 to the irreversible fixing of the national exchange rates of 31 December 1998) to make the best of all treaties. Indeed though the way to the Treaty was carefully drafted the negotiators forgot to discuss how to enforce it once it is in force. Therefore Vinegar was not banned out of the euro. It was still there with its destroying power when the euro started.

In the retrospect one may ask: Why has nobody warned the politicians? Where were the professional economists who should have known better? The fact is that economists did not remain silent. In February 1998 155 German economics professors (including the author of this paper) launched an open petition to the German government entitled: "The euro comes too early." They wanted to say that the euro project needs more rethinking (*Frankfurter Allgemeine Zeitung*, 9 February 1998). The petitioners' opinion was shared by a large part of their academic community in Germany and worldwide. The most prominent support was given by Milton Friedman whose opinion has been recorded in 1999:

> *"I am very negative about the euro and I am very doubtful about how it will work out... What most troubles me ... is that members of the euro have thrown away the key [no revision clause]. Once the euro physically replaces the separate currencies, how in the world do you get out? It's a major crisis. As a result, I would strongly agree ... that the euro should be abandoned before January 1, 2002. At the same time, the odds are very great that it will not be abandoned. The defects of the euro will take some time to show up; nothing happens very rapidly in this area. There are fewer than three years to go. Even if difficulties deriving from the euro occur in those three years, the political system is unlikely to react quickly enough to end the euro. As a result, I think it would be very desirable for some systematic thought to be given to devising some way to get out of the straitjacket of the euro after 2002." (Martino 2008)*

Once it is understood that the euro is the result of a process, one arrives at the conclusion that it is irreparable. If we want to restore the friendship among the European people as it was until the appearance of the euro it does not make sense to repair the ill designed euro. For as long as Vinegar cannot be eliminated as a player the euro remains a permanently defective institution.

It is also wrong to say that an exit out of the euro is too expensive. Most politicians agree that, could they step back to the year 1990 and had they the knowledge of 2014, they would vote against the euro because they expect a larger rate of growth of GDP without the euro than with the euro (Krämer 2014). If their calculus was right for 1990 it is likely to be right also right today, only that we have to account for the transitory switching costs. We can conclude: Whatever the switching costs are, there is a point in the future where the GDP without the euro (including transitory switching costs) crosses the development path of the GDP with the euro from below and then permanently exceeds the GDP with the euro ceteris paribus. In this case, the present value of all future GDPs is larger without the euro than with the euro under the same rate of interest.

Thus, the task of the responsible policy makers in Brussels and Frankfurt should be to develop alternative ways of a least costs exit instead of exclusively searching for ways to save the euro. It is indeed paradoxical to see how much money is invested in research that is exclusively directed to repair the failed construction of the euro, while practically no public money is directed into Milton Friedman's problem of how to get out of it. Some private researchers propose that leaving the euro needs the same procedure as entering the euro: parallel currencies and slowly adjusting exchange rates (Die Parallelwährung 2012). It is not claimed that parallel currencies are the best and unique way of an exit. It is rather suggested that policy makers – Council, Commission, Member State Governments and ECB – should stop to negate the exit question. Improvements can only be come from comparative economic studies of all alternatives, not from their one-sided exclusion. Therefore the great philosopher Karl Popper warns that no issue must be a political Tabou in an Open Society (Popper 1945).

IV. Learning from History: The Emergence of the German and French National Fiscal Systems

The central argument of this paper is a theoretical one. It is argued that Oil and Vinegar countries cannot coexist in a monetary union because they exert mutual externalities leading to a permanent crisis with high social costs, inimical excesses and political unrest. Oil and Vinegar continuously destruct each other.

In this section (IV) Oil and Vinegar will be identified in history. The histories of Germany and France are shown to come close to Oil and Vinegar, but not from the beginning, only since the French revolution of 1789. Section V describes the destinies of earlier monetary unions from the Latin Monetary Union of 1869 up to European Monetary System (EMS) of the 1980ies and 1990ies. Section VI explains the political reasons of the euro, the Maastricht Treaty, the subsequent destruction of the Maastricht Treaty and the emergence of the status quo. Section VII proposes the conclusions of the paper and the consequences for the euro.

Looking back to the Middle Ages, there existed no difference in the fiscal regimes of Germany and France. In fact, Germany and France did not exist as nations. Instead the region North of the Alps was split in many small domains of regional and local vassals who protected the peasants in their domain from attacks by roaming and robbing hordes of Normans and Huns. In return for protection the peasants provided labour services to the vassals. The vassals, in order to protect their domain from larger attacks, were reinsured by their seigneurs who could mobilize additional vassals for support (Volckart 2002).

This tripartite system of seigneurs, vassals and peasants functioned from 700 until about 1500. As literacy, contract and money slowly reappeared after about the year 1000 the seigneurs begun to arrange themselves with the vassals at the costs of the peasants who became assessable for the seigneurs whereas the vassals became functionless paladins at the courts of their seigneurs. So the appearance of the seigneurial system survived beyond the Middle Ages.

A real break, however, came with the French Revolution of 1789, when the French National Assembly formally abolished the seigneurial system on 4 und 5 August 1789 and replaced its taxes by a unitary national tax system which financed the unitary central national budget. The idea was that centralization should make the budget of public expenditures and taxes more rational. The contrary was the case. The central budget of France became the nation's common pool which was never sufficient to fulfill the demands of all interest groups. Therefore, a permanent shortage of means was built in the French system. Increasingly more resources were needed from outside sources, from secularized Church property, from money creation and from plundering in wars. So France became a "Vinegar State" dependent of attracting off-budget resources from wherever it was possible. As inflation played an important role, the French came out of the revolutionary wars with a smaller public debt than England.

The French system of government was admired for its Cartesian logic by the political leaders of the emerging national states of 19th century Europe. They enthusiastically followed the French example and established centralized Vinegar states, in particular in Italy, Spain, Portugal and Greece. Only Germany was an exception. Germany was unified in 1871 as a Federal State whose subcentral state governments had and still have to pay for their budget by own means. So Germany played and plays Oil, whereas France and the other States play Vinegar. Still, however, French Vinegar did not come into conflict with German Oil. For both countries were sovereign and financially independent states. Germany and France had trade, but they operated on their own costs. "They went Dutch." Each government had to break even. A mutual bailout was out of question.

V. The Forerunners of the Euro

The euro is not a unique historical example of a monetary union in Europe. There were many previous monetary unions allowing politicians of today to learn from history. In all cases it can be seen that monetary unions collapsed if politicians tried to mix Oil countries with Vinegar countries.

V.1 The Latin Monetary Union

In the 19th century the Latin Monetary Union brought Europe very close to a true monetary Union had not Vinegar interfered and destroyed the union. In these times cross-border flows of gold or silver regularly compensated trade balance disequilibria. There was no escape from this logic. All countries had to play Oil. In France the idea emerged that an international standardization of gold and silver coins would facilitate these transactions and could in fact establish a monetary union. In 1865 France, Belgium, Italy, and Switzerland agreed to mint their national currencies in a standard of 4.5 grams of silver or 0.290322 grams of gold (a ratio of 15.5 to 1) and make them freely interchangeable. A monetary union was established. But the drafters forgot Vinegar. Vinegar's first attack came from the fixed price ratio between gold and silver. As the international free market price of gold increased compared to the international free market price of silver towards the end of the century, speculators sold silver to the union member states in exchange of gold at the officially fixed Union exchange rate of 15.5 to 1. Thus, countries like Switzerland had to accept large amounts of silver and lost gold until the international market prices recovered. A second and ultimate attack against the Latin Monetary Union came from paper money which begun to circulate towards the end of the century. Now, vinegar governments could simply print money and refuse or postpone its conversion into gold or silver. This attack was no more sustained by the Latin Monetary Union. It collapsed in 1926.

The conclusions are obvious: If in a monetary union one or several countries permanently play Vinegar by printing paper money while the other countries play Oil, the system reaches a point where it cannot be repaired and collapses.

V.2 The System of Bretton Woods

But the dream of a worldwide monetary union remained awake despite of the repercussions of World War II. In 1944 the world monetary system of Bretton Woods has been established. It required each participant government to maintain a fixed exchange rate of its currency to the US Dollar which was priced at 35 Dollars per ounce of gold. So, Bretton Woods was close to a monetary union. If a government decided to finance its budget by money creation (Vinegar) it soon had not enough Dollars to maintain the fixed exchange rate to the US Dollar and was therefore constrained to return to a balanced budget policy. Hence, each country had an incentive to practice budgetary discipline and so to play Oil.

This rule was, however, not binding for one country: the United States. If the US decided to go off balanced budget policy, they could simply print Dollars without consequences. In particular after they gave up their promise to convert dollars into gold at the fixed rate of 35 Dollars per ounce of gold in the 1960s the US could play Vinegar without consequences while the other countries still had to play Oil. In fact the other countries bore the costs of the US fiscal deficit. In 1973 the participant countries of Bretton Woods refused to buy any longer dollars at the statutory exchange rate and hence caused the collapse of the system.

Again, the conclusion is that a monetary system cannot survive when one country permanently plays Vinegar and generates externalities which are shifted on the Oil countries. Such a monetary system cannot be repaired and it is determined to collapse. In fact, the collapse is the best remedy because it facilitates to adopt an alternative system as the existing system is irreparable.

V.3 The European Currency Snake

In 1972 when the Bretton Woods system was already in disarray the heads of the EU central banks decided to establish a system of limited exchange rate fluctuations between their currencies and the US Dollar illustrated by a "snake creeping in the tunnel" (of Bretton Woods). After the ultimate collapse of Bretton Woods in 1973 the snake crept out of the tunnel. It was decided among the European governments that each central bank had to buy or sell its own currency in order to maintain the exchange rate within a band of +/-2.5%.

In the so called "Werner Plan" the EU governments opened further talks on harmonizing the fiscal policies underlying their common exchange rates. However, no binding decision has been reached. Therefore, the Werner Plan could not work. The policy makers missed to make the underlying fiscal systems compatible.

Germany practiced a fiscal breakeven, whereas France did not. Therefore, Germany was able to maintain its exchange rate and to stay in the snake, while France and most other countries have lost foreign reserves and dropped out. Eventually only Germany, the Benelux, Denmark and Norway were able to keep their exchange rates within the snake, while all other member states dropped out.

V.4 The European Monetary System (EMS)

The European currency snake was amended by a three months monetary assistance mechanism of 1.4 bn. European Currency Accounting Units (later ECU) (Bernholz 1998: 792). This help was enough to cope with frictions on the foreign exchange market, but insufficient to absorb asymmetries as those between the German and French fiscal systems.

Therefore, President Giscard d'Estaing came to Germany in 1978 in order to convince Chancellor Helmut Schmidt to extend the existing currency assistance program open-endedly in anticipation of a future monetary union whose central bank should be equipped with enough money to balance all member states' fiscal accounts comparably to the Banque de France which balanced the fiscal accounts on the French national level. This conception of a central bank was initiated by the Belgian-American economist Robert Triffin (1960) who, as an advisor to the European Commission in the 1960s, pleaded for a European reserve pool to support national Governments' budgets. Germany's central bankers, in contrast, pointed to the Bundesbank law which strictly prohibited such support programs as the Bundesbank had to maintain price stability in the first place. This view of a central bank was, however, completely alien to French politicians who thought that a central bank without the capability of balancing budgets is useless. The Bundesbank again rejected this view.

After some negotiations the German and French governments agreed jointly with the other member state governments on a financial support program for countries which had difficulties in maintaining exchange rate stability. The resulting European Monetary System (EMS) should consist of the following four stages:

a) First stage: A short term repayable financial support program as known from the European Currency Snake extended to 11 bn. ECU.
b) Second stage: A medium term repayable financial support program of another 11 bn. ECU.
c) Third stage: A realignment of the exchange rates should take place in case of a fundamental exchange rate disequilibrium.
d) Fourth stage: An automatic exit occurs if the first three options do not succeed.

The EMS was a good compromise to unite Oil and Vinegar countries.

Germany caused no problem with its exchange rate because it had balanced budgets. France was not constrained to abandon its fiscal system inherited from the past, but was nevertheless warned not to overdraw it.

It could count on monetary support, but it was made clear that support was limited.

It is often said that the currency crisis of 1992-93 was a crisis of the EMS. However, this view is not correct. The crisis occurred because the UK and Italy who were hit by balance of payment deficits resisted against realignments according to the third stage and therefore had to leave according to stage four. France was in a similar situation, but it achieved a broadening of the exchange rate bands to +/-15% and therefore escaped from a realignment. All in all, the EMS was a success. The exchange rate volatility has declined within the EMS since the Sterling crisis of 1993 as shown in Blankart (2013).

VI. The Political Reasons of the Euro

The decision to abandon the EMS and to go towards the euro was purely political. No economic need required to give up the EMS. The political problem was the dominance of the German Bundesbank. If n-1 countries of n participant countries of a fixed exchange rate union intervene to maintain their exchange rates at the agreed level, the exchange rate of the n-th country is also fixed regardless of its monetary policy. The n-th currency will be the reserve currency. Which country's currency will turn out to be the reserve currency depends on its reputation. In order to be on the safe side, the countries attached themselves at the country with the highest reputation for price stability. Accordingly, the D-Mark became the reference currency for all other currencies. Whenever the Bundesbank increased the rate of interest, France had to follow and, hence, experienced a restraint of economic growth. Therefore, France wanted to get rid of the so called "diktat allemand" and demanded a European Monetary Union in which all EU governments were allowed to take part in the monetary decisions.

At the summit of Hanover in 1988 the Heads of State or Government decided to draft a road map, the so called Delors Plan, indicating the necessary steps to get from the status quo to the European Monetary Union. The Delors Plan was adopted a year later at the summit of Madrid in 1989. On the one hand all participating states will lose their monetary and some of their fiscal autonomy, on the other hand they will have to comply with the monetary regulations of the European Central Bank and with the fiscal rules of the stability and growth pact. The principles of the ECB were closely aligned to those of the Bundesbank. So the monetary order of the Bundesbank which the French government wanted to get rid of reappeared in the European Monetary Union. The French government was not amused. It avoided an open conflict by adopting a "yes-but-wait-and-see" position.

With these reservations in mind, President Mitterrand of France signed the Maastricht Treaty on 7 February 1992. The other Heads of State or Government signed as well. But President Mitterrand of France immediately recognized that the Maastricht Treaty lacked an enforcement mechanism once it is in force. Therefore three mental reservations have to be remembered:

(1.) The central bank should not be independent, but under political control

(2.) The political control should be French.

(3.) Mutual fiscal bailout should make sure that national governments cannot go bankrupt.

President Mitterrand expressed his *first reservation* already 7 months after the solemn signing of the Treaty of Maastricht. In an important and politically decisive television talk of 3 September 1992 just before the French referendum on the Maastricht Treaty he revoked the core principle of the European Monetary Union, central bank independence. When the President came to the issue of central bank independence he said: "No, this is not true. [...] The monetary policy belongs to the European Council and the application of the monetary policy belongs to the Central Bank within the decisions of the European Council."[3]

But words had to be followed by deeds. Mitterrand's *second reservation* was the control of the ECB. The European Central Bank (ECB) had to be brought under French control. Though, Wim Duisenberg (the governor of the Bank of the Netherlands), has already been elected as President of the European Monetary Institute (EMI) and the subsequent ECB, with approval of the heads of State or Government in 1996 the new French President Jacques Chirac insisted thereafter on a second vote in which he injected a veto (despite of the already existing decision and despite of the vote by qualified majority rule). For he wanted the Frenchman Jean-Claude Trichet to become President of the ECB and not Wim Duisenberg. Chirac coerced Duisenberg to step down more or less involuntarily of his office after four years of his presidency and to be replaced by Jean-Claude Trichet.[4] The procedure enforced by Chirac was a clear violation of the Treaty: First an existing decision has been cancelled (outside the rules) and second a new decision of a four year presidency is inconsistent with the Treaty (art. 109a(2) (b) EC = art. 283 TFEU) which states that

3 Quoted from Issing (2008).

4 In fact Trichet could not become president of the European Central bank immediately because he had to survive a court trial on a financial scandal of the state owned bank Crédit Lyonnais which he was in charge to control as a part of his political office in the French Government.

the President of the ECB is elected for eight years and not for four years (Warleigh 2002). This was a very bad start for the euro, but a consequence of the Maastricht Treaty for whose enforcement nobody is responsible.

Trichet, once in office, was not able to change the statutes of the ECB alone. But with the banking crisis of 2007-2008 the Southern members of the governing council became hungry for credits whatever the Treaty required. Their political demand for liquidity and their majority in the Council encouraged Trichet to start his securities markets programme (SMP) monetizing public debt of some States at the costs of all States. Some say that Trichet did not violate art. 123 TFEU because he intervened on the secondary and not on the primary market of government bonds. But in 1993 already, the European Council has clarified that this separation must not be misused for monetizing public debt. The Council said: "Purchases made on the secondary market must not be used to circumvent the objective of that Article".[5] Though SMP was inconsistent with the Treaty, it has nevertheless created a new status quo, which once in existence could no more be defined away. Indeed SMP can be seen as the trailblazer of ECB's later Outright Monetary Transaction Program (OMT).

Trichet has transformed the ECB (following Mitterrand's political testament) into a bailout institution for member states with balance of payments difficulties. He legalized Vinegar for some while the others had to play Oil.

Mitterrand's last reservation was the abolition of the no-bailout clause of art. 125 TFEU. Here again Trichet was the driving force. As Greece has become insolvent in the end of April 2010 the European Council decided that the no-bailout clause shall not be applied in this specific case. But a week later (on 7 and 8 May 2010) Trichet convinced the European Council that the situation is so dramatic that the no-bailout clause had to be abolished immediately for the euro zone as a whole and that it had to be replaced by a general bailout fund financed by all member states off-budget via a private company located in Luxembourg (Ludlow 2010). Obviously the Council was not empowered to de facto abolish the no-bailout clause of art. 125 TFEU. But Trichet was satisfied that the financial burden of the crisis has been distributed from some member states on all euro states collectively. The paying Member States were the Oil states. Their citizens were reluctant because they had to pay taxes for other member states. The receiving member states were the Vinegar states which were disappointed too because they received the money only under the condition of an austerity policy generating hardship and unemployment at home.

5 Council Regulation (EC) No. 3603/93.

VII. Summary and Conclusions

Friendship cannot be bought by money. But it can very well be destroyed by money. This danger highlights the problem of the euro. Friendship has grown in the European Union as long as the EU has promoted trade in private goods and every citizen could participate at private costs and private benefits.

European leaders believed that this success story will automatically continue with the euro. But they forgot that the euro is first of all a public good which has to be generated by coordinated action, not by trade. The public good offers an invitation to shirking because the more of the burden some participants contribute, the less have to be contributed by the other participants. Insofar as some member states are able to shift the burden of the monetary Union to others, the more the monetary union deteriorates into a transfer union.

If the participants of a monetary union consist of Oil and Vinegar governments such burden shifting seems to be nearly unavoidable. But a monetary union based on shirking and burden shifting cannot work. It is cause of distrust and hate and should therefore be dissolved to prevent a further deterioration. It is also impossible to improve the results ex post because the design at the outset is improper. This hypothesis is confirmed by history which shows that monetary unions consisting of Oil and Vinegar nations always collapsed. Their collapse was not a disaster, but an opportunity to a new start under a proper design.

Transfer unions cannot survive unless under dictatorship. But a dictatorship does certainly not improve the friendship among the European peoples. Therefore the alternative of a dissolution of an existing Oil-Vinegar Monetary Union and a new start seem to be reasonable alternatives to restore European friendship.

References

Bernholz, P. (1998). "Die Bundesbank und die Währungsintegration in Europa". In Deutsche Bundesbank (ed.), *Fünfzig Jahre Deutsche Mark. Notenbank und Währung in Deutschland seit 1948*. München: Beck, 773-833.

Blankart, Ch. B. (2013). "Oil and Vinegar: 'A Positive Fiscal Theory of the Euro Crisis'", *Kyklos*, Vol. 66, No. 4: 497-527.

Die Parallelwährung (2012). *Bundesverband Mitteständische Wirtschaft*, Düsseldorf u.a.

Issing, O. (2008). *Der Euro. Geburt – Erfolg – Zukunft*. München: Vahlen.

Krämer, W. and Müller H. (2014). "Hat der Euro eine Zukunft?" Discussion paper Nr. 25/2014, University of Dortmund.

Ludlow, P. (2010). "The European Council and the euro crisis". *Eurocomment 7* (7/8, Spring, 17 June): 1-59.

Martino, A. (2008). "Milton Friedman and the euro". *Cato Journal*, 28 (2, Spring-Summer): 263-72.

Poettinger, M. (2014). "Introduction", in: Monika Poettinger and Antonio Varsori (eds.), *Economic Crisis and New Nationalisms*. Brussels, P.I.E. Peter Lang: 9-34.

Popper, K.W. (1945). *The Open Society and Its Enemies. The Spell of Plato*. London: Routledge.

Savona, P. (2014). "Letter to German and Italian Friends", in: Monika Poettinger and Antonio Varsori (eds.), *Economic Crisis and New Nationalisms*. Brussels, P.I.E. Peter Lang: 49-62.

Triffin, R. (1960), *Europe and the Money Muddle: From bilateralism to near convertibility 1947-1956*. New Haven: Yale University Press.

Volckart, O. (2002). *Wettbewerb und Wettbewerbsbeschränkung im vormodernen Deutschland. 1000–1800*. Tübingen: Mohr.

Warleigh, A. (2002). *Understanding European Union Institutions*. London: Routledge.

How to Escape from the Crisis

The Divergent Opinions of Italian Economists

Piero Bini[1]

1. Introduction

This paper focuses on the analyses and remarks carried out by Italian economists concerning the nature and causes of the current economic crisis and its negative effects on the Italian economy and society.

From the perspective of the Italian debate, we can distinguish two phases within the six year-period since the beginning of the Great Recession. During the first phase, i.e. the first two year-period starting from 2008, the scholars' interest was mainly focused on explaining the causes of the Global financial crisis and on the responsibilities of those economists, with few exceptions, who failed to predict it. In this first period, the participation of Italian economists to the international debate, despite being qualitatively high, was quantitatively irrelevant[2].

We will not examine this first phase, instead we will focus only on the second one, which spans from 2011 to the present. During the latter the number of Italian economists who discussed this topic has increased exponentially. The reasons behind this growing interest can be traced

---

[1] Department of Political Sciences, University of Rome Three: piero.bini@uniroma3.it. Throughout the various drafts of this paper, we have benefited from the comments of several scholars that we would like to collectively thank here. Some of these comments were expressed at three scientific meetings, the first held in Florence on November 15th, 2012 with the title "Economic Crisis and New Nationalisms. German Political Economy as perceived by European partners"; the second one at the University of Florence on February 21st-23rd, 2013, as part of the XII scientific meeting of the Italian Association for the History of Economic Thought (AISPE); the third one at the University of Trieste on June 6th-7th, 2013, as part of a scientific meeting organized by the "Manlio Resta" Foundation, with the title "Growth and economic development in the 5° year of the crisis: how to change". A special thanks to Mariano D'Antonio, Cosimo Magazzino and Paolo Ramazzotti for their criticisms and suggestions. Responsibility for any errors or gaps is obviously ours alone.

[2] We particularly recommend the several works devoted to the crisis during the two year-period that goes from 2008 to 2009, written by Guido Tabellini and Alberto Alesina, as well as the specific essays written by Michele Fratianni (2008), Luigi Spaventa (2009), and Moro (2012).

back to the fact that the global crisis has acquired a specific European declination raising the level of the theoretical and ideological debate in Italy as well, which goes along with an intensification of the country's social illness.

This paper has been organised in the following way. After recalling some intellectual antecedents of the current debate (par. 2), we will employ an explanatory model divided into four sections (from par. 3 to par. 6 included) to describe the various perspectives held by Italian economists. These four sections are matched by as many critical orientations which highlight respectively:

a) the flaws of the European institution and Euro design, which are unable to solve the contradictions originating from a currency area that still lacks political unity;
b) the co-presence both of diversified forms of capitalism considered to be not compatible with each other and different geopolitical views within the Eurozone;
c) the intrinsic contradictions that some authors ascribe to market capitalism as such, which would explain the deterioration of workers' and poorest social classes' living conditions;
d) the misgovernment which is observed, not accidentally, in those countries hit harder by the crisis. In this paper, we will consider only Italy and some negative expressions of its cultural anthropology.

In the seventh and last section, we will draw some short conclusions. The sources used are those typical of the time we are living in. Besides books and articles published in scientific journals and in specialised newspapers, we will employ e-books, blogs and websites, some of which have been established to partake with greater agility and fervour to this ongoing battle of ideas.

2. The Missing Debate at the Origins of the European Monetary Union

Let us open this paragraph by making a significant observation. The number of Italian economists who expressed critical and often pessimistic considerations about the inner imbalances of the Eurozone in the past two or three years, is substantially greater than that of the Nineties when the project of the European Monetary Union (EMU) was still in progress. Had perhaps both public decision-makers and economists been short-sighted and superficial? Or has an event arisen which substantially modified the terms of convenience of the initial project?

It needs to be remembered that at the time of the EMU's planning, the opinions on the matter were essentially and largely positive. It was rightly said, but perhaps with a too much optimistic evaluation, that the exchange rate "certainty" guaranteed by the Euro would have decreased transaction costs. It was also stated, without any certain grounds (subsequently proved to be wrong), that an increase of foreign trade and capital flows within the Eurozone, which were to be expected thanks to this new economic and institutional context, would have favoured mainly the economies of the "weak" countries of the Union facilitating their convergence towards those of the "strong" countries.

At that time, the theoretical debate was further characterised by a positive connotation (both in Italy and on the international level) thanks to the contributions of a series of Italian scholars. Their analyses allowed to offer in advance a favourable, or rather a far-sighted interpretation of the European monetary agreement which anticipated an homogenizing process of the adhering countries towards standards of greater rigour both in terms of monetary policy and public finance. A brief account of these views is shown below.

Alesina and Tabellini (1987) considered an economy in which two party coalitions with different programs of fiscal policy alternate in Government as a result of democratic elections. According to Alesina and Tabellini's public choice approach, in this situation of strong political competition, Government debt becomes a strategic variable used by each party to influence negatively the choices of his successor in charge. Therefore, the equilibrium level of Government debt is larger than it would be with a social virtual planner which was sure to be elected. In a nutshell, Alesina and Tabellini's analysis shows that a deficit and inflation biases occur in this kind of competitive democracy, which raises the question of how to realise more effective controls and ties to these partisan Government activities.

Following rational expectation hypotheses, Giavazzi and Pagano (1988) pointed out that the advantages achievable through an inflationary policy in terms of income growth and devaluation of the public debt, would prove to be in short quite apparent. By contrast, they envisioned the benefits attainable by a high inflation prone-country to "tie its hands" by entering a monetary system with fixed exchange rates. Indeed, these authors consider this operation to be necessary as to bring credibility gains to policy-makers, thus overcoming the inefficient stemming from the usual public's mistrust of the authorities.

The normative meaning of these two articles is that if a country, because of its own historical and institutional characteristics, fails to get an effective regulation of its economic and monetary policy, it can then decide to obtain it from an external authority.

Giavazzi and Pagano (1990) hypothesised subsequently a significant scenario where a restrictive spending policy – designing a permanent tax reduction in the future and thus improving positive expectations in the households about their life-cycle income – could determine growth via an increase of the current and planned consumption[3].

Alesina and Perotti (1995) introduced a successful series of studies intended to explain the (expansionary or, alternately, recessionary) effects resulting from a given operation of fiscal consolidation. Indeed, these effects can change according to the composition of this very operation (public spending cut and/or tax increase). The aim was to propose economic policy decisions which could reduce recessionary effects in the short term and maximise the expansionary ones in the long term[4]. Alesina and Perotti's more significant conclusion was that "any fiscal adjustment hoping to be successful, cannot avoid dealing with cuts in the welfare state" (Alesina and Perotti 1995: 21), so laying the groundwork among liberal economists – as Blyth says critically – for expansionary austerity to be seen as the new normal rather than policy exception: "Keynes, it seems, had it all backwards" (Blyth 2013: 171).

All these studies, many of which are of an econometric nature with an empirical foundation, have certainly contributed to strengthen the EMU's incoming economic philosophy, concerning its aversion to inflation and its disagreement to several practices of public intervention in economy. These researches represented also a paradigmatic alternative compared to several theoretical and doctrinaire orientations still highly regarded in Italy at that time, which indicated:

a) the exclusively recessionary effects of restrictive fiscal policies;
b) the lack of a specific centre to support the aggregate demand among the tools envisaged by the Maastricht Treaty;
c) the impossibility of being able to consider the Eurozone as an optimum currency area. This fact raised the question of integrating the EMU's original structure with a series of *ad hoc* policies oriented to compensate the imbalances caused by possible asymmetric shocks in the single countries of the European Union.

However, the introduction of the Euro silenced, so to speak, all these last critical evaluations. Indeed, the consensus built around this operation of monetary unification was so high and widespread as to discourage any dissident voice. One of these voices, in commenting the Euro's building process, which had been completed by 1999, stated:

---

3 See also Giavazzi and Pagano (1996).

4 See also Alesina and Ardagna (1998), Ardagna (2004), Alesina and Ardagna (2010).

> "It seems as if there is a fear that expressing uncertainties and doubts on the contents of the Treaty could be interpreted as a display of anti-European scepticism or that the emergence of these critiques could contribute to worsen Euro's difficulties on the financial markets, since they would signal a return, broadly speaking, to Keynesian concepts which were responsible for the troubles and weaknesses of European economies. When these doubts are expressed, they are answered by hoping for an evolutionary interpretation of the EMU text and rules" (La Malfa 2011 [2000]: 110).

Nevertheless, in the wake of recent events, the number of economists who started to criticize the inflexibility of the monetary Union's agreement has increased rapidly. This is not surprising. The Euro crisis has advanced so much that it is far more recognizable now than it was fifteen years ago (at the time of La Malfa's critiques), or even than it was two or three years ago. Unfortunately, in the meantime the effects of this damage have become more traumatic and its possible cures are more uncertain.

3. For a Different Implementation of the European Monetary Union

The first topic we are going to deal with concerns the flaws and omissions of the European institutional scheme. According to some economists, the weaknesses of public finance and real economy registered in those European countries which have been hit harder by the crisis (the well known *Piigs*: Portugal, Ireland, Italy, Greece, Spain), are not so much the result of their respective ruling classes' negligence, but rather the outcome of a wrong EMU's regulation. According to this interpretation, the Union is considered to be the main cause of the growing imbalances among those countries which are experiencing some hardships and the strong ones of Central and Northern Europe, such as Germany, Denmark, the Netherlands, Finland and Austria.

In order to illustrate these critical stances, it is worth to point out the effective summary provided by Giacomo Vaciago. According to him, EMU can be likened to a Nash game, where Germany and the other countries of Northern Europe play the role of guards, while the countries of Southern Europe are the thieves. If the rules are not modified, the game will end up badly for everyone, especially for the weak countries of Southern Europe, since both the costs to remain in the Eurozone and those to leave will increase over time (Vaciago 2012). To put it briefly, Euro's regulations will cause its end by rewarding non-cooperative behaviours.

However, some economists who focused on the flaws of the Euro's building process, believe that the latter could be fixed effectively given that the following reforms will be undertaken:

a) the implementation of a more expansionary monetary policy, along with the appointment of the role of lender of last resort to the European Central Bank (ECB);
b) the achievement of a greater fiscal integration policy among the countries of the Eurozone, both to mutualise a part of their overall public debt and to finance projects for infrastructural investments on a European scale. Hence, the proposal of issuing European debt securities such as Eurobonds and Europrojects is advanced to meet this purpose.

Even though the economists considered in this section generally agree with these proposals, they differ from one another because of their divergent interpretations of these reforms or variations within the latter, which witness at the same time their diversified social and cultural backgrounds.

3.1 Economists who advocate a Social Market Economy

These economists usually support a free market economy as the essential mechanism of resources' allocation and the central role played by private entrepreneurship as guarantor of innovations and economic growth. Meanwhile, they believe that the normative framework of the economic system needs to be strengthened in order to make welfare's institutions less bureaucratic and more effective. Furthermore, they wish to bring income inequalities towards more acceptable parameters and to extend competition even to those sectors where it is not practised enough.

Among the economists who support this type of social liberalism, Alberto Quadrio Curzio is currently the most representative one. His proposal (Quadrio Curzio 2012) aims at launching a European Financial Fund (EFF) to issue ten-year or more EuroUnion Bonds. The funds raised through this issue of European public debt should be used partly to decrease the public debt of the Union's single countries in a non-deflationary way. The remaining part should be employed to make big public investments for the production of basic goods and services aimed at raising the performance and the level of competition in the European economic system[5]. He is also keen to point out that: "thanks to these

[5] The specific points of this proposal are the following ones. The European Financial Fund should have 1000 billion Euros bestowed by the EMU member States, which should make their golden reserves and part of their real assets available to the Fund to meet this end. Through a leverage of 3, the collected funds would be used to buy out 2300 billions of Government bonds from the EMU countries and by doing so the average of the public debt on the Eurozone's GDP would drop around 60% (in Italy this ratio would decrease to 95% circa). The remaining funds would be used to make large European investments in the following fields: energy, telecommunication, water, railway and harbours.

provisions the German fear of paying others' debts should be appeased" (Quadrio Curzio 2012: 67).

According to Quadrio Curzio, a specific value of this developmental operation is that of not resorting to Keynesian policies of increasing public spending, which may lead to an excess of welfarism and dirigisme[6].

Paolo Savona is another scholar who is inspired by social market economy and its ethical values. His view is characterised by the attempt to combine conditions of free initiative and competition in the marketplace with "an increased level of civil society, not only of material wellbeing". Specifically, he believes it is necessary to decrease the current and great inequality of income distribution. We cannot consider that this phenomenon could "be regulated by the hypothesis that the market is a perfect system which behaves as written in economic textbooks, but it needs to be entrusted to Parliaments and to the private negotiation between labour and capital" (Savona (2012a: 87-8).

3.2 Keynesian Economists

Differently from the authors mentioned above, other economists, who support a change in the procedures' implementation of the EMU, follow a (largely) Keynesian orientation. Even in this case, however, we are faced by a different degree of views[7].

For instance, Terenzio Cozzi points out a cautious Keynesian solution which does not require an increase of the deficit to GDP ratio. His proposal is based on a re-modulation of the tax burden in favour of low incomes with an elevated propensity to consume, to be financed by higher taxes imposed on real property owners and financial income holders who have presumably less propensity to consume. Hence, the Italian council tax *Imposta Municipale Unica* (IMU) introduced in 2012 is in line with Cozzi's thought. However, the recessionary impact of this measure has

6 "Public spending supports the demand, but it does not necessarily produce development and growth" (Quadrio Curzio 2012: 33).

7 This is inevitable if we consider the different orientations that Keynesian thought has developed over time. For the purpose of our research, we will use the term "Keynesian" without any further specification, every time that the interpretative context justifies the reference to one or more point of views expressed by the Cantabrigian economist. For instance, they may refer to the presence of market failures which hinder the achievement of short-term equilibria, to the uncertainty as a cause of markets' endemic instability, or to the inequality of income distribution as a possible cause for an insufficient aggregate demand and the need for a broad State intervention in economy following the above mentioned market's macroeconomic failures. For those who are interested in clarifying the differences between mainstream Neo-Keynesian theoretical approach and the heterodox Post-Keynesian one, we recommend D'Ippoliti (2012a, 2012b).

been amplified by a further general increase in taxation, instead of being compensated by the same amount of tax reliefs as suggested by Cozzi (2011, 2013).

According to Keynesian economists, it is generally wrong to ascribe the specific seriousness of the Italian economic crisis to the imbalances of public finance. The attempt to eliminate these imbalances by decreasing public spending or increasing taxes or both, triggers a vicious circle of cumulative deflation, that is well known in scientific literature[8]. A wrong diagnosis – they affirm – originated a self-defeating cure.

According to these economists, the crisis that hit Italy and the other *Piigs* should be attributed above all to the unsuitable logic of the Euro's structure[9]. Indeed, the Euro (which does not allow to adjust the exchange rate) and the free capital flow with its high degree of destabilizing effects, have determined the progressive imbalances of the Eurozone countries' current accounts. On the one hand, the less competitive countries are increasing their foreign debt, on the other hand, the more competitive Northern European countries are experiencing a parallel increase of foreign credit. This cumulative and divergent process prevents the implementation of effective economic policies in deficit nations, and it is turning the European economic area in a battlefield of winners and losers.

Keynesian economists devise the following operational scheme from this type of analysis. Surplus nations should implement expansionary public spending; they should also favour a domestic wage dynamics higher than that of labour productivity and possibly agree to transfer resources towards deficit nations, as it happens among the regions of a Federal State. It is basically a matter of compensatory framework to support the aggregate demand in surplus countries so to increase their import demand

8 An effective theoretical summary of these deflationary causes has been provided by De Grauwe (2009), who lists the four basic types: 1) Keynesian savings paradox; 2) Fisher's Debt-Deflation theory; 3) cost cutting deflation; 4) bank credit deflation. The common feature of these four types of deflation is that of creating a self-defeating downward spiral. Hence, De Grauwe affirms that policy-makers should employ expansionary fiscal policy without too much diffidence.

9 With regards to this matter, we point out some bibliographical references which fully or in part support the type of debate related here: Bagnai (2012a), Brancaccio and Passarella (2012), Fassina (2012), De Cecco (2013a), La Malfa (2013), Piga (2012, 2013). See also the several contributions which can be found in Cesaratto and Pivetti (2012). Clear Keynesian elements can be found both in the *Lettera degli Economisti* (Economists' Letter) which was formulated in 2010 by many Italian academic economists, and in *Piano del Lavoro* (Plan of Work) which was drafted recently by the Italian General Confederation of Labour (CGIL 2013). Many debates of a Keynesian nature are also hosted by Keynesblog.

towards (presumably[10]) deficit countries, thus boosting their economic growth. A collateral goal of this intra-European macroeconomic policy is also that of stopping the process of domestic devaluation undertaken *de facto* by strong countries of Central and Northern Europe during the first decade of 2000.

The ultimate meaning of these proposals is that if Keynesian expansionary policies have been overlooked by the economic policies of countries with a weak public finance[11], they would become feasible again thanks to a European economic policy.

These topics based on the rational and convergent coordination of economies that otherwise could not coexist spontaneously within the same monetary area, recall Kenen's (1969) theoretical point of view. Among those, since Mundell (1961) onward, who contributed to formulate the theory of optimum currency areas, Kenen is the one who has greatly argued about the need for institutions and *ad hoc* compensatory measures to overcome the unbalancing effects of asymmetric shocks which hit countries belonging to the same area[12].

Nonetheless, the effective way European decision makers have been operating in these recent years of crisis, is very far from the Keynesian model of integration described above.

Indeed, the attempt to shift the solution of the "weak" countries' problems to a European level clashes with the suspicion of the "strong" countries' Governments and their citizens to be asked to support financially recovery policies which do not concern them. Whether this suspicion is real or not, the sole fact of being politically relevant induces "strong" countries' governmental authorities to support only those mechanisms of adjustment which exclude any logic of "mutual assistance"[13]. Given that,

---

10 The dubitative construction is needed here, since the success of this operation is not guaranteed, given that the increased import demand of surplus nations could favour countries which do not belong to the EMU, because of their greater competitiveness.

11 Actually not all the authors who follow the Keynesian orientation, share this way of thinking, on the contrary they believe that national policies of public spending are required and achievable in this deteriorated state of the economy. Later on we will go back to the reasons behind their views.

12 See how Krugman (2013b) highlights positively Kenen's contribution, for the fact that it would favour "an automatic equilibrating process in case of asymmetric shocks". At the same time, Krugman criticises Mundell's point of view on the optimum currency areas, because it is based on productive factors' flexibility – of labour in particular – since the migrant flows of young workers who leave their crisis-stricken countries, contribute to further impoverish their homelands: "once these youngsters left, who is going to pay the taxes to support pensioners?". To sum up, according to Krugman, Kenen's contribution is the "best guide to face Europe's current issues". Iodice and Palma's (2013) contribution is in line with Krugman's.

13 See Bini Smaghi's (2013) remarks on this matter.

it becomes tautological that this lack of trust can be restored only after the "weak" countries have proved that they are able to become autonomously "strong" countries just like the others. In other words, the exchange of trust can occur only when it has zero cost, i.e. when it is not needed de facto. It is also clear that this point of view shifts the economic policy's emphasis from the measures of the aggregate demand to those which implement the supply-side and from the fiscal aspects to the structural ones. In short, the Keynesian plan of European integration would break against the so called "material" constitution of the Euro.

Several reasons have led to this negative result, starting from the actual datum represented by the different financial and economic situation faced by the 17 EMU countries. Indeed, crisis-stricken countries accuse Central and Northern European surplus nations to assume a little less than a sort of imperialist guardianship towards them. While the latter read the difficulties experienced by the former as proof of their inability or lack of willingness to adopt some criteria for a good administration of their public finances. As a result, the Euro crisis has turned into a crisis of trust by questioning once again the existence of the most valuable common good, i.e. the idea of a European identity.

The argument that considers the traumatic event of the crisis as an opportunity to make – as it has sometimes been said – a "jump forward" in the process of European integration appears currently weaker than ever as much as it might be appealing. Indeed, during crisis periods the national interests' point of view and populist movements usually prevail on the ideals embodied by the pursuit of a common fate.

Ultimately, the major limit of EMU's formulation in this phase is that of being unable to disentangle itself from this basic vicious circle. On the one hand, it would call for a sharp procedure to obtain a vigorous fiscal and monetary integration encompassing all the 17 EMU countries, but on the other hand, this procedure is only attainable thanks to a European political unity which is yet to be achieved[14].

In the following section we will go back to the meaning of this *impasse* and to the reasons that might even make it unsolvable.

4. Rhenish capitalism vs European Semi-Periphery Capitalism

It is well known that there are different types of capitalism. This knowledge has fostered a specific field of studies dedicated to

14 Rossi's (2013) point of view on this subject is less problematic. He sees the process of European political unification as a pragmatically gradual one.

elaborate "the varieties of capitalism paradigm". By interpreting the productive outcomes of a specific geographic area, these studies not only consider economic data, but also underline the various local, cultural, social and anthropological characteristics which distinguish that area from others. After taking into account these traits and trying to achieve a suitable mediation among them, the political authority of the analysed area should be concerned with creating the most adequate institutional structure. Thus, the economic system of that area could achieve the highest possible level of positive performance. It follows that if the political process of several geographic regions with different institutional inclinations is unified, the achievement of optimal results will be precluded to all or some of them.

Regarding the Euro crisis, the above mentioned approach has been employed by some authors who state the existence of a Southern-European (Mediterranean) capitalism as opposed to the Rhenish (continental) one. The former encompasses Italy, Spain, the Southern regions of France, Portugal and Greece, which present characteristics and perspectives significantly different from the Central and Northern European countries where the latter is spread[15].

In Italy, the negative effects of this theme had already been perceived since 1987 when a new phase of the European Monetary System was launched which was characterised by the freeze of nominal exchange rate ratios among the countries belonging to it (the so-called "strong EMS"). This new arrangement entailed a major surrender of the monetary policy's autonomy and the risk of a real revaluation of the EMS weak currencies which discriminated against their exports, as it happened in Italy. This subject was perceived even more strongly some years later in regard to the Maastricht Treaty. Indeed, the Treaty's strict parameters of convergence along with a conception of the European Central Bank which aimed only at price stability, could have determined a further imbalance among the adhering countries and could have caused the phenomenon of unemployment from "hysteresis" in some of them[16].

From another perspective, the varieties of capitalism paradigm promotes the idea of the existence of a dualistic dynamics among regions belonging to a same broad geopolitical area. This dualism is shown by the concentration of high value-added activities in some regions (i.e. the

15 See on this matter the analyses – even of a bibliographical nature – provided by Rangone and Solari (2012a, 2012b).

16 Franco Modigliani, to whom we can ascribe the recounted critical stance, played a pivotal role in the debate we are referring to; see, for instance, Modigliani (2007) and the overview given by Asso (2007).

"central ones"), as opposed to their poor spreading in other regions of the area (i.e. the "periphery" or "semi-periphery" ones)[17].

These analyses are usually complex and have an interdisciplinary approach which employ at the same time issues such as the weight of local traditions, the cultural degree of political liberties witnessed by different communities, the level of corruption which characterise them, and so on. From this specific perspective, the creation of the EMU could have introduced paradoxically a new element of fracture among the regions that are part of it.

Some recent data relating to Italian economy compared with the rest of Europe and world economies, could be read consistently with this type of critical consideration. In particular, we refer to the dynamics of added-value for unit of labour, registered during the past fifteen years, which shows clear difficulties in Italy.

> "In other countries – it is observed – this value has increased more greatly than in ours. This rise is due to the greater value of high technology products, in comparison to the medium-low technology ones, obtained thanks to the change of technological specialization in the production procedures of those countries" (Ferrari 2012: 50).

On the one hand, the meaning and direction of these dynamics witness that high technology products represent a growing quota of foreign trade; on the other hand, they explain the reduction of the Italian exports' quota in relation to the Euro area and to the rest of the world.

In the light of the centre-periphery paradigm, a part of Italy's lesser competitiveness could be attributed to the fact that the reforms introduced to adjust the country to the Euro's normative framework produced an institutional structure which is unsuitable for its historical, geographical, cultural, anthropological and social characteristics.

The comparison between a before and after Euro helps to understand this type of argument. Before the EMU's formation, Italy's institutional structure was characterised by a strong presence of the State in economy and by a system of credit intermediation that relied on state-owned

17 Wallerstein (1979) and Arrighi (1985) have been pioneers of this territorial approach to political economy. They put Southern European countries (including Italy) in the world's "semi-periphery". The criterion for this arrangement, like the one to establish "central" and "periphery" countries, is determined by the position which they occupy respectively in the "international value chain". For instance, the "central" countries are considered as such, because they have a larger quantity of production processes which "control" a greater share of the total surplus. Several factors such as a country's more or less suitable institutional structure and a lack of interests pursued by its ruling class contribute to determine its rise or fall in the "international value chain".

banks. Another distinctive trait was constituted by the fragmentary, dualistic and sometimes conflicting industrial relations, but which were also supported by institutional mechanisms that blocked their most uncertain developments. Moreover, Italy's institutional framework was marked by a high inflation rate whose redistributive implications and reduction of social tension were appreciated. Another important characteristic was the welfare system which had both modern aspects (i.e. the National Health Service) and other more backward features which did not guarantee against the risks typical of modern industrialised systems, such as unemployment. Finally, other aspects of welfare relied on the family's solidarity circuit and on a generous pension system.

Italy's attempt to adapt to the Maastricht model implied the implementation of an almost opposed institutional philosophy characterised by a much more market-oriented structure than the previous one, high labour-market flexibility, and monetary stability.

The interpretative current that we are analysing stresses the fact that this institutional change failed to devise more effective forms of economic coordination, as it was expected to do. Indeed, the greater operational space left to markets (through privatizations, liberalizations, or the 1997 labour market reform) accentuated inequalities, made the access to credit more difficult for small and medium enterprises (SMEs) and increased job insecurity.

Later on, according to this interpretation, the disappointing results achieved until now are not caused so much by the mistakes made in the European integration process as such, as by the non-conformity of the enforced reforms with the structural characteristics of Italian society or of other countries in Mediterranean Europe.

This negative view found its matching in the economic analysis described by Alberto Bagnai in some of his recent works (Bagnai 2012a, 2012b, 2013). According to this author, since 1996 Italian authorities and the Bank of Italy reached a turning point in comparison to the previous devaluation policy. Indeed, they stabilised the lira at a revaluated exchange rate in view of the application of the Maastricht Treaty. Bagnai believes that this measure determined a negative shock on the foreign demand for Italy's products, which in turn was at the origin of a decreased productivity in the sectors open to foreign trade. This negative tendency became generalised as a consequence of the Treu reform of 1997 which aimed at labour market flexibility that favoured low added-value productions and discouraged the applications of technological progress. Another factor which contributed to the generalisation of the above mentioned tendency was wage moderation implemented by income policy during the Nineties which depressed the domestic demand, creating a situation of long-term deflationary bias that was new to Italy.

Looking back through today's eyes, it is quite easy to identify a fundamental divarication in the way of thinking in the second half of the Nineties.

The majority of scholars saw the process of monetary unification as a crucial opportunity to overcome the distorted, corrupted, backward, ineffective and often iniquitous forms ascribed, not without reason, to the Italian "way" of governing economic and social relations. This belief was supported despite the sometimes expressed awareness of short-term problems that the entry to the Maastricht Treaty would have caused by imposing a new discipline of individual behaviours and collective decisions.

At the same time however, there were those (almost more virtual than real) authors who, by considering the great lack of homogeneity between the Italian institutional system and the one to aim at, saw the risk that the measures imposed by the Maastricht Treaty would inhibit Italy's institutional defences by compromising its growth's potentialities.

Going back to the present situation, even the analysis carried out recently by De Cecco and Maronta (2013) fosters this second interpretation of the Eurozone as an anomalous currency area, even though their point of view cannot be strictly included within the varieties of capitalism paradigm.

These authors' main reflection is that Germany is fulfilling two conflicting roles in recent EMU's events. The country's inclination towards Rhenish capitalism explains its aversion to inflation, wage moderation along with a high productivity of the manufacturing system, its ability of employing an effective control on public spending which does not prevent the possibility of achieving a high level of welfare. As a consequence, Germany has increased its economic and financial stability over time, as opposed to Southern European countries and it has become a point of reference for all the countries within the Eurozone.

However, being the most efficient economic system under the aegis of the Euro, Germany has also increased its role as net creditor to Southern European countries.

Following the examples of what happened historically in Great Britain and later on in the USA, De Cecco and Maronta point out that a country can play a leading role in an economic and political system of a large area, if beyond the military and diplomatic aspects, it is also able to favour the growth of the other countries of that area. In order to do so, the leading country should import more than export, thus creating liquidity instead of reducing it; it should also tolerate inflation at least at moderate levels rather than fighting it as its top priority. The contradiction of a "central" country considered as such from an economic point of view which however does not recognise the need of making its developmental model compatible with that of semi-periphery countries, will inevitably lead to question both its economic and political centrality. The ghost of Germany which is pleased by its own power (even if it is only an economic one) appears once again. It is worth to mention that this type of interpretation makes the several hints which appear in today's literature about German politics' renewed imperialist temptations[18] more believable than they would be otherwise.

Is this way of thinking excessively pessimistic? We believe it is, or rather: by following this type of interpretation the authors of the varieties of capitalism paradigm tend to adopt a deterministic and almost fatalistic approach on the theme of European integration which seems to suggest that things will only get worse. Moreover, they tend to underestimate the logical context of the opposite argument, which warns that it is not surprising if the entry and permanence of European semi-periphery countries in the Eurozone made their *already existing* institutional flaws to a certain extent more visible. This epiphany-effect should have raised the reformist determination of these countries for their improvement. However, this was unfortunately not the case which led us to affirm today that it would be partial to attribute all responsibilities to the system's flaws. Indeed, at least a part of them was surely caused by the negligences of human beings and in particular by European "semi-periphery" countries' ruling classes.

At the same time, we believe that the intellectual strength of the arguments on the varieties of capitalism paradigm should be neither minimized nor overlooked. It is true that an awareness is growing among European ruling classes concerning the rigidity of views which risks to degenerate in a new "mini" (i.e. only on a European scale) version of something similar to a clash of civilizations. This outcome would be exactly the opposite of the original and more genuine purpose of the Maastricht Treaty.

Nevertheless, some compromise solutions have been implemented following the more interventionist role played by the ECB (e.g. on the secondary market of securities) or certain declarations come from Brussels regarding an eventual future issue of Euro debt securities.

However, this process of mutual acknowledgement between these two European areas is exasperatingly slow, as those processes which involve habit and lifestyle changes usually are. This fact provides new evidence

---

18 We recommend Savona's pamphlet (2012b) for its clarity on this matter. You can see the English edition in this book.

to the varieties of capitalism paradigm. Hence, our point of view is that the latter – by foreseeing the negative scenarios of a virtually impossible unification – should at least represent, rather than being an excuse to leave the project, a further incentive to better understand its complexity and difficulties and a stimulus to make incisive decisions on this matter.

5. Europe and the Left-Wing "Critical" Thought

Moving on to the third topic concerning the Euro crisis, we encounter a long standing fault, whose related arguments point out not only the deeply unstable nature of the economy, but also the irrationality of the free market capitalist system. Consequently, the politico-philosophical tendency showed by those scholars who support this point of view is that of tracing the current imbalances of the Eurozone back to the contradictory and incurable expressions of this system as such.

Obviously, as economists, they attempt above all to offer analytical in-depth studies concerning the above mentioned imbalances. For instance, their attention is mainly focused on showing the self-destructive outcome of an austerity economic policy, the destabilizing effects of capital flows within the Eurozone and the need to change the status of the European Central Bank (ECB). Their further characteristic is that of adopting heterodox theoretical approaches, an inclination which is made even clearer by their strong criticism toward neoclassical theory.

These scholars have particularly focused on the topic concerning labour market and wages. In this regard, they support a point of view in opposition to that of the mainstream economists. The latter attribute the loss of competitiveness of the enterprises' system and low employment rates to the excessive regulation of labour market and propose measures aimed at its flexibility. The economists discussed in this section reply to this view as follows:

a) Sraffa's theory proved that an inverse relation between real wages and employment does not exist. Hence, the downward wage flexibility (caused by the measures of labour market deregulation) does not ensure an increase in employment *per se*[19];
b) in a situation such as the one they ascribe to Italian economy, where the price level decreases less (or increases more) than how much nominal wages decrease (or increase), the wage share reduction on production value restrains the aggregate demand and – through its

19 See, among others, Brancaccio and Passarella (2012), particularly p. 71: "the paradigm of producibility [of Sraffian derivation]" states that "employment depends mainly on the effective demand for goods and services, not on labour's flexibility".

negative effects on labour productivity (this relation is known as Kaldor-Verdoorn's law) – growth as well[20];

c) by inducing greater flexibility in the employment of the workforce and lower wages, labour market deregulation discourages enterprises from introducing innovations and technological progress, which are the main factors to increase productivity (on the supply-side) at international level[21].

By following this critical apparatus, these authors aim at defining a current of heterodox economics where several theoretical orientations could merge. The approaches taken into account are the Keynesian one for the relevance given by demand-side economics to the effects of growth, and the Sraffian economics, which is valued for its understanding of capitalistic accumulation process as not limited by a shortage of resources, but by distributive conflicts and wastes[22]. Other relevant theories are Hyman Minsky's scientific contribution, which is based on the financial fragilities' analysis of the capitalistic process (Minsky 1982), and Mickail Kalecki's doctrine (Kalecki 1971), which gives importance to the socio-political elements of income distribution and to a link between the latter and the effective demand (because of wages' and profits' influence respectively on consumptions and investments).

Therefore, what emerges from all these currents of economic thought is that market economy cannot avoid situations of unemployment in the long term[23].

For the purpose of this research, these various point of views express a perspective which is strongly critical of the process of European economic integration. Indeed, it is seen – as an economist belonging to this orientation affirmed – as "a tool of control and oppression, rather than cooperation and integration" (Bagnai 2012b: 58).

In other words, the economic thought analysed in this section tends to trace institutional anomalies and weaknesses, economic imbalances, wrong normative applications and the EMU's out-of-control mechanisms,

---

20 See Cesaratto and Stirati (2011), Stirati (2012) and Perri's (2013) observations as well. Kaldor-Verdoorn's law connects labour productivity growth (dependent variable) with output growth (independent variable). Read from the demand-side, the law states that productivity growth is determined by the growth of the aggregate demand.

21 See Bagnai (2013). A review of the main theoretical arguments employed by Italian economists in the debate of the last twenty years concerning the relation between labour flexibility and growth can be found in Pacella, Realfonzo and Tortorella Esposito (2013).

22 The basic reference is Sraffa (1960).

23 As it has been noticed, these heterodox currents could be the bases for a new macroeconomics, even though, to reach this synthesis – as Roncaglia (2011: 131) affirmed – "much still needs to be done".

back to a deeper cause, i.e. the exploitation of labour relations which are typical of the capitalistic system[24]. In brief, it is an economic orientation which draws from the original source of Marxist thought and in general from a conflictual idea of the economic process.

Some citations from the following economists provide the outlines for this interpretation. Cesaratto: "I very much sympathise with the old Marxist idea of an 'industrial reserve army': capitalism works well only with a pool of unemployed at its disposal and if it wants to change things it will increase the size of that pool" (Reichlin and Cesaratto 2013: 115). And Pivetti: "What has happened since the first decade of the Eighties to the present, the same turning point endured by the process of European economic and monetary unification, was the result of a conscious project of weakening the contractual force of wage earners[25], [being at stakes the] change of distributive and power conditions taking place during the last three decades in favour of capital and enterprises" (Pivetti 2012: 19).

Based on comments like the ones cited above[26], all the categories of Brussels' economic doctrine and ECB's monetary policy are dialectically declined as a "critique of political economy". The cut of public spending is judged negatively not only for its recessionary effects, but also because it would assume the connotation of a public intervention's withdrawal from economy, which in turn would be a sign of strengthening industrial bourgeoisie's positions as opposed to workers' (Barba 2012: especially p. 120). The proposal of selling State-owned properties and companies which has been advanced in order to decrease public debt stock, is criticised for its lack of realism, but even more so because it represents a hypothesis of recovery which would not undermine the distributive and powerful position of the wealthiest social classes (De Vivo 2012: 26; Zezza 2012: 113). Likewise, ECB is criticised because of its high interest rates which hinder real economy's recovery, but even more so for its control of intra-capitalist conflict, which tends to make a selection

24 According to this interpretation – devised by Brancaccio and Passarella (2012) – austerity has its own rationality insofar it weakens workers and shifts power relations in favour of capital. Therefore: "by contributing to further control the workforce, the policy of sacrifice is worth a crisis" (Brancaccio and Passarella 2012: 86).

25 See Mattei and Pivetti (2013: 237).

26 These opinions are often linked to those expressed against those economists who follow a pro-market orientation and who are defined as "in bad faith" scholars (Cesaratto and Pivetti 2012: 11), or "authors of theoretical restoration" (Pivetti 2012: 16), or still as scholars who act like "props, mere ideological supports of a seriously compromised mechanism of production and distribution, functional to an ever more limited and concentrated core of private interests" (Brancaccio and Passarella 2012: 13). Furthermore, these scholars are likened to those called by Marx "vulgar economists" since they are more interested in gaining consensus in favour of capitalist institutions rather than producing science.

process of solvent capitalists to the detriment of those who risk to be insolvent, by achieving a Marx-like process of capital centralization (Brancaccio and Passarella 2012: 75 and ff.).

The interpretation concerning Italy's peculiar situation is formulated in a similar way to the above mentioned one, i.e. as an alliance among dominant interests which would explain why the public spending "party" cannot prevail as it used to do during the period that goes from the Fifties to the Eighties. Indeed, during that time public spending was supported both by large sectors of public opinion which aimed also to stop communist propaganda, and by private capital's representatives, who saw the increased supply of public goods (e.g. motorway network) as a prospect of new outlets for private goods. Nowadays, the absence of the communist "threat" and the different nature (compared with the past) of required public goods (e.g. environmental goods) would have weakened the consensus on public spending, determining a new type of alliance to support capital's hegemony[27].

The authors of these interpretations point out that these models of capitalistic logic will inevitably originate contradictions which will prevent the achievement of set goals. For instance, many of them observe that the idea of turning the Eurozone into a big export enterprise – as the only way to compensate the low levels of domestic demand caused by austerity policies – will clash with similar hostile strategies adopted by the rest of the world. The final predicted scenario is that of a European unification's project which will crash under the weight of the disastrous results of Brussels' economic policies.

From the point of view of the evolution of ideas, those described in this section show sometimes a continuity with the concepts formulated during the Sixties and Seventies by a group of Italian economists who tended to orient decisions of economic policy following the "conflict paradigm". This theoretical core has multiple derivations (Keynes, Sraffa, Marx) with the vision of a new kind of society freed by the logics of market capitalism. Under the circumstances of the Italian economic crisis during the Seventies, this paradigmatic attempt, despite the initial success of adhesions, did not succeed in its purpose since it lacked an adequate scientific and political consensus in the end (Bini 2013). Nowadays, this attempt is brought again

[27] See what Barba (2012) argues on this matter. However, his point of view is not confirmed by the data relating to Italy's public spending which go from the post-war period to the present. These data show a public spending's resistance to decrease compared with the GDP in the last two decades when this restructuring was deemed to be necessary by the official documents of Italian economic policy. Remaining within the same interpretative framework, it should be said, unlike what Barba affirms, that the "public spending party" was stronger than those Governments which alternated from the Nineties onwards. In regard to this see Giarda (2012).

to the attention of the scientific community, the public opinion and policy-makers. However, unlike the past, these collective subjects are not only Italian, but at least European. Hence, it might be pointless to underline it, this debate is even more problematic today than it was back then[28]. According to this profile of historical dynamics, the economists' advice is to make Europe – after the turning point, achieved during the Eighties, of implementing an American-like economic policy based on the instruments of regulation rather than those of direct intervention – resuming its role as the seat of economic Governmental projects. In order to do so, they envision a greater presence of the State in economy, as well as State-owned companies, nationalizations and planning[29]. Given these same premises, the "Keynesian recipe" – based only on monetary and fiscal anti-cyclical measures – is labelled as "vulgar" (Brancaccio and Passarella 2012: 119). Indeed, it would show the serious limit of leaving "unchanged the role of market prices [...] by determining the level of composition of demand and production", thus being unable to influence substantially "the current system of accumulation led by private finance" (120-1). In brief, these economists who promote a left-wing "critical" thought, suggest to retrace backwards the path of the last thirty years, a proposal which – despite the endurance of the Eurozone crisis – is difficult to imagine in terms of practicability.

However, these deep-rooted ideas have their own inner strength which makes it impossible to predict their development with certainty. Surely, the concepts expressed by the economists analysed in this section are clear and incisive. According to them Europe will either adopt a left-wing political philosophy, or its union will never be achieved.

6. The Cultural Anthropology of Italians and the Controversial Effects of Austerity

In the previous sections the Euro crisis has been traced back to institutional flaws in the European constitution, to the almost impossible integration of two economic structures very different from each other (i.e. the Central-Northern one and the Southern-European one) or, finally, to the contradictions of market capitalism as such.

28 For instance, it is clear that to contrast "competitive and wage deflation" which is ascribed to Brussels's current economic policy, it will be necessary to implement a new internationalization of labour. The end of this measure should be that of achieving a wage standard common to all the EMU countries, which questions exactly the international approval foreshadowed by such an agreement.

29 The reader can find several debates on these topics in works by authors such as, for instance Cesaratto and Pivetti (2012), Cesaratto (2012), with a special attention to p. 46, and Brancaccio and Passarella (2012), particularly chap. 16 titled "Modernità della pianificazione".

The last theme that we are going to examine highlights the fact that the Italian crisis has its own profile, its own specific flaw which makes it *more* deep-rooted than the international one.

Paolo Savona refers to this "something more" typical of the Italian crisis as an overdose of flaws and responsibilities caused by decades of public policies opposed to rationality and sometimes even to economic common sense. These policies have been implemented by an inadequate political ruling class, often with the compliance of voters scarcely interested in understanding and making decisions coherently (Savona 2012: 65). The inspiration to title provocatively this section came from this overview on Italian anthropological vices.

6.1 Economists from the Italian tradition of Economics

This way of thinking is not isolated among economists. Suffice it to remember that Mariano D'Antonio – despite coming from a different academic background than Savona's – stigmatizes, as the latter does, Italy's many castes which range from the political one to that of high bureaucracy crossing a very large series of cases of patronage system and familism (D'Antonio 2013). Likewise, Alberto Quadrio Curzio – left aside the usual caution in expressing judgements – could not but be surprised by the "upsetting" Italian costs of politics, which are estimated to be 24.7 billion Euros per year[30].

Savona, D'Antonio and Quadrio Curzio are only few among many economists who share the idea of a situation which went to a certain extent out of control, seeing it as the end of a long sequence of mistakes and omissions made by Italian ruling classes since the Seventies and Eighties. This idea originates from the underestimation of the problem constituted by the qualitative and quantitative dynamics of public spending, the inability of formulating far-sighted industrial policies, unsatisfactory measures against tax evasion and corruption, the difficulties, that are still present, to find a solution to the dualism between North and South and so on.

In order to summarise the failure of Italian politics, these scholars often refer to some distinctive themes which are the excessive levels of public debt and tax burden currently reached by Italy.

Although they are not isolated voices, the names of these three authors have not been mentioned by chance. Indeed, we wanted to point out a type of liberal economist who considers the possibility of cumulative economic

30 See Quadrio Curzio (2012: 87). It is an evaluation that the author takes from a research made by the Italian Union of Labour (UIL) carried out in 2011 which verified that 1.3 million of people live off politics and that only 6.4 billion Euros would be actually necessary to make democracy work. See also UIL (2012).

dynamics and non-exclusive economic behaviours and the existence of imperfect markets. Hence, these economists adopt not only an economic but also a juridical conception of markets. They also stress the importance of the institutional datum and the historical context, rather than focusing only on aspects of pure logic. This is the reason why we linked the names of these three scholars to the Italian tradition of economic thought, which they are currently maintaining, despite their specific differences.

6.2 *Italian Economists from Bocconi University and American Universities*

Among those who share the idea that exists a specific Italian overdose of the crisis, there are some economists who come from a different scientific background than that of the above mentioned authors. A good part of them was educated, gained further specialisation and currently work at Milan's Bocconi University and/or in American Universities or Institutions. We mentioned some of these economists, namely Alberto Alesina, Silvia Ardagna, Francesco Giavazzi, Guido Tabellini, Marco Pagano, Roberto Perotti, in the second section when we discussed the theoretical researches which gave a prominent contribution to the development of economic philosophy at the time of the Maastricht Treaty. Moreover, some of these economists have been among the first ones to comment on the international crisis exploded at the end of 2008 following the bankruptcy of Lehman Brothers investment bank reading it as a serious incident of the capitalist system. Specifically, they highlighted a series of flaws such as cases of moral hazard, rating agencies' conflicts of interests, wrong schemes of top managers' remuneration, a regulation of markets and financial institutions that needed to be reviewed not because it was excessive or mild, but because it was pro-cyclical, i.e. it amplified shocks[31]. However, according to their opinions, none of these flaws, as much as they were serious, would have questioned the endurance of market capitalism. Their negative effects would have been temporary[32]. It is perhaps redundant to underline that the American economy was the main focus of their analyses dating back to 2008 and 2009.

Considering the Italian situation, it is important to point out that the interest of these economists towards it has increased over time. Alesina, Giavazzi, Perotti, Tabellini and others are frequent contributors to newspapers of widespread circulation such as *Corriere della Sera* and *Il Sole 24 Ore*. They are invited sometimes to participate in talk-shows in opposition to Italian economists who follow other orientations. Some of them established the blog *Fermare il declino* ("Stop the Decline"; from

---

31 See, for instance, Alesina (2009) and Tabellini (2009).

32 For further comments on this topic see Crescenzi (2010).

now on: FD) to comment on the main developments of economy and Italian politics[33]. The media success of this initiative – endorsed by a very well known economic journalist like Oscar Giannino – has also prompted some of these economists to get directly involved in the 2013 electoral campaign.

There are undoubtedly significant differences between the economists who follow more closely the Italian tradition of economic thought discussed in sub-section 6.1. and the group of authors treated in this sub-section. Broadly speaking, the economists belonging to this second group ascribe to the mechanisms of free market the ability of regulating effectively an area of economic and social relations which is much greater than it is considered to be by the economists of the first group. To be more specific, they are not so much inclined to deal with the issue of monetary sovereignty that Italy lost upon its entry in the Eurozone while an actual European political union had not yet been achieved (a topic which is instead central to Paolo Savona's interpretation of the Italian crisis). Likewise, they are not particularly fond of the principles of the social market economy (as it is typical of Quadrio Curzio). Finally, these economists do not seem interested in understanding the lesson that derives from the historical-sociological root of our current economic problems (an approach followed by D'Antonio).

At the same time, these two groups of economists share several common ideas which, in our opinion, justifies their placing within the same thematic field. In particular, within a liberal perspective which judges negatively a broad presence of State intervention in economy, both groups stigmatize the high public debt to GDP ratio as one of the main obstacles to growth. Furthermore, they think that the difficulties to implement structural reforms in Italy do not derive from the long-term characteristics of the Italian economy, as it is believed instead by those economists who are inspired by the varieties of capitalism paradigm. Once again the causes that hinder the enforcement of the above mentioned reforms can be found in the country's type of governance, whose low profile is responsible for the failed process of institutional market-oriented recovery, thought to be not only necessary, but also possible and feasible.

The main proposals of economic policy formulated by the economists of "FD" are two. The first one aims at the privatization of public assets (i.e. real properties and companies owned by the State or by other public authorities) for about 175 billion Euros over a five year-period to repay a part of the public debt. The second proposal aims at decreasing public spending by 1% per year throughout the entire legislation that goes from

33 We are referring to authors such as Luigi Zingales, Michele Boldrin, Sandro Brusco, Alberto Bisin and others still.

2013 to 2018, followed by a parallel tax reduction to be implemented over a six-year period. Overall, it would be a restrictive accounting measure (although a very mild one that may be calculated around 0, 17% per year) to which they ascribe expansionary net effects deriving from a low recessionary impact caused by spending cut and from a higher expansionary impact generated by tax reduction.

The main idea behind this macroeconomic supply-side model (known as "expansionary austerity") is that the ability of increasing income through a further increase of public spending (i.e. a typical Keynesian proposition) – in a situation characterised by an already excessive level of public spending – will tend to zero, if not to negative values via rational expectations. In economics, the assessment of these degrees of reactivity is carried out through the employment of the so-called "fiscal multipliers", a much studied and controversial subject within the current international debate, which deserves a brief digression.

6.3 Fiscal Multipliers and the Risk of Sovereign Debts

The concept of "expansionary austerity" has been formulated in some writings of the last 10/15 years (see section 2), and it has been further supported by a recent study carried out by Alesina and Giavazzi (2012) who have even provided some specific proposals. Let us recall them briefly: a) a fiscal adjustment implemented through spending cuts is less recessionary than an adjustment achieved through increased taxes; b) if fiscal consolidation, achieved through spending cuts, is combined with favourable collateral policies (i.e. an easy monetary policy, the liberalization of goods and labour markets and alike), it could have zero recessionary effects or it could even produce a positive impact on growth in the short-term; c) only an adjustment based on public spending reduction can eventually lead to fiscal consolidation, i.e. to stabilisation, if not to a reduction of the public debt to GDP ratio[34].

From this perspective it derives that Alesina and Giavazzi criticised the Fiscal Compact, because it was based on a purely quantitative measure of fiscal restriction, rather than on a different composition of public spending and taxation, according to the above mentioned criteria.

"Expansionary austerity" has gained a large consensus among the international community of economists and among Brussels' decision-making environments as well. Clearly, the idea shared by Alesina, Ardagna, Giavazzi and others, according to whom in certain specific circumstances a policy of fiscal consolidation can be pursued without

[34] Besides Alesina and Giavazzi (2012), this approach characterises also Alesina, Favero and Giavazzi (2012) and Giavazzi (2012).

incurring in disagreeable effects represented by the reduction of income and employment, could not but be welcomed by European policy-makers, who are always careful on how their decisions will affect their voters' consensus[35]. However, in the last couple of years, this approach has undergone a downsizing process, thanks to Paul Krugman who among others does not waste an opportunity to criticise the economists from Bocconi University (so-called "Bocconiani")[36]. Specifically, some researchers observed that in conditions of recessionary crises, the multipliers' value of several types of public spending increases with the possibility of being greater than one and greater than tax multipliers' values as well. Therefore, a restrictive policy based mainly on spending cuts produces a net recessionary effect which determines an opposed phenomenon to the one envisioned by Alesina, Ardagna, Giavazzi and others, i.e. an austerity policy that does not help to come out of the crisis, but which makes it worse[37].

What can be said on the current state of the debate on fiscal multipliers is that a synthesis is yet to come. Moreover, a self-critical connotation emerged from this same expansionary austerity's group of scholars. The reference is to Perotti's study (2011) which pointed out the several methodological problems to establish correctly the simulations of scenarios following the implementation of fiscal consolidation's policies. Perotti draws a conclusion which, coming from an author who has been involved in this sort of studies for a long time, has a certain relevance: "Economists have tried to shed light on multipliers for decades. The results, as usual in these cases, are neither black nor white: there are several shades of grey" (Perotti 2013).

35 A comment on this influence which aims at limiting the effectiveness of Alesina's contribution (2010) to the Econfin's conference held in Madrid in April 2010, can be found in Islam and Chowdhury (2012).

36 See, for instance, Krugman (2013c).

37 A clear depiction of this point of view has been carried out by a group of scholars who have been authors of the First Report of a research project titled *Independent Annual Growth Survey (iAGS) 2013 – Failed Austerity in Europe. The Way Out*; see IAGS (2012). Among the several studies cited in this report to support its thesis, there are those of three Italian researchers from the IMF and ECB (Batini, Callegari and Melina 2012). Piga's two speeches (from 2012 and 2013) are referred to this same study. He uses it to support his proposal in favour of a policy of increased public spending financed by higher taxes, founding it on the assumption that "public spending (which plays an expansionary role) has higher multipliers than taxes. If the sign of the two shocks (spending reduction and tax reduction as suggested by Alesina and Giavazzi) is inverted the debt on the GDP will increase, because less spending will depress the GDP more than less taxes will increase it" (Piga 2013: 2). A very much cited study carried out within the IMF that criticises the concept of expansionary austerity is Blanchard and Leigh (2013).

It is worth noticing that this declaration of uncertainty marks the passage of this author from a position that considers austerity as a strategy for growth, to another one which sees it as an almost forced choice in the short-term and in the absence of any possible alternatives. At the same time and even more so, he confirms his downgrading of the predictive values of fiscal multipliers on which a favourable assessment about expansionary policies is based. This fact originated angry replies from those who argue about the disastrous value of "expansionary austerity", in a crescendo of mutual controversies, as it happens every time that scholars of these two opposing fronts confront each other on the topic of fiscal multipliers' computation.

Another episode which raised the tension among opposed point of views is the one triggered by Reinhart and Rogoff's paper (2010). These two authors point out the presence, within the historical experience of several countries, of a negative correlation between growth and public debt, with the latter's level being greater than 90% of GDP. During the first phase of this debate, this correlation has sometimes been used with a propagandistic tone in terms of cause-effect, to support the certain recessionary effect caused by public debt levels which are greater than 90% of GDP. On the contrary, a second phase is characterised by the criticism received by these two authors on the methods employed in selecting and balancing data for their empirical study, and for making a mistake in calculating those same data[38]. The propagandist tone has marked also this second phase, but with an opposite meaning, i.e. to discredit the paper in its entirety without the support of any further in-depth analyses and clarifications. All these controversies give the feeling of a repetitive and unproductive debate, besides witnessing the animosity of a debate in which the ideological element has fiercely entered.

Certainly, the recent contribution given by Giancarlo Corsetti does not fall within this useless logic. Indeed, he proposes to integrate the computation of fiscal multipliers with the consideration of risk premium which weighs on sovereign debts (Corsetti, Kuester, Meier and Muller 2012 and Corsetti 2012). If risk premium is high (the thought goes obviously to Italy), pessimistic expectations on the vulnerability of a determined economic system will tend to become self-fulfilling, fostering the vicious circle of recession. Hence, Corsetti affirms that in the presence of a high risk premium, the recessionary effect of a public spending cut could be fully or partially compensated by the positive effect of a sovereign risk premium which decreases, thanks to the finance world's positive expectations generated by the eventual public spending cut.

[38] For a critical overview, see Zacchia (2013).

The interest for this type of formulation, besides its intrinsic content, derives from these two further reflections. The first one confirms the existence of a complex and hardly quantifiable interaction among multiple variables with the underlying advice of being cautious in computing *ex-ante* an optimal fiscal consolidation policy. Bearing in mind the weak framework of Italian public finance within the context of international speculative movements, the second observation concerns the argument based on the risk premium of sovereign debts which should not be undervalued, as it is widely witnessed by the fluctuating spread between Italian State Bonds (BTP) and German Bunds.

6.4 Stop the Decline: is it possible?

Let us now go back to the main issue of this section: i.e. the Italian overdose of the crisis. Once the expansionary austerity paradigm has been questioned, the founders of FD ("Stop the Decline") still consider as solid measures their main proposals aimed at decreasing the public finance sector.

FD's authors believe that privatizations and disposals of public assets for 35 billion Euros per year are practicable and realistic, given that they are supported by a strong political will. The latter is also needed to introduce legislative variations to enable the sale of public assets owned by town councils.

Sandro Brusco summarizes the main positive effects concerning public debt reduction as follows: a) a better allocation of resources which raises the general productivity of the economic system; b) an increase of the public debt's market value which causes positive wealth effects perceived both by families (increasing consumption) and banks (credit-crunch mitigation)[39].

The following citation from Adam Smith supports the thesis expressed by point a):

> "In every great monarchy of Europe the sale of the crown lands would produce a very large sum of money, which, if applied to the payment of the public debts, would deliver from mortgage a much greater revenue than any which those lands have ever afforded to the crown [...] In the course of a few years it would probably enjoy another revenue. When the crown lands had become private property, they would, in the course of a few years, become well improved and well cultivated. The increase of their produce would increase the population of the country, by augmenting the revenue and consumption of the people. But the revenue which the crown derives from the duties of customs and excise, would necessarily increase with the revenue and consumption of the people" (Smith 1976: V. 2.19).

39 See Brusco (2012) and Fare per Fermare il Declino (2012b).

With regard to a parallel public spending and tax reductions, FD founders advocate a significant spending review. Among several proposals, we point out three of them which have been recently advanced by the economist Michele Boldrin, the leader of this political movement. The first proposal recommends a 25% spending reduction of disability pensions out of its total amount which is around 40 billion Euros, bringing to the surface (what Boldrin assesses to be) the analogous percentage of pensioners who benefit illegally (as they are not disabled) from these compensations (Boldrin 2013a[40]). The second proposal is concerned with the progressive reduction of State grants to enterprises by decreasing them from the current 27 billion Euros per year to 7 billion Euros which should be reached by 2018[41]. The third proposal aims at decreasing the total number of Italian Government employees between 10% and 15%, based on the assumptions of public administration's low productivity and that "the State system is the main cause of stagnation" (Boldrin 2013b).

Broadly speaking, the logic behind these measures is that of re-modulating the Government budget in a productional way. The aim is that of identifying those cuts of a "highly unproductive and parasitic" public spending that, despite avoiding a "social slaughtering", will free resources "to decrease taxes on labour, especially for lower incomes" and on enterprises by abolishing the Italian Regional Production Tax (IRAP)[42].

Furthermore, it is a proposal that, although similar in its ends to those envisioned by the expansionary austerity theory, can gain a broader consensus than either the one based on the uncertain measurement of fiscal multipliers or the one found on the ideological belonging to the so called neo-liberism. Indeed, it re-introduces *de facto* the traditional issues about a good governance of the economy.

The recent proposal advanced by several economists aimed at a substantial exemption from social security contributions to be financed partly by Government budget's savings and partly by the temporary loosening of Brussels' fiscal restrictions, provides the example for a possible convergence among different point of views. For instance, the views expressed by "neo-liberists" Alesina and Giavazzi (2014), and the Keynesian Marcello De Cecco (2013b).

---

40 He does not reference the source of this assessment.

41 This significant reduction is justified by the fact that these grants "instead of supporting efficient [companies] [...] end up in almost their entirety to few big entities, which are scarcely efficient and almost fully controlled by the State [whose] end is that of fostering the unwieldy public apparatus and its countless clienteles" (Boldrin 2013a).

42 See Fare per Fermare il Declino (2012a) and the second part of Brusco (2012).

Moreover, this proposal is shared by those economists belonging to the Italian tradition of economics that we discussed at the beginning of this section. According to them, a serious spending review would have the great advantage to cut the umbilical cord that links Government budget to the inefficiencies of public administration, corruption, wrong incentives and rents.

However, this system of good governance, as every other one, requires the existence of an adequately efficient institutional setup and a virtuous action by the Country's ruling class. But these premises are lacking today in Italy, because of resistances to implement incisive financial recovery policies by the political parties' apparatus, lobbies and established interests. It is also for this reason that a feeling of dissatisfaction is growing among economists, which on the one hand it is useful to soften some of their notorious displays of cognitive pride, but on the other hand it determines negatively an essentially fruitless state of the public debate. It is as if the bridges of communication had been cut off between the world of economic thought and that of political action or as if it were temporarily proclaimed the irrelevance of theoretical knowledge on the effects of public policies.

The interpretative scheme which oversees this pessimistic view is as follows. We start observing that politicians are often characterised by a strong inclination to defer "actual" reforms, because they have a high political cost in terms of loss of electoral consensus. We proceed by noticing that the deferral method causes, in the long term, a decline of competitiveness in the country where this practice has become the norm in the political routine compromising at the same time the country's credibility in the international arena. Finally, a financial emergency (such as the one experienced in Italy) originates from these combined negative elements, which can be overcome by the affected country through the employment of the only available tools of immediate impact's interventions such as: an increase in tax burden, credit-crunch and the like, i.e. austerity measures. According to Bini-Smaghi, who has formulated more clearly this interpretative scheme, austerity is a self-destructive policy, but since we have not been able to avoid its constitutive conditions, it has become a forced way out (see Bini Smaghi, 2013). It means that no current Government, much as "clever" and watchful, can fix or remove the mistakes made by past bad Governments.

Hence, today we are only left with the nagging thought, or better with the hope for a country that at least in the future will be able to release itself from that historical law of *italianità* which always prevents us from learning from our mistakes in order to meet for once in a useful and timely way the challenges set by historical change.

7. Conclusions

The debate among Italian economists on the causes and nature of the Italian crisis is on-going; discussions on the most suitable measures are still open and their outcomes are uncertain. It is still too early to evaluate this debate in terms of an even approximate historiographic synthesis.

What has clearly emerged from this research is that since 2011, the numerous critical observations made by Italian economists can be grouped in four critical orientations. Let us recall them briefly.

The first orientation focuses mainly on the limits deriving from the existence of a currency area which lacks political unity. The second orientation highlights the great difficulty to implement an effective integration process among geopolitical economic areas, which are very different from each other, within the Eurozone. The third line is that of the left-wing "critical" thought which underlines the inner contradictions of market capitalism as such. Finally, the fourth field of observations criticises the inadequacy of Italian ruling classes as well as an insufficient level of civic and political maturity displayed by the national public opinion.

The competitive debate among these different ways of reading the serious current recession could not but lead to as many diverse indications concerning the most suitable public policies to face the crisis. Some of these views are strongly favourable to the State intervention in economy (including incisive forms of economic planning). By contrast, other economists consider to be essential to give more space to free market relations, which are considered to be the least imperfect and iniquitous ones in guaranteeing a process of growth.

Moreover, showing the main characteristics of these four orientations has enabled us to highlight the multiple concepts of "austerity" which originate from them. Let's summarize them briefly:

1. "foolish" austerity (according to Keynesian point of view), because those who ask for it seem to ignore the already established theories which have proved that it strengthens the perverse spiral of recession;
2. austerity of "conflicts" which expresses capitalism's inherent rationality aimed at weakening labourers and shifting power relations towards capital;
3. austerity of "good government" based on the re-modulation of Government budget aimed at increasing production and implementing the civic virtues of the Italians;
4. "expansionary" austerity considered to be as such, because it is able to positively overturn the economic people's expectations;

5. "forced" austerity, because it is the result of a financial emergency state risen as a consequence of the long-term inability of a country to implement the required "structural" reforms.

However, this paper has highlighted a further discrepancy, i.e. the lack of conditions of practicability which exists among the several proposals of economic policy advanced by many scholars and the actual possibility of implementing them. We have seen that these deficits of practicability can be attributed to several causes such as the existence of supranational institutional constraints and the EMU's countries' opposing perspectives and interests caused by their different economic realities. This situation often surfaces in those attitudes according to which each country claims only the goodness of those proposals which are tailor-made for its own national interests. Another cause which increases the above mentioned discrepancy is the resistance opposed by various social groups, sometimes along with the conservatism of Italian bureaucracies and political elites, to the implementation of fiscal adjustment policies and so on.

However, nowadays it seems that economists are growing aware of this discrepancy between their respective optimal projects and the related difficulty to implement them. As a result, a more flexible intellectual attitude is arising from this process. Let us consider, for instance, those economists who state the absolute necessity to adopt Keynesian fiscal expansion policies to come out of the current recessionary phase. Nowadays, some of these economists are more cautious in supporting their stance, once they realised the growing public opinion's intolerance towards high levels of tax burden and public spending which characterise Italy's public finance. Likewise, a greater caution in advancing suggestions is shown by those who believe it is essential to implement drastic measures of fiscal restraint. In the previous section 6.4, we mentioned a proposal that despite being placed within this doctrinaire context, considers also a temporary loosening of Maastricht fiscal strictness as a short-term step to achieve more easily an increase of growth potential in the long-term[43].

In general, the long and deep-rooted crisis that began in 2008 is also highlighting an intellectual process which is evolving in several phases. The first phase was characterised by an attitude of cultural disorientation among the majority of Italian scholars. The second phase – which coincides with the period analysed in this paper – was marked instead by a considerable scientific and designing liveliness. During this second phase, heterodox positions concerning both basic assumptions, analytical

43 See Alesina and Giavazzi (2014). See also the proposal advanced by Bini Smaghi (2014) in his conclusions.

tools and modelling processes, emerged more precisely marking a clearer difference with orthodox views.

Moreover, we can envision a third phase of this evolving process – which will be achieved only by a definitive overcoming of the current period of Great Recession – where some heterodox positions, formulated at the borders of the economists' profession, could be included in mainstream economics[44]. But this is purely a conjecture based on what has sometimes happened in the past. In regard to this matter, it is worth to recall the inclusion of Keynes theory in mainstream economics following the elaboration of neoclassical synthesis. Another example is provided by the articulated debate which took place in Italy in the Seventies between Keynesian, Sraffian and Marxist economists on the one hand, and monetarism and New Classical Economics on the other hand, concerning the ways to escape from the crisis during that decade. It needs to be noticed that the high levels of heterodox design which took place in that period, decreased once the traumatic event of crisis, which paved its way, was overcome.

Similar observations might be applied to the phenomenon known as "return to Keynes". It seems reasonable to believe that this outcome can acquire new scientific and cultural relevance only if it is declined consistently with the current historical context. This is witnessing a shift in the geopolitical barycentre of economic policy's decision-making from single nations to the European Union. Moreover, the historical context underlines the need to reconsider the tools of Keynesian economic policy to support the aggregate demand (e.g. fiscal multipliers) in the light of the global scenario in which finance operates.

As mentioned above, it is still too early to develop an historiographic synthesis of this on-going debate. Nevertheless, we think that the four scientific and interpretative lines identified in this paper could offer a basis for an effective implementation of these point of views and, perhaps, for their future convergence about some points. Considering the long-term projections pointed out by these economists, we believe that they could help us gaining a better understanding of the historical and economic essence of the age started by the worldwide process of globalization and the Maastricht Treaty.

44 In regard to this process of co-optation of heterodox theories within mainstream economic thought, see Colander, Holt and Rosser Jr. (2004).

References

Alesina, A. (2009). "La crisi del '29 e le sue false morali". *Il Sole 24 Ore*, May 20.

Alesina, A. (2010). *Fiscal adjustments: lessons from recent history*. Paper prepared for the Ecofin meeting in Madrid, April 15.

Alesina, A.; Ardagna, S. (1998). "Tales of Fiscal Adjustment". *Economic Policy*, 27 (October): 489-585.

Alesina, A.; Ardagna, S. (2010). "Large Changes in Fiscal Policy: Taxes versus Spending". *Tax Policy and the Economy*, ed. by J. R. Brown, University of Chicago Press, 24 (1): 35-68.

Alesina, A.; Favero, C.; Giavazzi, F. (2012). *The output effect of fiscal consolidations*. Innocenzo Gasparini Institute for Economic Research W. P., n. 450, August.

Alesina, A.; Giavazzi, F. (2012). "The austerity question: 'how?' is as important as 'how much'?". In Corsetti, G. (2012): 11-6.

Alesina, A.; Giavazzi, F. (2014). "La soluzione tre per cento". *Corriere della Sera*, January 5.

Alesina, A.; Perotti, R. (1995). *Fiscal Expansions and Adjustments in OECD Countries*. Department of Economics, Columbia University, Discussion Paper Series, n. 754.

Alesina, A.; Tabellini, G. (1987). *A Positive Theory of Fiscal Deficit and Government Debt in a Democracy*. National Bureau of Economic Research W. P., n. 2308, July.

Ardagna, S. (2004). "Fiscal stabilization: when do they work and why". *European Economic Review*, 5: 1047-74.

Arrighi, C. (1985) (ed.). *Semiperipheral Development. The Politics of Southern European in the Twentieth Century*. London, Sage.

Asso, P. F. (2007). "Franco Modigliani e l'Italia". In Modigliani, F. (2007): 9-49.

Bagnai, A. (2012a). *Il tramonto dell'Euro. Come e perché la fine della moneta unica salverebbe democrazia e benessere in Europa*. Reggio Emilia: Imprimatur editore.

Bagnai, A. (2012b). "Le aporie del più Europa". In Cesaratto, S.; Pivetti, M. (2012): 49-60.

Bagnai, A. (2013). *Declino, produttività, flessibilità, euro: il mio primo maggio* (http://goofynomics.blogspot.com/2013/05/declino-produttivita-flessibilita-euro.html).

Barba, A. (2012). "Le illusioni del Keynesismo antistatalista", in Cesaratto, S.; Pivetti, M. (2012): 117-24.

Batini, N.; Callegari, G.; Melina, G. (2012). *Successful Austerity in the United States, Europe and Japan*. IMF W. P., n. 190, July.

Bini, P. (2013). "The Italian Economists and the Crisis of he Nineteen-seventies. The Rise and Fall of the Conflict Paradigm". *History of Economic Thought and Policy*, 1: 73-102.

Bini Smaghi, L. (2013). *Morire di austerità. Democrazie europee con le spalle al muro*. Bologna, Il Mulino.

Bini Smaghi, L. (2014), *33 false verità sull'Europa*. Bologna, Il Mulino.

Blanchard, O. J.; Leigh, D. (2013). *Growth Forecast Errors and Fiscal Multipliers*. IMF W. P., n. 1, January.

Blyth, M. (2013). *Austerity. The History of a Dangerous Idea*. Oxford, Oxford University Press.

Boldrin, M. (2013a). *Ecco dove trovare 14 miliardi per tagliare le tasse*. June 5 <http://www.fermareildeclino.it/articolo/michele-boldrin-ecco-dove-trovare-14-miliardi-per-tagliare-le-tasse>.

Boldrin, M. (2013b). *Taglierei il 10-15% dei dipendenti pubblici*. July 4 <http://www.fermareildeclino.it/articolo/michele-boldrin-taglierei-il-10-15-dei-dipendenti>.

Brancaccio, E.; Passarella, M. (2012). *L'austerità è di destra e sta distruggendo l'Europa*. Milano, Il Saggiatore.

Brusco, S. (2012). *Un altro rapporto debito/PIL è possibile*. August 27 and 29 (http://noisefromamerika.org/articolo/altro-rapporto-debitopil-possibile-1 and http://noisefromamerika.org/articolo/altro-rapporto-debitopil-possibile-2).

Cesaratto, S. (2012). "Il vecchio e il nuovo della crisi europea". In Cesaratto, S.; Pivetti, M. (2012): 29-48.

Cesaratto, S.; Pivetti, M. (2012) (eds.). *Oltre l'austerità*. Gli eBook di MicroMega.

Cesaratto, S.; Stirati, A. (2011). *German and the European and Global Crisis*. Quaderni del Dipartimento di Economia Politica dell'Università degli Studi di Siena, quaderno n. 607.

CGIL (2013). *Il piano del lavoro 2013. Creare lavoro per dare futuro e sviluppo al paese, Conferenza di programma CGIL del 25-26 gennaio 2013* <www.cgil.it/Pagine Speciali/ConferenzaProgramma2013.aspx>.

Colander, D.; Holt, R.; Rosser, B. Jr. (2004). "The changing face of mainstream economics". *Review of Political Economy*, 16 (4): 485-99.

Corsetti, G. (2012) (ed.). *Austerity: Too Much of a Good Thing?, A VoxEU.org eCollection of views by leading economists*. London, Centre for Economic Policy Research <http://www.voxeu.org/epubs/cepr-reports/austerity-too-much-good-thing>.

Corsetti, G.; Kuester, K.; Meier, A.; Muller, G. (2012). *Soverign risk, fiscal policy and macroeconomic stability*, IMF W. P., n. 33.

Cozzi, T. (2011). "Debito e crescita". *Moneta e Credito*, 255: 291-6.

Cozzi, T. (2013). *Austerità e crisi*. June 20 (http://sviluppofelice.wordpress.com/2013/06/20/austerita-e-crisi/).

Crescenzi, A. (2010) (ed.). *La crisi mondiale. Storia di tre anni difficili*. Roma, Luiss University Press.

De Cecco, M. (2013a). *Ma cos'è questa crisi. L'Italia, l'Europa e la seconda globalizzazione (2007-2013)*. Roma, Donzelli.

De Cecco, M. (2013b). "Unless we boost demand we will stay bogged down". *Review of Economic Conditions in Italy*, 2: 23-27.

De Cecco, M.; Maronta, F. (2013). *Berlino, Roma e i dolori del giovane euro*. May 20 (http://keynesblog.com/2013/05/20/berlino-roma-e-i-dolori-del-giovane-euro).

De Grauwe, P. (2009). *Keynes' Savings Paradox, Fisher's Debt Deflation and the Banking Crisis* <http://www.eurointelligence.com/article.581+M5c1f8fa62ab.0.html>.

De Vivo, G. (2012). "Molto rigore per nulla". In Cesaratto, S.; Pivetti, M. (2012): 21-8.

D'Antonio, M. (2013). *La crisi dell'economia italiana. Cause, responsabilità, vie d'uscita*. Soveria Mannelli, Rubbettino.

D'Ippoliti, C. (2012a). *Crisi: (come) ne usciamo?*. Roma, L'Asino d'oro edizioni.

D'Ippoliti, C. (2012b). "Introduction. There is more to Keynesianism than public spending alone". *PSL Quarterly Review*, 260: 3-10.

Fare per Fermare il declino (2012a). *Come e quanto tagliare la spesa pubblica* <http://www.fermareildeclino.it/fermareildeclinoit/come-e-quanto-tagliare-la-spesa-pubblica>.

Fare per Fermare il declino (2012b). *Ridurre il debito pubblico. Ecco come* <http://www.fermareildeclino.it/ridurre-il-debito-pubblico-ecco-come>.

Fare per Fermare il declino (2013). *Ridurre il rapporto Spesa Pubblica/PIL di 6 punti*. January <http://www.fermareildeclino.it/sites/default/files/users/fabio.lazzari/punto02programmacompleto.pdf>.

Fassina, S. (2012). *Il lavoro prima di tutto. L'economia, la sinistra, i diritti*. Roma, Donzelli.

Ferrari, S. (2012). "Crisi internazionale e crisi nazionale". *Moneta e Credito*, 257: 49-58.

Fratianni, M. (2008). "Financial Crises, Safety Nets and Regulation". *Rivista Italiana degli Economisti*, 13 (2): 169-207.

Giarda, P. (2012). *Dinamica, struttura e criteri di governo della spesa pubblica: un rapporto preliminare*. Rapporto presentato per gli incontri di lavoro delle parti sociali su "Bilancio e patrimonio pubblico", e promosso dal Ministro dell'economia e delle finanze nell'ambito delle iniziative finalizzate alla riforma del sistema fiscale.

Giavazzi, F.; Pagano, M. (1988). "The Advantage of Tying One's Hands". *European Economic Review*, 32: 303-30.

Giavazzi, F.; Pagano, M. (1990). *Can Severe Contractions Be Expansionary? Tales of Two Small European Countries.* National Bureau of Economic Research W. P., n. 3372, May.

Giavazzi, F.; Pagano M. (1996). "Non-Keynesian Effects of Fiscal Policy Changes: International Evidence and the Swedish Experience". *Swedish Economic Policy Review*, 3: 67-103.

Giavazzi, F. *et al.* (2012). *Analisi e raccomandazioni sui contributi pubblici alle imprese. Rapporto al Presidente del Consiglio e Ministro dell'Economia*, July 30.

Independent Annual Growth Survey – IAGS (2012). *First Report 2013: Failed Austerity in Europe. The Way Out* <http://www.iags-project/documents/iags_report2013.pdf>.

Iodice, G.; Palma, D. (2013). *Una critica alla teoria delle Aree valutarie ottimali come spiegazione della crisi dell'euro* <www.keynesblog.com>.

Islam, I.; Chowdhury, A. (2012). *Revisiting the evidence on expansionary fiscal austerity: Alesina's hour?* February 28 <http://www.voxeu.org/debates/commentaries/revisiting-evidence-expansionary-fiscal-austerity-alesina-s-hour>.

Kalecki, M. (1971). *Selected essays on the dynamics of the capitalist economy.* Cambridge, Cambridge University Press.

Kenen, P. B. (1969). "The Theory of Optimum Currency Areas: An Eclectic View". In Mundell, R. A.; Swodoba, A. K. (eds.), *Monetary Problems of the International Economy*. Chicago, Chicago University Press, 41-60.

Krugman, P. (2013a). "Draghi non si faccia tentare". *Il Sole 24 Ore*, July 15.

Krugman, P. (2013b). "La moneta unica mette a rischio i sistemi di Welfare più deboli". *Il Sole 24 Ore*, June 14.

Krugman, P. (2013c). *Paul Krugman contro i bocconiani Alesina e Ardagna: "Colpa loro se l'Europa ha puntato tutto sull'austerity"*. May 20 <http://www.huffingtonpost.it/2013/05/20/paul-krugman-contro-i-boc_n_3304823.html>.

La Malfa, G. (2011 [2000]). *L'Europa in pericolo. La crisi dell'Euro*. Firenze, Passigli editore.

La Malfa, G. (2013). "Più deficit per ripartire". June 6 (Keynesblog.com).

Lettera degli economisti (2010). *La politica restrittiva aggrava la crisi* <http://www.letteradeglieconomisti.it/>.

Mattei, U.; Pivetti, M. (2013). "La rivolta dei beni comuni". *MicroMega*, 3: 225-38.

Minsky, H. P. (1982). *Can 'it' happen again? Essays on instability of finance*. Armonk, NY, Sharpe.

Modigliani, F. (2007). *L'impegno civile di un economista. Scritti editi e inediti sull'economia e sulla società italiana,* ed. by P. F. Asso. Siena, Fondazione Monte dei Paschi di Siena.

Moro, B. (2012). "The Theoretical Debate on the Recent Great Crisis". *Rivista Italiana degli Economisti*, 1 (April): 3-42.

Mundell, R. A. (1961). "A Theory of Optimum Currency Areas". *American Economic Review*, 5: 657-65.

Pacella, A.; Realfonzo, R.; Tortorella Esposito, G. (2013). *Flessibilità e crescita. Il dibattito in Italia negli anni delle riforme del mercato del lavoro (1990-2010)*. Mimeo.

Perotti, R. (2011). *The "Austerity myth": Gain without Pain?*, Bank for International Settlements W. P., n. 362, November.

Perotti, R. (2013). "Se l'austerità non ha alternative". *Il Sole 24 Ore*, June 15.

Perri, S. (2013). *La bassa domanda e il declino italiano*. April 5 (Keynesblog.com).

Piga, G. (2012). *Toh, chi si rivede! Il moltiplicatore Keynesiano*. October 17 (Keynesblog.com).

Piga, G. (2013). *Ecco le prove. Si può fare. Si deve fare*. February 14 <http://www.gustavopiga.it/2013/ecco-le-prove-si-puo-fare-si-deve-fare/>.

Pivetti, M. (2012). "L'austerità, gli interessi nazionali e la rimozione dello Stato". In Cesaratto, S.; Pivetti, M. (2012): 13-20.

Quadrio Curzio, A. (2012). *Economia oltre la crisi. Riflessioni sul liberalismo sociale*, ed. by S. Natoli. Brescia, La Scuola.

Ramazzotti, P. (2013). *Shared economic thought and the neglect of social costs. Why progressive economists often stick to conventional wisdom*. Mimeo.

Rangone, M.; Solari, S. (2012a). "From the Southern-European model to nowhere: the evolution of Italian capitalism 1976-2011". *Journal of European Public Policy*, 19 (8): 1188-206.

Rangone, M.; Solari, S. (2012b). "'Southern European' capitalism and the social costs of business enterprise". *Studi e Note di Economia*, 1: 3-28.

Reichlin, P.; Cesaratto, S. (2013). Egualianza? Dipende. *MicroMega*, 3: 99-116.

Reinhart, C. M.; Rogoff, K. S. (2010). "Growth in a Time of Debt". *American Economic Review*, 100 (2), "Papers and Proceedings of the One Hundred Twenty-Second Annual Meeting of the American Economic Association": 573-8.

Roncaglia, A. (2011). "Macroeconomie in crisi e macroeconomie in ripresa". *Moneta e Credito*, 254: 115-33.

Rossi, S. (2013). *Processo alla finanza*. Roma-Bari, Laterza.

Savona, P. (2012a). *Eresie, esorcismi, e scelte giuste per uscire dalla crisi. Il caso Italia*. Soveria Mannelli, Rubbettino.

Savona, P. (2012b). *Lettera agli amici tedeschi e italiani. Come funziona il meccanismo economico europeo*. Roma, Cromografica.

Smith, A. (1976). *An Inquiry into the Nature and Causes of the Wealth of Nations*, ed. by R. H. Campbell, A. S. Skinner and W. B. Todd. Oxford, Clarendon Press.

Spaventa, L. (2009). "Economists and economics: What does the crisis tell us?". *CEPR Policy Insight*, 38: 1-7.

Sraffa, P. (1960). *Production of Commodities by Means of Commodities. Prelude to a Critique of Economic Theory*. Cambridge, Cambridge University Press.

Stirati, A. (2012). "Crescita e 'riforma' del mercato del lavoro". In Cesaratto, S.; Pivetti, M. (2012): 148-60.

Tabellini, G. (2009). "Il mondo dopo la crisi". *Il Sole 24 Ore*, May 7.

UIL (2012). *Secondo rapporto sui costi della politica*, July <http://www.uilpensionati.it/Documents/Iniziative/Costi_della_politica/2costi-politica2012%20(1).pdf>.

Vaciago, G. (2012). *A che gioco giochiamo?*. October 23 <http://www.rivistailmulino.it/news/newsitem/index/Item/News:NEWS_ITEM:1839>.

Wallerstein, I. (1979). *The Capitalist World Economy*. New York, Cambridge University Press.

Zacchia, P. (2013). *Il debito pubblico deprime la crescita? Il clamoroso errore di Carmen Reinhart e Kenneth Rogoff*. April 18 (http://keynesblog.com/2013/04/18/il-debito-pubblico-deprime-la-crescita-il-clamoroso-errore-di-carmen-reinhart-e-kenneth-rogoff/).

Zezza, G. (2012). "La crisi dell'euro: invertire la rotta o abbandonare la nave?". In Cesaratto, S.; Pivetti, M. (2012): 99-116.

The Genealogy of German Ordo-Liberalism and the European Project[1]

Gerhard WEGNER

1. Introduction

The fiscal crisis in the European Union has revealed the diversity of approaches to economic policy which characterizes the European project from its beginning. These approaches originate from different political experiences but also from different intellectual cultures. Accordingly, they shape the perception of crises and instruct the search for their causes and appropriate political measures to remedy them in divergent ways. The cultural spectrum is frequently described as a North-South divide: on the one hand a pro-market, free trade, pro-competitive and anti-interventionist political culture favoured in the UK, the Scandinavian countries, the Netherlands, and Germany; on the other hand an interventionist, regulative, redistributive economic policy preferred in the Mediterranean countries such as Italy, Spain, Greece or France.

This divide is a stereotype rather than a fair description of reality: the Northern States in the EU and Germany maintain highly developed welfare states (in spite of reforms in the past decade), and some of them have supported a large public sector for nearly a century (UK, Germany) and regulate their economies quite heavily. Indeed, Keynesian economic policy has been practiced in all European countries including the UK, Germany and the Netherlands. In the same vein, excessive public debt was considered an issue in the UK and in Germany, whereas Spain had quite a consolidated budget before the outbreak of the crisis.

This qualifies the dichotomy between the alleged pro-competitive North and the anti-competitive South. Nevertheless, a divide of political cultures in Europe cannot be ignored, and during European integration, it has become relevant at several points in time. Compromises, namely between France and Germany, were repeatedly required in order to bridge different stances to economic policy and the role of Government in a market economy.

1 I thank Erik Grimmer-Solem and Marie-Luise Heinrich-Mergui for their critical comments and suggestions.

The fiscal crisis in 2010 shed new light on the divide of political approaches in the European Union. From the perspective of some of its EU partners, the German approach to economic policy settled in the post-war period lacks understanding. Historically, the Ordo-liberal school plays a key role in shaping the thinking of economically relevant elite groups in Germany. In what follows, I will delineate this approach with brush strokes in order to explain some of the assumptions and approaches of German economic policy. Even though the recent history of economic thought has taken notice of the Ordo-liberal school and has occasionally attracted the attention of international scholars, its relevance for present-day debates is underestimated by European partners[2]. The main reason for this disregard is the fact that Ordo-liberalism represents a national school of economic thought rather unknown in the international arena; unlike Austrian economics, it has only spread to a few US economists or to economists in other countries. Furthermore, Ordo-liberalism is hardly linked to the post-war debate of liberalism (such as the progressive movement) despite the fact that many of its representatives were members of the Mont Pelerin Society. One reason is the early death of its outstanding figure, Walter Eucken in 1950. A further reason can be seen in the national orientation that emerged with the Cold War divide between market-oriented and centrally planned economic systems, which promoted research in comparative economics; the outcome of this "Systems Competition" was far from being taken for granted even among leading economists[3]. However, comparative economics has become a marginal sub-discipline in economics for a long time now.

Present day economics in Germany does not make explicit reference to Ordo-liberalism, nor would many economists present themselves as followers of this tradition. The internationalization of the discipline has widely removed theoretical schools which are rooted in national intellectual cultures. Moreover, the academic relevance of the Ordo-liberal school expired in the 1970s. Nevertheless, much evidence suggests that the tradition of the Ordo-liberal school implicitly shapes the thinking of German economists, legal scholars, and economic journalists in important newspapers and thus still exerts influence on the national debate. For a long time – to some extent even today – it has formed the corporate identity of the German Ministry of Economic Affairs, the Council of Economic Experts as well as the thinking of leading figures of the German Bundesbank such as Jens Weidmann and its representatives in the ECB,

2 See Sally (1998: part III) who gives an excellent overview of German Ordo-liberalism; for an Italian version of this chapter see Sally (2012).

3 Acemoglu and Robinson (2012) remind us that even Samuelson's famous textbook argued that the economic order of the Soviet Union will overpass Western economies "possibly by 1984, but probably by 1997" (Acemoglu and Robinson 2012: 127-8).

such as Ottmar Issing. To this day, legal scholars make reference to the Ordo-liberal idea of an "economic constitution" (*Wirtschaftsverfassung*) in order to create a legal framework for an operating market economy[4]. Time and again they have been outspoken in their criticism of European law making when the European *Wirtschaftsverfassung* was about to interfere with the guiding principles of the Ordo-liberalism. One of the most influential voices for such critiques has been the renowned newspaper *Frankfurter Allgemeine Zeitung* which regularly comments on issues of national and European economic policy from a perspective that traces back to the Ordo-liberal school[5]. Its editors and contributors strongly dispute neo-Keynesian positions put forward by the US Government or the IMF, which recommend a "transfer union" or suggest that German Government should overstretch public budgets in order to overcome the current economic crisis in Europe.

In the following pages, I will first sketch the philosophy of Ordo-liberalism and its key ideas as succinctly as possible. Theoretically it is not as outdated as it may appear at first sight. Quite the contrary, recent work in institutional economics takes up key Ordo-liberal ideas pertaining to the relationship of political and economic freedom; in the same vein, constitutional economics parallels Ordo-liberal ideas (see below). I will then delineate how Ordo-liberalism expands on key questions of European integration. Besides some general reflections, namely those of Wilhelm Röpke who commented on the early stage of European integration, the Ordo-liberal school did not develop a political conception for the European Union. However, this task has been accomplished by German scholars who updated Ordo-liberal ideas and combined them with Hayekian elements within constitutional economics. The building blocks for a theory of Systems Competition with an application to the European integration process was thus created. In contrast to many other contributions in the field of constitutional economics the theory of Systems Competition is highly informed about the legal framework of the European Union. Hence I will argue that it is the only coherent institutional conception for the EU which holds out the chance of strengthening both democracy and economic competition within the Union.

2. The Ordo-liberal Genealogy

In the first half of the 20th century a small group of German economists and legal scholars launched what has become known as "Ordo-liberalism" (Zweynert 2008). The concepts and theories of Ordo-liberalism began

4 Böhm (1966) coins the term "Wirtschaftsverfassung" ("economic constitution").

5 See Streit and Mussler (1995); Mussler left academia and is now a leading journalist of the *Frankfurter Allgemeine Zeitung* and comments on the Euro crisis.

to take shape in the aftermath of the First World War but had some precursors, e.g. in the work of Lujo Brentano in the late 19th century. While in retrospect Ordo-liberalism reminds us of economic sociology or institutional economics, its important scholars, such as Walter Eucken, intended a more rigorous approach to economics as compared to the younger German Historical School of Brentano and others. Unlike some dogmatic representatives of this School, who insisted on methodological inductivism and rejected abstract economic theories, Walter Eucken and his followers (such as Adolf Lampe) strongly supported a theoretical approach in economics[6]. On a practical level, the Ordo-liberal school strongly criticized the course of economic policy in the Weimar Republic. In many aspects the German economic order, as in many other countries at the time, was inconsistent with the principles of a market economy by channeling manifold political constraints to free competition. These restrictions were not entirely home-based: Post-war protectionism reflected tense foreign relationships between former wartime combatants; accordingly, protectionism directly ensued from the absence of political cooperation among the major European powers. After the outbreak of the Great Depression in 1929, protectionism intensified. Besides protectionism, many other domestic reasons for constrained competition lingered. Of key significance was the cartelization and monopolization of the German economy which was considered a major obstacle for the market economy by Eucken and Ordo-liberal colleague Franz Böhm. The existence of cartels resulted from a far-reaching decision of the Reichsgericht (supreme court) in the end of the 19th century which considered even formal price-fixing agreements of suppliers to accord with the freedom of contract. This decision gave cartels and industrial syndicalism legal sanction. Monopolies and industrial conglomerations, namely in the steel and the chemical industry, became a salient feature of the German economy. Interestingly, the constraints for free competition also found political support. Given the prevalent opposition against capitalism and support for a socialist order by Weimar-era intellectuals and political groups, industrial syndicalism was favored since it was considered the third way between central planning and capitalism[7]. Additionally, strong unions in the heavy industry availed themselves of their bargaining power and thus participated in monopoly gains[8].

6 See the standard version of Ordo-liberal economic policy in Eucken (1952).

7 For this reason, the first chancellor of the Weimar republic, Walther Rathenau (who later was assassinated by an anti-Semite right wing group), preferred industrial syndicalism; see Gall (2009).

8 This bargaining power was gained through the Stinnes-Legien agreement in the immediate aftermath of the 1918 Revolution which prevented nationalization of heavy industries in exchange for concessions to key trade unions (8 hour day, works councils) which

Eucken and Böhm strongly opposed the positive view on monopolies and deemed them to be a major obstacle for prosperity and economic growth (Böhm 1933). Thus, the control of economic power by means of effective competition assured by anti-cartel policy became the major theme in the Ordo-liberal debate. Its proponents saw the major task for economists in the analysis of the institutional requirements for effective competition (Eucken 1952). In so doing they sought to "translate" (as they termed it) the economic conditions for free competition into legal norms. Franz Böhm, a legal scholar, researched into the consequences of free competition for private law, commercial law and cartel law; the latter still needed to be introduced (Böhm 1966).

During the Nazi-Period it became increasingly difficult for Ordo-liberal scholars to publish and canvass support for their ideas. Franz Böhm was prohibited from teaching because of his pro-Jewish attitude, which he explicitly defended against a public prosecutor; Walter Eucken bore the consequences of Martin Heidegger's repressive presidency of Freiburg University and ceased to express his preferred conception of an economic order in public[9]. Together with Böhm and some trustworthy intellectual allies he retreated into a private circle and held seminars at home. Eucken and Böhm escaped persecution and imprisonment only narrowly; other members of the group such as Röpke or Lutz taught in Switzerland; Rüstow emigrated to Turkey. The personal experience of suppression by a totalitarian regime explains why the control of power, whether in politics or in the economy, gained top priority for the leading figures of Ordo-liberalism.

The opposition against the power of the totalitarian State puts some early remarks into perspective that are liable to misunderstanding. If we leave aside Müller-Armack who revealed support to the Nazi-movement in the beginning and did not belong to the inner circle of the Ordo-liberals, the plea for a "strong State" before 1933 should not be interpreted as a form of support for Nazism[10]. Rather, it meant the strong *Rechtsstaat*, that is the State committed to the rule of law. In line with Hegel's conception of the State as the representation of a higher morality, the representatives of Ordo-liberalism demanded that the State be aligned to public interest. Rather than offering a playground for interest groups, the State was conceived to be the "arbiter" who sets the rules of the game and

was then enshrined in Weimar-era corporatist policy (Verordnung über Tarifverträge, Arbeiter- und Angestellten-Ausschüsse und Schlichtung von Arbeitsstreitigkeiten vom 23. Dezember 1918) and the Weimar Constitution (Artikel 165).

9 For a detailed analysis see Hansen (2009).

10 Indeed, Hayek considered Müller-Armack to be of minor importance for the theoretical renewal of liberalism.

guarantees freedom and competition. Hence, the rules should be universal and should not privilege certain groups or persons, which accords with Kant's political philosophy.

Like many other conservative (but notably also leftist) intellectuals of the Weimar period, the Ordo-liberals held strong misgivings about democracy in the beginning. One reason for this skepticism is that anti-liberal economic policies emanated from the influence of interest groups which had made use of their enlarged political power in the Weimar Republic in order to satisfy their self-interest. The collective bargaining of the Government with different interest groups was seen to be the plague of politics in democracy and believed to be the major obstacle to any rule-based economic policy. This thought became a recurrent theme of mid-century economic liberalism as well as Ordo-liberalism. Although it may appear utopian at first glance, the independence of the State towards interest groups remained a core ideal of Ordo-liberalism.

Critical stances to democracy notwithstanding, Walter Eucken did not sympathize with the idea of capitalism without democracy. Quite the contrary, he stressed what he called the "interdependency of orders". In his textbook *Grundsätze der Wirtschaftspolitik* he asserts that economic freedom depends on political freedom, while a centrally planned order will be unsustainable as long as political freedom prevails (Eucken 1952: 127). This argument opposes Schumpeter's reflections on capitalism, socialism and democracy (Schumpeter 1950); unlike Schumpeter, Eucken did not see the political and the economic order as interdependent but advocated a combination of economic and political freedom. It is worth stressing that the idea of an interdependency of orders has re-emerged in economic theory and plays a key role in contemporary institutional economics (Acemoglu and Robinson 2012; North, Wallis and Weingast 2009).

After the Second World War, the Ordo-liberal school has played a major role in the conceptualization of economic policy in West Germany (Rieter and Schmolz 1993). Even though recent history has made clear that Ordo-liberalism competed with socialist ideas in the early post-war period, its outstanding role and political influence is beyond doubt. The main reasons were that Ordo-liberalists had developed a coherent, up-dated theory of the market economy and conceptualized a suitable institutional framework for its realization. Furthermore, the first minister of economic affairs, Ludwig Erhard, became a practitioner of Ordo-liberal policy. He convinced the commander of the American occupational troops to lift fixed prices and thus introduced free market prices into the entire economy (with few exceptions such as accommodation rents). While the European victors Britain and France kept fixed prices and the rationing of goods for some more years and also nationalized key industrial sectors, West Germany paved the way towards a market economy. Though the early 1950s have not yet seen a fully fledged market economy, the economic success of the first policy measures testified to the superiority of Ordo-liberal principals; it encouraged Ludwig Erhard to continue his Ordo-liberal policy agenda which amongst others included the introduction of the cartel law in 1956 as the most significant policy measure. At the same time, the economic policies of the other European countries, namely the planification in France and the politics of nationalization in Britain, failed to present themselves as attractive alternatives.

Looking at its underpinnings, Ordo-liberalism is a rule-based conception of economic principles. Reflecting the major obstacles for a market economy, Walter Eucken attempted to find solutions to the following problems:

- interventionism in the economy, e.g. through price controls, price ceilings or lower limits for prices,
- the restriction of competition, e.g. via cartels and barriers to market entry, and generally the problem of economic power,
- protectionism and the restriction of foreign trade
- insufficient working conditions and poor living conditions for workers,
- inflation.

In search for a solution, Eucken fundamentally reflected upon the operating conditions of a market order and identified principles of the relationship between the market and the State. In general, Ordo-liberal scholars distanced themselves from what they called "Manchester-Liberalism" and tried to find a solution to the social question that is compatible with the principles of economic freedom. Nevertheless, Wilhelm Röpke's qualification of Ordo-liberalism as a "third way" between Capitalism and Socialism (as recently termed by Anthony Giddens) is misleading since the entire conception aimed at an improvement of the standards of living by economic dynamics (Röpke 1979). Rules for economic policy included:

- the principle of accountability as a pillar for the market economy, which rules out that economic decision makers can shift the consequences of their actions to others,
- a monetary constitution in order to secure stable money which gives rise to an independent, rule oriented central bank,
- competition policy as an instrument to restrain economic power (cartels, monopolies)
- the style of policy making which necessitates stability instead of rampant policy changes,

- occasional regulations of the economy in order to protect workers or to balance requirements of the market economy with social standards and ethical, namely Christian norms (prohibition of working on Sunday, reduction of labor hour etc.) (Eucken 1952: Ch. XVI and Ch. XVII).

In *Grundsätze der Wirtschaftspolitik*, Eucken condensed the solutions into the so called constitutive and regulative principles for economic policy (Eucken 1952). It gets clear of discretionary economic policy or any form of "economic government", which includes the rejection of (neo-) mercantilist policies or industrial policy in order to influence the structure of the economy. Specifically, the Government should refrain from promoting an export industry or producing a balance of payment surplus by means of protectionism. This conception is in opposition to industrial policy which plays a key role in French economic policy. As a consequence, German and French Governments have maintained divergent views on the role of EU institutions in the past. For instance, throughout the European integration process, the French Government intended to establish an "economic government" alien to Ordo-liberalism: Its advocates view any political prerogative over the economy to be the backdoor for political failure and untrammelled interventionism caused by influential interest groups. Rather, the State should withdraw from economic activities whenever private coordination is a conceivable alternative. Misgivings about State monopolies result from the key idea of a neutral arbiter and enforcer of the rules of the market economy. According to Ordo-liberal thinking, the State lacks neutrality as an economic player when it becomes engaged in the promotion of private industries (e.g. in the export sector).

In the context of the national debate, rule orientation has become a cornerstone of the corporate identity of the German Ministry of Economic Affairs. Until the late 1960s, it was impossible to apply for a job in the ministry without being familiar with Eucken's constitutive and regulative principles of economic policy. As of the late 1960s the influence of Ordo-liberalism diminished due to the rise of Keynesianism. Theoretically, it was widely regarded as an outdated conception which opposes to the management of the economy (namely some key macroeconomic variables in terms of "fine tuning") by fiscal policy, monetary policy, taxation or industrial policy. However, this was the exact message of Ordo-liberalism which conceived the central task of Government in the pursuit of *Ordnungspolitik* (the policy of establishing economic order), a term which badly translates to English but points to the institutional framework securing economic freedom given the modifications sketched above. *Ordnungspolitik* opposes Keynesianism if one concentrates solely on its macroeconomic version. However, it is worth noting that Karl Schiller, the successor of Ludwig Erhard who was a professor of economics and became the first Social

Democratic minister of economic affairs, advocated a synthesis between *Ordnungspolitik* and Keynesianism; despite the fact that he was the first minister to launch Keynesian deficit spending in the late 1960s, he refused to consider Keynesian fiscal policy a viable alternative to *Ordnungspolitik*; even according to this renowned practitioner of Keynesianism, deficit spending could only supplement *Ordnungspolitik*. This accords to Wilhelm Röpke's stance to Keynesian economic policy some decades earlier; while he was willing to accept violations of a balanced budget rule in a particular situation such as the World Economic Crisis, he refused to make Keynes' *Theory* a general approach to economic policy.

Ordo-liberalism never has been applied straightforwardly. Complaints about violations of the principles of *Ordnungspolitik* abound. However, these complaints indicate that *Ordnungspolitik* remains a point of reference for the critical assessment of current economic policies. The Council of Economic Experts of the Ministry of Economic Affairs in particular, time and again, reviews German economic policy from this perspective. In addition, the editors of the influential *Frankfurter Allgemeine Zeitung* are strongly committed to this view and have offered the newspaper as a national stage for economists who argue from the viewpoint of Ordo-liberalism.

Nevertheless, the significance as well as the reputation of *Ordnungspolitik* with regard to German economists has been subject to ups and downs. The 1980s have witnessed a remarkable rise of *Ordnungspolitik*, which corresponded to the on-going problems of Western economic policy such as stagflation and excessive public debt. Moreover, the revival found a new theoretical foundation in Buchanan's constitutional choice theory (Buchanan 1975 and Brennan and Buchanan 1985). Buchanan argues from the perspective of a completely different political theory which is at variance with the philosophical background of Ordo-liberalism. However, he deals with the same problem as Ordo-liberalists, i.e., the penetrating influence of interest groups on economic policy, which Buchanan made responsible for the economic crisis in the US of the late 1970s. His response echoed Ordo-liberal scholars insofar as Buchanan sought to constrain public policy by a set of rules that are to expand on current constitutional rules. While Ordo-liberalism derives these rules from economic expertise and thus belongs to a substantial version of economic liberalism, Buchanan seeks to establish a new social contract ("constitutional revolution") for citizens to ponder on reasonable rules for democratic economic policy. Liberal economic policy is thus conceived as resulting from a special procedure, as opposed to standard welfare economics[11]. In spite of the different theoretical perspective

11 For the difference between substantial and procedural economic liberalism and a detailed discussion see Wegner (2009).

which integrates democracy into the conception of liberal economic policy, Buchanan's approach underscores the guiding principle of Ordo-liberalism that is the rule-oriented policy.

3. Ordo-liberalism and the European Union

The conception of rule-oriented policy has become relevant at several stages of the European integration process and has led to conflicts with EU-partners. For instance, German experts in cartel law and competition policy were initially highly skeptical towards the growing influence of European competition policy which appeared to be abandoning German economic policy as of the 1990s (Möschel 1996). Specifically, the guiding principle of workable competition has found criticism because it was likely to undermine the German standards. Namely, the efficiency defence clause of Article (101, 3) of the Treaty and merger control were deemed a backdoor for French style industrial policy, which is likely to thwart the intention of the prohibition of cartels. Furthermore, the integration of the cartel authority into the European Commission (which promotes industrial policies in various forms) was interpreted as an institutional failure. Only lately have German scholars of cartel law and competition policy toned down their skepticism and now largely appreciate European competition policy. A further example concerns the debate on the Maastricht Treaty in the early 1990s (see below). This debate in the remainder of the analysis is instructive for the thinking of economists following the principles of Ordo-liberalism.

In the 1990s, German economists intensively discussed globalization and the future of the European Union. A group of economists affiliated with the Max-Planck-Institute into the Research of Economic Systems in Jena (now: Institute of Economics) employed the Maastricht Treaty as an opportunity to reflect on the appropriate institutional framework for the European Union. This discussion also contributed to research on the impact of globalization on economic policy in general.

The debate highlighted that the Maastricht Treaty represents a watershed of the European integration project as compared to the Rome Treaty. Streit, Wohlgemuth and others stressed that in retrospect, the Rome Treaty comes close to an ideal framework for the European economic integration if one takes the Ordo-liberal school as a point of reference[12]. For a long time this development has been put in the shade of European agricultural policy which displayed an expensive type of subsidization and market regulation. Since this policy measure (to this date) absorbed the lion's share of the EU

12 See Streit and Mussler (1995) and Streit and Wohlgemuth (1999) for a comprehensive study of the ideas of the Jena Group.

budget, it attracted liberal criticism throughout the 1970s and 1980s. On top of that, EU agricultural policy was unjustifiably interpreted to be the typical mode of European integration. Nevertheless, the concept of "New Systems Competition" suggests an alternative interpretation.

Early Ordo-liberal contributions have revolved around the question whether a common market depends on a central political authority that sets the rules at the European level. This type of political strategy bears a key problem that echoes Weingast's (1995) diagnosis of the central State: a European State which is strong enough to set the rules for the common market will also be strong enough to distort these rules. Tumlir (1983) discussed this problem in the journal *Ordo* and expressed his skepticism towards a central authority that sets and controls the rules for the common market. From this perspective there is not much hope that the central rule setter will live up to Ordo-liberal expectations and thus differ significantly from the economic policy of a nation State. Agricultural policy is a telling example for the influence of interest groups who try to "capture" the central regulator and to close markets on their behalf. In the 1990s, the former President of the Commission, Jacques Delors, envisaged the idea of a "Fortress Europe" which confirmed Ordo-liberal fears regarding the centralization of the European Union. According to Delors, the Common Market in Europe needed to be paralleled by market entry barriers for economies outside from the EU. In so doing, a European economic Government to be installed would have more leeway to intervene in the markets according to political priorities. Since protectionism is complementary to industrial policy, the European Government could perform a neo-mercantilist policy reflecting political priorities which could not be thwarted by international competition.

By nature, the European integration process so far does not rest on a central political authority. The Treaties establish basic economic rights (free trade for goods, services, capital and the right of abode) as subjective rights of the European citizens. These rights are directly applicable and in principle do not depend on the implementation of the governments of the member States. Rather, European citizens can sue the governments of the member States for their economic rights laid down in the Treaties. Ultimately, the European Court interprets the content of the Treaty, which it has done in a very liberal way so far. In the same vein, the Court has transformed the ban of discrimination on the basis of national status into a ban of restrictions for transnational trade. In so doing, the jurisprudence in the Cassis-de-Dijon case has established a common European market for goods that extends free trade: the member States are obliged to accept the regulations of their partners since trade restrictions would discriminate due to national status (the so called measure with equivalent effect of Art. 34 of the Treaty). Unlike free trade outside the EU, which commits exporting producers to the country of destination principle, the EU establishes the country-of-origin principle. The governments of the member States are committed to this principle: the European concept of market integration is "revolutionary" (Streit and Mussler 1995) in the sense that European law overrides national law. Hence, interest groups in the member States have lost some of their power at erecting market entry barriers by regulations.

Given the legal arrangement of the EU, Ordo-liberal economists have come around to a positive interpretation of the institutional design of the Union. Instead of a constructivist "big bang", the integration process works smoothly and rests upon civil courts instead of government actions. Protectionist relapses on the level of the member States are forestalled unless the governments call upon the European Council in their interventionist intentions (they have done so in response of the "Bolkestein-proposal" for the opening of the service sector along the lines of the markets for goods). Thus, the institutional design of the integration process comes close to Tumlir's (1983) Ordo-liberal conception for an international trade order: for being effective, the institutional arrangement has to put national governments on the sideline.

In their in-depth analysis, the Jena Group of Ordo-liberal economists has shown that the extant constitution of the Union has a chance of bringing about undistorted competition and remedying "political failure" caused by interest groups capturing their governments[13]. Since firms still are exposed to the regulations of their own governments, different regulations of the member States compete on the European market. The verdict in the Cassis-De-Dijon case has pointed out that firms cannot freely adopt the regulations of other member States but instead have to relocate if they want to escape too-narrow regulations of their own nation State. Relocation, in turn, does not face any legal obstacles due to the free movement of capital. If the relocation of capital from member States with restrictive regulations to less restrictive systems makes for unemployment, labor will follow suit. Of course, free movement of labor has been restricted for a long time within the EU and is practically restricted for many reasons (language and cultural differences, problems concerning the recognition of occupations etc.). Unlike the international order of the WTO, the European Union has established a type of Systems Competition that has not yet been attained any other transnational region in the World. Neither the country-of-origin-principle for goods nor the fully established free movement of capital and labor as actionable subjective rights present a realistic option to regions outside the EU within the foreseeable future. In contrast to the widely held beliefs about

13 See the contributions in Streit and Wohlgemuth (1999).

globalization in the world economy, only the European Union provides the necessary legal requirements for its institutional establishment. Unlike other regions in the world, the European Union has sufficient competences to cope with transnational collective good problems such as the distortion of competition in the Union or the overexploitation of the environment by European environmental policy. Member States cannot gain an economic advantage by damaging the environment unilaterally or by distorting competition e.g. through subsidies for their domestic industry or protectionist measures. By now, this type of fully-fledged workable competitive order is not a realistic option for other transnational regions.

The EU institutional arrangement just discussed are likely to solve the main problem of the Ordo-liberal school, namely the absence of policy-makers that are interested in the introduction of rules for an open market economy. The competition for goods, the threat of relocation of capital and the movement of labor create unprecedented exit options for economic agents. Exit, in turn, holds out the chance to re-align the economic policies of the member States with rules that are constitutive for a market economy. Governments who depend on powerful interest groups will bear the consequences of restrictive regulations and interventions in markets through firm and labor exit. A decline in investment, employment and tax revenues will undermine the standing of the government and its outlook for re-election. Hence, economic reforms that are suitable to attract investors and to keep the workforce at home make up a possible outcome of New Systems Competition. At least to some extent, New Systems Competition supplants market oriented rules for economic policy.

The institutional framework of the European Union has not been the result of a deliberate conception. Rather, it emerged "spontaneously" from judicial decisions of the European Court. It is doubtful whether the European Court has fully foreseen the economic consequences of its decisions or intended the emanation of Systems Competition within the Union; Hence, Streit and Mussler (1995) describe the "unconscious discovery" of New Systems Competition by the European Court. There is little doubt that the European Commission as well as the governments of the member States did not embrace this development. For instance, after the path-breaking Cassis-De-Dijon verdict, the Commission made a proposal for an unifying regulatory framework for all products in the EU. Due to practical reasons which made it impossible to harmonize all regulations from scratch, the country-of-origin-principle has not been abandoned. Since that time, the Commission has made various efforts to halt the variety of legal norms in the Union by introducing a unitary European norm. Cases in point are the proposals for European civil law or a European commercial law. The obvious strategy is to create a European norm as an additional legal option which is likely to drive out the norms of the member States in the long term. However, these attempts time and again suffer from practical impediments, which is why the institutional framework for institutional competition is largely intact to this day.

Not only regulations but all institutions that are related to production and impinge on costs or the flexibility of firms as to the workforce are subject to New Systems Competition. Cases in point concern the labor law which regulates the terms of labor contracts, including the dismissal of the workforce and the extent of the welfare state which defines supplemental labor costs. In the aftermath of re-unification for instance, the German economy came under pressure due to high supplemental labor costs and the low productivity of the former GDR. As the social frictions of Eastern Germany's extensive de-industrialization were cushioned by the extension of the welfare state, labor became too costly compared to its productivity. Mounting unemployment up to more than 5 Mio in 2005 was the consequence of excessive (total) labor costs. Government and unions reacted to this development by settling on a combination of budget cuts, tax reductions and reforms of the labor market which increased the incentives to accept jobs. In view of high unemployment, the unions merely pursued a compensation for inflationary losses in the first decade after 2000. The reactions of the government and the unions resulted from the undermined competitiveness of the German economy and the outflow of capital. Economists and politicians who interpret this policy as a neo-mercantilist approach ignore the former situation of the German economy and its burden from re-unification. (Furthermore, the interpretation ignores the fact that all members of the currency union have to cope with economic crises without the key instruments of neo-mercantilist policy since exchange rates, interest rates as well as foreign trade policy are exclusive competences of the European Union)[14]. Besides, in Germany wages are not set by the government but negotiated by unions and entrepreneurs associations. In view of high unemployment and undermined productivity, the unions saw little room to demand wage increases.

The remarkable recovery of the German economy after 2005 resulted from the New Systems Competition in the EU and the reactions of the government and the unions. In this context, economic policy

14 Keynesian economists or influential policy makers demanding Germany to raise its wages they ignore that a collective actor called "Germany" setting wages does not exist. Rather, wages are the outcome of individual and collective bargaining which responds to micro- and macroeconomic conditions.

makers came under pressure since the owners of mobile resources were able to relocate into regulatory regimes that were beneficial for profit making. The labor market reform ("Hartz IV legislation") but also substantial reductions in income and corporate taxes took into account that economic agents had more options to relocate than before. In a competitive environment that constrains government actions, nascent European federalism becomes "market preserving" (Weingast 1995): it works as a surrogate for market preserving constitutional rules since any type of economic policy that inhibits profit making is sanctioned.

Nevertheless, the route to European integration is open. The current European crisis has reinforced proposals for "more Europe", which apparently implies shifting political competences from the member States to the Union. According to a widely held belief it is necessary to "co-ordinate" economic policies since economic integration is purportedly impossible without political integration. The Ordo-liberal perspective strongly opposes this claim if posed without qualification. Rather, the centralization of the European Union would run the risk of undermining the current pro-competitive order.

The Maastricht Treaty points to an alternative route for future European integration that rivals the conception of the Treaty of Rome. Following the Ordo-liberal perspective, the Jena Group analysed this tendency and advocated that the Treaty of Rome be the most suitable conception for the EU. By contrast, the Maastricht Treaty attenuates the clear conception of the Treaty of Rome by expanding the goals of the union. Namely, industrial policy became part of the Treaty rivalling the goal of "undistorted competition" in the Union, whilst the Lisbon-Treaty formally removed that goal from the agenda (although legal scholars argue that the legal status of undistorted competition is undisputed). In the Lisbon-Process which had its follow-up in the Agenda 2020, industrial policy became manifest in the institutional framework of the European Union. "Helping the losers and picking the winners" in the industry heavily contradicts the principle of undistorted competition since it necessitates the introduction of privileges for industrial sectors and firms[15]. Expanding the goals of the European Community poses a problem because some of the goals rival each other: to what extent is distortion of competition acceptable in order to pursue industrial policy? In contrast to the Treaty of Rome, the Council and the Commission have become policy-makers instead of a rule setters. These changes have significantly altered the nature and the design of the European Union. To the extent that discretionary economic policy becomes institutionalized,

15 For a critical analysis from the perspective of law school see Scherzberg (2010).

the market preserving character of the Union is challenged. The strategy of the German government during the fiscal crisis obviously relied on a rule-oriented approach which avoids strengthening the competences of the Commission. However, the talk of "more Europe" is extremely vague and suggests an alternative interpretation favored by those European partners which prefer discretionary policies. The foreseeable outcome of this interpretation would be an increase in conflicts between the member States because its governments will become embroiled into the formation of a winning coalition.

4. Outlook: Rules for European Economic Policy

It is necessary to stress that a rule oriented approach to the renewal of the European Union does not imply that all partners need to harmonize their policies or to adopt the same type of economic policy. Rather, the arguments for New Systems Competition emerge from an evolutionary theoretical framework which stresses the lack of knowledge as to the best economic response to the challenges of globalization. If these answers cannot be objectively determined, European institutions have to create a framework which enables experimentation and learning on the level of the member States. Accordingly, each country has to find its own specific economic answer to the challenges of international competition and adapt its economic and social policies accordingly. Furthermore, the outcome reflects the political preferences of the respective member States, e.g. the willingness to pay for certain social policies in terms of growth losses. By contrast, the more political competences are transferred to the Union, the more political preferences of some of the member States are compromised. Namely small member States would undergo severe restrictions of their national sovereignty if the Union acquires political competences beyond the requirements of a competitive order. Ordo-liberal thought requires the member States to be the sovereign of their policies. This also implies that they bear the consequences of their preferences and actions. Joint accountability, by contrast, violates the operating conditions of Systems Competition. For instance, if a member State prefers a huge public sector, it makes use of its political sovereignty. Depending on the willingness to pay for this public sector (which may correspond to its effectiveness), the size of the public sector will be sustained or undergo reforms. In order ensure functioning Systems Competition, the principle of accountability is necessary for a feedback mechanism in politics. For that reason the no-bail-out clause of the Maastricht Treaty is essential. It assures that the member States act autonomously but nevertheless bear the consequences of their political decisions. If the partners were liable for decisions other than their own, the European Union would generate a common pool resource problem and political failure would multiply. In this case, it is likely that liberal intellectuals and policy-makers in Germany who have supported the European integration for decades would turn away from the EU in the future. For that reason, the rescue operation resulting from the fiscal crisis has put the Union to a test. By no means is it taken for granted that the liberal camp in Germany will stick to the European integration process if the rescue operation is interpreted as a starting point for further joint liability (e.g. in terms of Euro bonds).

Hence, the political autonomy of the member States should remain a building block of the Union. It will recreate political diversity rooted in different political cultures and in turn contribute to a specific variety of capitalism. In correspondence to its different political cultures, the member States maintain different sizes of their public sector, different levels of taxation for income or firms, different regulations for goods, services, and production or dismissal rules on the labor market and different dimensions of the welfare state. Since this diversity reflects both a variety of political preferences and a varying influence of interest groups ("government failure"), decisions about political reforms should be established at the level of the member States. Even though currently the capacity for political reforms might be overstressed for some member States, a feasible alternative is not in sight. Otherwise, European polities will become embroiled into political conflicts of their partners without having sufficient insight into the specific political and cultural characteristics.

In conclusion, Systems Competition within the EU represents a feasible update for Ordo-liberal ideas. In my view it cracks the code of how to combine political autonomy, democracy and undistorted economic competition. Open competition in the Union is supportive to political learning because it establishes a feedback mechanism between political decisions and economic consequences. This in turn guarantees the competitiveness of the Union as a whole. As a by-product, Systems Competition in the EU, as any type of competition, will reproduce alternate "laggards". However, in view of European history this is not a disquieting fact. From the roots of modern capitalism in late 17th century in England, European countries took turns in obtaining the laggard position. In a competitive surrounding, backwardness only provides the starting point for a catch-up process. A "harmonization" or centralization of politics in Europe would endanger the advantages of political variety and competition. Within the European institutional framework, peaceful political and economic competition among the European partners, is not determined to end up with homogeneous policies. In contrast to popular comments on the current crisis, political variety within the EU is not the problem. It is rather the solution to a problem.

References

Acemoglu, D.; Robinson, J. A. (2012). *Why Nations Fail. The Origins of Power, Prosperity, and Poverty*. New York, Crown Business.

Böhm, F. (1933). *Wettbewerb und Monopolkampf*. Berlin, Heymans.

Böhm, F. (1966). "Privatrechtsgesellschaft und Marktwirtschaft". *Ordo*, 17: 75-151.

Brennan, G.; Buchanan, J. M. (1985). *The Reason of Rules. Constitutional Political Economy*. Cambridge, Cambridge University Press.

Buchanan, J. M. (1975). *The Limits of Liberty: Between Anarchy and Leviathan*. Chicago, Chicago University Press.

Eucken, W. (1952 [2004]). *Grundsätze der Wirtschaftspolitik*. Tübingen, Mohr.

Gall, L. (2009). *Walther Rathemau. Porträt einer Epoche*. München, Beck.

Hansen, N. (2009). *Franz Böhm mit Ricarda Huch. Zwei wahre Patrioten* (Forschungen und Quellen zur Zeitgeschichte; Bd. 57), Düsseldorf, Droste.

Mestmäcker, E.-J. (2004). *Wirtschaft und der Verfassung in Europäischen Union. Beiträge zu Recht, Theorie und Politik der europäischen Integration*. Baden-Baden, Nomos.

Möschel, W. (1992). *Unity and Diversity in Europe. An Argument for less Harmonisation and Centralisation*. Bad Homburg, Frankfurter Institut.

Möschel, W. (1996). "Gutachten des Wissenschaftlichen Beirats beim Bundesministerium für Wirtschaft, Anpassung des deutschen Kartellgesetzes an das europäische Recht?", *BMWi-Studienreihe*, No. 93, Bonn.

North, D. C.; Wallis, J. J.; Weingast, B. (2009). *Violence and Social Orders. A Conceptual Framework for Interpreting Recorded Human History*. Cambridge, Cambridge University Press.

Olson, M. (1982). *The Rise and Decline of Nations. Economic Growth, Stagflation and Social Rigidities*. New Haven and London, Yale University Press.

Rieter, H.; Schmolz, M. (1993) "The Ideas of German Ordoliberalism 1938-45: pointing the way to a new economic order". *The European Journal of the History of Economic Thought*, 1: 105-6.

Röpke, W. (1942). *International Economic Disintegration*. London, William Hodge.

Röpke, W. (1979). *Civitas Humana. Grundfragen der Gesellschafts- und Wirtschaftsreform*. Bern und Stuttgart, Haupt.

Sally, R. (1998). *Classical Liberalism and International Economic Order. Studies in theory and intellectual history*. London, Routledge.

Sally, R. (2012). *L'ordoliberalismo e il mercato sociale. Il liberalismo che salvò la Germania*. Istituto Bruno Leoni Occasional Papers, No. 89 <http://www.brunoleonimedia.it/public/OP/IBL-OP_89-Sally.pdf>.

SCHERZBERG, A. (2010). *Die EU-Innovationspolitik im Rahmen der Lissabon-Strategie*. In Blanke, H.-J.; Scherzberg, A.; Wegner, G. (2010). *Dimensionen des Wettbewerbs. Europäische Integration zwischen Eigendynamik und politischer Gestaltung*. Mohr, Siebeck, 455-79.

SCHUMPETER, J. A. (1950 [1987]). *Kapitalismus, Sozialismus und Demokratie*. Einleitung von E. Salin, 6. Aufl. Tübingen, Francke.

SINN, H.-W. (2003). *The New Systems Competition*. London, Blackwell.

STREIT, M. E.; MUSSLER, W. (1995). "The Economic Constitution of the European Community: From Rome to Maastricht". *European Law Journal*, 1: 5-30.

STREIT, M. E.; WOHLGEMUTH, M. (1999) (eds.). *Systemwettbewerb als Herausforderung an Politik und Theorie*. Baden-Baden, Nomos.

TUMLIR, J. (1983). "International Economic Order and Democratic Constitutionalism". *Ordo*, 34: 71-83.

TUMLIR, J. (1989). "Franz Böhm and the development of economic-constitutional analysis". In Peacock, A.; Willgerodt, H. (Eds.). *German Neoliberals and the Social Market Economy*. London, Macmillan, 127, 131, 134, 139.

WEGNER, G. (2009). "Substantive versus Procedural Liberalism: Exploring a Dilemma of Contemporary Liberal Thought". *Journal of Institutional and Theoretical Economics*, 165: 535-557.

WEINGAST, B. (1995). "The Economic Role of Political Institutions: Market Preserving Federalism and Economic Development". *Journal of Law, Economics and Organisation*, 7: 1-31.

ZWEYNERT, J. (2008). "Die Soziale Marktwirtschaft als politische Integrationsformel". *Wirtschaftsdienst*, 88 (5): 334-7.

Index of Names

Contributors

Charles Beat Blankart, professor at Humboldt University of Berlin since 1992, emeritus since 2010, is Permanent Guest Professor at University of Lucerne Switzerland. Dr. rer. pol. of University of Basel (1969), he received postdoctoral lecture qualification (Habilitation) at University of Konstanz (1976). He was professor at the Free University of Berlin, at the University of the German Armed Forces in Munich, at the Berlin Polytechnic University. He was fellow and guest professor at University of Munich, Bucerius Law School Hamburg, Andrassy University Budapest, the Center for Study of Public Choice VPI, Blacksburg, Va., at the Science Center Berlin, the Center for Study of Public Choice, George Mason University, Fairfax, Va., the University La Sapienza in Rome and at Wirtschaftsuniversität Vienna. Some publications: "Land, Men and Taxation", in *Constitutional Political Economy* 2014. Oil and Vinegar: A Positive Fiscal Theory of the Euro Crisis, in Kyklos, *International Review for Social Sciences*, Vol. 66, November 2013, No. 4 Wie finanzieren sich Völkergemeinschaften? Vom Kaiserreich zur Eurokrise, erscheint in: *Zeitschrift für Wirtschaftspolitik*, 3/2012. Public Choice: A Survey, CESifo Working Paper No. 4102, February 2013, Federal Transfer Programs in Germany, in J. Clemens and Niels Veldhuis, Vancouver, Fraser Institute, Canada 2013, p. 57-68.

Piero Bini is full professor of History of Economic Thought and also teaches Political Economy and History and Theories of Public Intervention in the Economy at the Faculty of Political Sciences of the University of "Roma Tre". He has been the scientific director of the six-monthly review "Storia del Pensiero Economico" from 2004 to 2010. Since 2012 he is the Editor of the international review "History of Economic Thought and Policy". He is member of the editorial and scientific committees of other journals. Since 2001 to 2008 he has been the President of the Italian Association for the History of Economic Thought (AISPE). Besides AISPE, he is affiliated to various other national and international scientific associations: SIE – ESHET – STOREP – SISE. As for his research areas, the main lines pursued in past years are these: 1) International spread of economic ideas; 2) Methodological, analytical and historical relationships between economic theory and public policies; 3) Italian economic thought and style. In connection with these research areas, he elaborated more than 80 publications (volumes, essays, articles and so on).

Monika Poettinger is qualified associate professor for Economic History and currently teaches economic history and history of economic thought at Bocconi University and University of Florence. She has published many articles and book chapters on the industrialisation of Lombardy, merchant networks and German entrepreneurial migrations. Recent publications include: *Deutsche Unternehmer im Mailand des neunzehnten Jahrhunderts. Netzwerke, soziales Kapital und Industrialisierung*, Casagrande Editore, Lugano, 2012 and as editor *Firenze e l'Europa liberale. L'Economista (1874-1881)*, Polistampa, Firenze, 2013. Her research interests comprise the role of merchants in society from Babylonia to the nineteenth century, European liberal economic thought and its diffusion, and entrepreneurial migrations and the role of merchant networks in industrialization.

Paolo Savona is emeritus professor of Political Economy at the LUISS Guido Carli University of Rome. From 1963 to 1976 he worked at the Research Department of the Bank of Italy as member of the team of the first econometric model of the Italian economy (published in 1970 as M1BI); after he becomes Director of the Financial Market Section. In 1976 he was awarded a chair at the University through a national competition, teaching Political Economy in various Italian Universities until 2010. During this period he performed as Director General of the Italian Confederation of Industry, Secretary General for Economic Planning at the Ministry of Budget, Minister for Industry in the Ciampi Government, Director General for the European Policies at the Premier Office and Chairman of the Italian FDIC. He also had a wide experience as chairman of major domestic banks and companies and he published many books and papers, particularly on international monetary problems.

Bertram Schefold was born 28.12.1943 in Basel (Switzerland). He studied at Munich, Hamburg and Basel, 1962-1967; and obtained the diploma in mathematics, physics an philosophy. He continued with doctoral studies in Cambridge (GB) and Basel, Ph.D. in economics 1971. He then lectured at Basel and was Research Associate at Harvard University, Cambridge/Mass. He became full professor (C 4) at the Faculty of Economics, Johann Wolfgang Goethe-University, Frankfurt, March 1974 and was Dean, Faculty of Economics, J.W. Goethe-University, 1981/2. He has published more than 40 books and 250 articles on economic theory, history of economic thought, energy policy and general economic policy. He edited the series Klassiker der Nationalökonomie. Honours: Dr. iur. h.c. Tübingen, Dr. rer. pol. h.c. Macerata, Thomas-Guggenheim Prize. A first Festschrift from his pupils is published as: Caspari, Volker (ed.), *Theorie und Geschichte der Wirtschaft: Festschrift für Bertram Schefold*, Marburg: Metropolis 2008. A second Festschrift from his colleagues is published as: Caspari, Volker (ed.), *The Evolution of Economic Theory. Essays in honour of Bertram Schefold*, Abington and New York: Routledge 2011.

Antonio Varsori is full professor of International History at the University of Padua where he is also the Director of the Department of Politics, Law and International Studies. He is the vice-President of the Liaison Committee of historians of contemporary Europe at the European Commission, member of the editorial boards of several journals, President of the Italian Society of International History. He has published extensively on the Cold War, the European integration, Italy's foreign policy. Among his most recent publications in volumes: *La Cenerentola d'Europa? L'Italia e l'integrazione europea dal 1947 a oggi* (Rubbettino, 2010); *European Union History Themes and Debates*, ed. with W. Kaiser (Palgrave/Macmillan, 2010); *L'Italia e la fine della guerra fredda. La politica estera dei governi Andreotti 1989-1992* (Il Mulino, 2013).

Gerhard Wegner is professor at the University of Erfurt and holds a chair for Institutional Economics and Economic Policy since 2000. He received his PhD from the University of Mannheim and taught economics at the University of Bochum from 1997 to 2000. He has published several books on institutional economics, institutional competition, constitutional economics and liberal thought. He is engaged in many projects directed to the research into the political economy and institutions of the market economy, e.g. as a fellow of the post graduate programme "Social Market Economy" of the Konrad-Adenauer-Foundation. His recent monographs include: *Ökonomischer Liberalismus als Politische Theorie. Befund, Kritik, Rekonstruktion* (Tübingen, Mohr), 2012, 300 p.; *Political Failure by Agreement. Learning Liberalism and the Welfare State* (Cheltenham, Edward Elgar), Series: New Thinking in Political Economy, 2008; *The Evolutionary Analysis of Economic Policy* (edited with P. Pelikan) (Cheltenham, Edward Elgar), 2003; *Nationalstaatliche Institutionen im Wettbewerb - Wie funktionsfähig ist der Systemwettbewerb?* (Berlin, De Gruyter), 2004.

EUROCLIO – Published Books

N° 81 – *The European Community and the World. A Historical Perspective.* Giuliana Laschi (ed.), 2014.

N° 80 – *Christian Democrat Internationalism. Its Action in Europe and Worldwide from Post World War II until the 1990s. Volume II: The Development (1945-1979). The Role of Parties, Movements, People.* Jean-Dominique Durand (ed.), 2013.

N° 79 – *Christian Democrat Internationalism. Its Action in Europe and Worldwide from Post World War II until the 1990s. Volume I: The Origins.* Jean-Dominique Durand (ed.), 2013.

N° 78 – *Investment Banking History. National and Comparative Issues (19th-21st centuries).* Hubert Bonin & Carlo Brambilla (eds.), 2013.

N° 77 – *Citizenship and Solidarity in the European Union. From the Charter of Fundamental Rights to the Crisis, the State of the Art.* Mariana Canotilho, Pedro Madeira Froufe & Alessandra Silveira (eds.), 2013.

N° 76– *The OSCE: Soft Security for a Hard World. Competing Theories for Understanding the OSCE.* Roberto Dominguez (ed.), 2013.

N° 75 – *Euroscepticism, Europhobia and Eurocriticism. The Radical Parties of the Right and Left vis-à-vis the European Union.* Cesáreo Rodríguez-Aguilera de Prat, 2013.

N° 74 – *Fermer les mines en construisant l'Europe. Une histoire sociale de l'intégration européenne.* Nicolas Verschueren, 2012

N° 73 – *Reflets de la construction européenne. Réflexions, références et refus du débat sur l'Europe.* Bertrand Vayssière (dir.), 2012.

N° 72 – *The International Relations of Local Authorities. From Institutional Twinning to the Committee of the Regions: Fifty Years of European Integration History.* Fabio Zucca, 2012.

N° 71 – *Histoire du Conseil de l'Europe (1949-2009).* Birte Wassenberg, 2012.

N° 70 – *The EU, Security and Transatlantic Relations.* Finn Laursen (ed.), 2012.

N° 69 – *Européanisation au XX*e *siècle. Un regard historique/Europeanisation in the 20th Century. The Historical Lens.* Matthieu Osmont, Émilia Robin-Hivert, Katja Seidel, Mark Spoerer & Christian Wenkel (dir./eds.), 2012.

N° 68 – *Consensus and European Integration. An Historical Perspective/Consensus et intégration européenne. Une perspective historique.* Daniela Preda & Daniele Pasquinucci (eds./dir.), 2012.

N° 67 – *Générations de fédéralistes européens depuis le XIXe siècle. Individus, groupes, espaces et réseaux.* Geneviève Duchenne et Michel Dumoulin (dir.), 2012.

N° 66 – *Raymond Aron, penseur de l'Europe et de la nation.* Giulio De Ligio (dir.), 2012.

N° 65 – *Europe Twenty Years after the End of the Cold War. The New Europe, New Europes?/L'Europe vingt ans après la fin de la guerre froide. Nouvelle Europe, nouvelles Europes?* Bruno Arcidiacono, Katrin Milzow, Axel Marion & Pierre-étienne Bourneuf (eds./dir.), 2012.

N° 64 – *Aux origines de la diplomatie européenne. Les Neuf et la Coopération politique européenne de 1973 à 1980.* Maria Gainar, 2012.

N° 63 – *Europe and the Middle East. The hour of the East?* Birte Wassenberg & Giovanni Faleg (eds.), 2012.

N° 62 – *Quelle architecture pour un code européen de droit international privé ?* Marc Fallon, Paul Lagarde, Sylvaine Poillot-Peruzzetto (dir.), 2011.

N° 61 – *La construction d'un espace euro-méditerranéen. Genèses, mythes et perspectives.* Houda Ben Hamouda et Mathieu Bouchard (dir.), 2012.

N° 60 – *Innovations et transferts de technologie en Europe du Nord-Ouest aux XIXe et XXe siècles.* Jean-François Eck et Pierre Tilly (dir.), 2011.

N° 59 – *Novel Outlooks on the Marshall Plan. American Aid and European Re-Industrialization.* Fransceca Fauri & Paolo Tedeschi (eds.), 2011.

N° 58 – *Europe in the International Arena during the 1970s. Entering a Different World/L'Europe sur la scène internationale dans les années 1970. à la découverte d'un nouveau monde.* Antonio Varsori & Guia Migani (eds./dir.), 2011.

N° 57 – *Cultures nationales et identité communautaire. Un défi pour l'Europe ?/National Cultures and Common Identity. A Challenge for Europe?* Marloes Beers & Jenny Raflik (dir./eds.), 2010.

N° 56 – *Les trajectoires de l'innovation technologique et la construction européenne. Des voies de structuration durable ?/Trends in Technological Innovation and the European Construction. The Emerging of Enduring Dynamics?* Christophe Bouneau, David Burigana & Antonio Varsori (dir/eds.), 2010.

N° 55 – *L'OTAN et l'Europe. Quels liens pour la sécurité et la défense européenne ?* Birte Wassenberg, Giovanni Faleg et Martin W. Mlodecki (dir.), 2010.

N° 54 – *The Road Europe Travelled Along.* Daniele Pasquinucci and Daniela Preda (eds.), 2010.

N° 53 – *Vivre et construire l'Europe à l'échelle territoriale de 1945 à nos jours.* Yves Denéchère et Marie-Bénédicte Vincent (dir.), 2010.

Euroclio European Network

together with the SEGEI Network

Coordination: Chaire Jean Monnet d'histoire de l'Europe contemporaine (Cehec)
Collège Erasme, 1, place Blaise-Pascal, B-1348 Louvain-la-Neuve

Germany

Jürgen Elvert
Wilfried Loth

Belgium

Julie Cailleau
Jocelyne Collonval
Yves Conrad
Gaëlle Courtois
Pascal Deloge
Geneviève Duchenne
Vincent Dujardin
Michel Dumoulin
Roch Hannecart
Pierre-Yves Plasman
Béatrice Roeh
Corine Schröder
Caroline Suzor
Pierre Tilly
Arthe Van Laer
Jérôme Wilson
Natacha Wittorski

Spain

Enrique Moradiellos
Mercedes Samaniego Boneu

France

Françoise Berger
Marie-Thérèse Bitsch
Gérard Bossuat
Éric Bussière
Jean-François Eck
Catherine Horel
Philippe Mioche
Marine Moguen-Toursel
Sylvain Schirmann
Matthieu Trouvé
Laurent Warlouzet
Emilie Willaert

Hungary

Gergely Fejérdy

Italy

David Burigana
Elena Calandri
Eleonora Guasconi
Luciano Segreto
Antonio Varsori

Luxemburg

Charles Barthel
Etienne Deschamps
Jean-Marie Kreins
René Leboutte
Robert Philippart
Corine Schröder
Gilbert Trausch

The Netherlands

Anjo Harryvan
Jan W. Brouwer
Jan van der Herst

Poland

Józef Laptos
Zdzisiaw Mach

Switzerland

Antoine Fleury
Lubor Jilek